ENGLISH BARDS

AND GRECIAN MARBLES

THE TEMPORARY ELGIN ROOM AT THE
BRITISH MUSEUM IN 1819

The figure in profile at the extreme left is Haydon; the seated figure in front,
with hand extended, is Benjamin West.

STEPHEN A. LARRABEE

ENGLISH BARDS
AND GRECIAN MARBLES

THE RELATIONSHIP BETWEEN

SCULPTURE AND POETRY

ESPECIALLY IN THE ROMANTIC

PERIOD

KENNIKAT PRESS, INC./PORT WASHINGTON, N. Y.

ENGLISH BARDS AND GRECIAN MARBLES

FOR THE ANONYMOUS FRIEND

WITHOUT WHOM THIS BOOK COULD NOT

HAVE APPEARED "FOR THE DURATION"

PREFACE

THIS BOOK presents a critical and historical study of that English poetry, up to and including the Romantic period, which is inspired by ancient Greek sculpture. I examine a considerable body of poetry both for its own merits and for its relationship to a somewhat loose yet easily discernible tradition of interest in ancient art. Before the Romantic period, not every poem is reviewed; but I consider most of the important poets, and in any case I have sketched the major strands in the development of poetic interest in Greek sculpture.

Complete by itself, the book nevertheless looks ahead to several others. It implies, first of all, a sequel (already planned in part), which will continue the account of Grecian marbles in English poetry throughout the nineteenth and into the twentieth century, with at least a side glance at American poetry. I also hope this work may encourage various studies of Hellenism in England, both by itself and in relation to similar movements in other countries. In contrast to Continental scholars, English-speaking writers have done surprisingly little in this interesting field.

Two matters of chronology need some explanation. I have placed Milton after his proper time, not to remove him from the "Renaissance tradition" with which, perhaps, he has most in common, but in order to suggest the elements in his works and thought which contributed to the Hellenism of the eighteenth-century and the Romantic poets. The chapters on individual Romantic poets follow movements of ideas, unless, as in the cases of Wordsworth and Keats, something is gained by following a chronological sequence. I have not scrupled to treat works by Romantic poets which appeared as much as two decades after the close of the Romantic period.

My obligations are numerous and heavy. I am indebted more than

I can properly say here to Professor Charles Grosvenor Osgood of Princeton University, who first suggested the field of this wide-spreading investigation and then guided my efforts with never failing discrimination and patience. Professor Erwin Panofsky of the Institute for Advanced Studies has encouraged this study almost from its inception. On many occasions he has given information about the fine arts, especially in connection with the earlier periods discussed here. Professors Morris W. Croll and Donald A. Stauffer of Princeton suggested improvements in the first or "thesis" draft of Chapters II, III, IV, and VIII, and, in the case of the latter, Chapter I. Professor Rensselaer Lee of Smith College generously read the full manuscript and made many valuable criticisms. Professors Robert K. Root, Theodore M. Greene, W. B. C. Watkins, and Edward L. Hubler, Dr. Carlos H. Baker, and Mr. Robert H. Super, all of Princeton, and Professor Hoyt H. Hudson of Stanford University and Ensign E. D. H. Johnson, U.S.N.R., have read portions of the manuscript. Dr. James M. Osborn of Yale University kindly allowed me to see his still unpublished bibliography of Hellenism in England, especially of travels in Greece.

The staffs of the British Museum, the Bodleian Library, the Harvard College Library, and, above all, the Princeton University Library gave their usual kind assistance. To the Graduate College at Princeton University I owe a year as a Charlotte Elizabeth Procter Fellow, during which a considerable portion of the reading was done.

The special circumstances under which this work was finally prepared for publication deserve mention. When I was suddenly sent to Northern Ireland on military service, with only telegraphic warning, Dr. Allen T. Hazen, then of the Yale University Library, accepted the burden of supervising the final revisions of the manuscript and of helping with the proof. Most of the labor in connection with the illustrations fell to him, too. My sisters, Misses Elizabeth and Catherine Larrabee, teachers of English literature and the classics in East Hartford High School, spent many vacation hours on the manuscript and the proofs and attended to numerous other matters in my absence. Professor Osgood increased my debt to him by helping with the proof and in other ways. I wish to thank also the staff of Columbia University Press, especially Mr. Henry H. Wiggins and Miss Thelma Sargent, for their intelligent and patient solution of the peculiar problems created by an author in the Army.

STEPHEN A. LARRABEE

Camp Barkeley, Texas
September, 1942

CONTENTS

ILLUSTRATIONS

I. POETS AND SCULPTURE

> Medici manuscripts have told of places
> Where common sense was wedded to the graces,
> Doric temples and olive-trees and such,
> But broken marble no longer goes for much.

SO LOUIS MACNEICE has written in explaining why W. H. Auden and he chose some years ago to visit Iceland rather than the shores of the Mediterranean in search of 'both poetry and pleasure.[1] Broken—or, for that matter, unbroken—marble of Greece and Rome apparently "goes for" little among contemporary poets. Yet MacNeice's phrase "no longer" rightly indicates that in the past ancient marbles went for a very great deal among the poets. With the "much" that Greek sculpture has meant to English poets, particularly in the Romantic period, this study is concerned.

The poetry which in some measure takes its origin from the finished works of the fine arts is somewhat unusual and specialized poetry, perhaps. But who shall say that poets may not be inspired by statues ànd paintings as well as by sunrises, daffodils, or deserted lovers? Furthermore, who can confidently assert what the poetic potentiality or content of any object is, or arbitrarily announce what use poets can, or should, make of works of art in other media?

From the history of literature it is clear that, while most poets have been moved to write primarily by the infinitely varied feelings and activities of mankind and by "nature" (mountains, fringed gentians, nightingales, and so forth), a surprisingly large number of them have also drawn inspiration from paintings, statues, books, and buildings. Moreover, separate works by an individual poet have variously sprung from his physical surroundings, his observation and com-

[1] *Letters from Iceland* (1937), p. 33. Throughout the text and notes the place of publication of all books is London, unless some other reference is given.

mentary upon himself and other human beings, his sense of relationship to supernatural powers, and his pride and delight in the cultural achievements of man, such as man's communal institutions and the fine arts. The materials for the present book belong almost entirely to the last-named source of poetic inspiration.

The amount of interest in Greek sculpture among English poets from the time when the ancient masterpieces began to be known until the present, but above all in the Romantic period, constitutes a literary phenomenon worthy of extended consideration. Some of the poetry inspired by sculpture, as well as by the other fine arts, is, to be sure, merely the verse of the artist and of the man of taste or connoisseur—the commonplaces of the studio and the cant of the critic and dilettante presented in more or less metrical form. In all but the most "art-less" ages there will probably be some verses of this nature. In England "learned" poetry dealing with sculpture appeared most often in the eighteenth and nineteenth centuries. The interest in Greek sculpture among English poets has come in part, as we shall see, from other than literary considerations.

On the other hand, many of the important poets, since the late seventeenth century in particular, have been seriously attracted to and inspired by ancient Greek sculpture. Taken all together, they have produced a considerable body of poetry associated with the Antique. The significance of that poetry for both critic and reader resides, of course, not in the number of lines, but in the pleasure and in the understanding of poetry which may come from studying the responses of poets to works of art in another medium. The appreciation of the relationship between a poet's "experience" of Greek sculpture and his finished poetry demands a careful analysis of his temperament, tastes, and achievements, in themselves and in respect to the spirit of the age in which he wrote.

One recognizes, too, at the outset that little is to be learned about the Greek masterpieces from examining English poetry, since the dissemination of information about any art or special skill is scarcely the function of poetry. For example, who wishes to listen to a poet paraphrasing a handbook of art? In the seventeenth century, to be sure, a number of English poets versified what they knew concerning the statues of Greece and Rome, by common consent the greatest works of art in existence. Nevertheless, their accounts were of necessity limited and sketchy. Then, too, certain poets of the eighteenth century revealed glimmerings of a historical sense. The same may be said of such Romantic poets as Wordsworth, Coleridge, Shelley, and Landor. Yet none of them showed what approaches an adequate conception of the different periods of Greek sculpture. For these poets, moreover, an acquaintance with Greek sculpture could include only a fraction of the works on which is based our encyclopedic knowledge of the arts of antiquity and of the various movements and schools in the gradual mastery of materials and techniques and in the expression of anatomical form and inward sentiment.

To the poets treated in this book the Antique signified, rather, a few works seen in galleries (often in copies) or in prints, or the aggregate of ancient statues lumped together somewhat uncritically as a kind of abstract and vaguely Platonic Idea of Grecian statuary. To the poets in England, up to and including the Romantic period, Greek sculpture therefore meant either the individual statues, reliefs, or vases which excited feelings and thoughts to be put into verse, or else all the ancient statuary of Greece as a unified body of works expressing Beauty. The qualities associated with that enticing abstraction were varied: the "breathing life" or counterfeit of nature admired by medieval and Renaissance poets; "the affections of the mind" sought in the seventeenth century; the Grecian purity and simplicity of eighteenth-century taste; in aesthetics of the Romantic period, the spiritual impulse shining through external appearances. Greek sculpture was the Venus de Medici, the Apollo Belvedere, the Elgin Theseus; or it was

> the marble fairness of old Greece;

or

> those permanent and perfect forms,
> Those characters of heroes and of gods,
> Which from the crude materials of the world,
> Their [the sculptors'] own high minds created;

or

> The intelligible forms of ancient poets,
> The fair humanities of old religion.

In writing of specific statues and of the Idea of Grecian sculpture, the poets revealed a good deal about themselves and the ages in which they lived. Their evaluations of works of art, which generations of poets, critics, and gentlemen have thought to be among the best things made by human hands, inevitably showed more about their own standards and values than about the sculptures. Their responses to Grecian statues agreed with their intellectual and aesthetic views. Hence, in all but a few cases poets found in ancient sculpture the qualities which they admired elsewhere. Since the Grecian works early became symbols of the perfection of the artistic power, poets discovered in them what they considered the characteristics of all great art, however far those qualities might be from the original purpose or significance of the sculptures or from the accounts in books of reference.

In the tradition of interest in Greek sculpture among English poets through the Romantic period, the most significant trend was the gradual increase in the personal and emotional and imaginative—that is, poetic—response. From the Renaissance to the early nineteenth century the concern of the poets with Grecian statuary exhibited the shifting of interest from description to interpretation; from admiration of counterfeits of nature to speculation on Ideal Beauty; from disquisitions on the best proportions of the Grecian models to considerations of the "inner meaning" or significance of the ancient forms. The Renaissance and eighteenth-century poets praised the Laocoön, the Venus de Medici, the Apollo Belvedere, and the Antinous. To those works of "fine proportions" and Ideal Beauty some of the Romantic poets added the Parthenon figures, though one of the curiosities in the history of taste, as it is related to poetry, was the failure of the Elgin Marbles to elicit poetry from other poets than Keats and Landor and a few minor Romantics.

The poet's approach to the finished works of another art through his emotions is obviously not that of the archaeologist, the historian

of art, or the critic. As the imaginative presentation and interpretation of emotional experience, poetry must express the sensations
and thoughts aroused either by a single work of art or by the Idea
of an art. Yet the poet is neither a critic nor a historian of art. His
historical and critical senses (so far as he possesses them) will be in
abeyance, to a great extent, in the poem, or at least during the experience giving rise to the poem. This fact does not prevent the poet from
studying and perhaps writing formal or "technical" criticism of the
arts in his letters or essays or, it may be, in his verse. In such activity,
however, he is for the time being primarily not a poet. One may
admit, too, that poetry is a kind of criticism—even of a most subtle
nature sometimes—without going to the extreme of Baudelaire,
who said, "The best account of a picture [or of any work of art?]
would be a sonnet or an elegy." [2]

The poet's interest in Greek sculpture as the stimulus or material
of poetry is of much the same character as his poetic interest in other
works of art. To the poet, painting is not an encyclopedia of men
and schools but Titian's Bacchus and Ariadne or the "power" of
painting as a whole; architecture is not a handbook of styles and
influences but King's College Chapel or the principle of design;
and poetry is not the *Cambridge History of English Literature* but
Lycidas or the "spirit" of Poesy. The great masters in all the arts
influence other artists similarly. Shakespeare, for example, is not the
Variorum but Cleopatra or passages like "The lunatic, the lover, and
the poet" or *Romeo and Juliet;* or he is an idea, Shakespeare plain,
Shakespeare stripped of the bobs and trinkets of criticism about his
historical-comical-tragical-pastoral stages.

Since the sculpture of the Greeks is, then, a field for the emotional
and imaginative activity of poets, one wonders that critics like R. H.
Wilenski refer disparagingly to Keats's use of Greek statues as "emotive fragments." [3] How else, one is tempted to inquire, is the poet to
use the works of other artists? Unless a statue is emotive, that is,
unless it arouses the emotions and stimulates the imagination of

[2] See Frank P. Chambers, *The History of Taste* (New York, 1932), p. 150.
[3] See *The Modern Movement in Art* (1927), p. 184.

the beholder, how can it lead to a poem? Yet if an imaginative presentation of an emotional experience is regarded as constituting the first essential, at least, of poetry, and if the poet's acquaintance with sculpture is often slight, inadequate, and based on inferior works, would it not be wiser for poets to leave Greek sculpture to the specialists? That, for good or ill, the English poets have been unwilling to do—until the twentieth century at least. As Mr. Mac-Neice suggests, classical marble has gone "for much," and the sensations and thoughts evoked by antique works surviving as "emotive fragments" have found their way into many English poems.

The poet who responds to Greek sculpture and then uses it in his poetry may follow several procedures. First, he may give a rather unemotional or factual account of certain figures that he knows and that are popular at the time. In this spirit Samuel Rogers in 1802 wrote a sonnet on the Torso Belvedere, which had long been admired by connoisseurs, partly on account of its fame as "the school of Michelangelo." Such use of works of sculpture frequently reflects the poet's virtuosity, vanity, or pedantry; the naming of works and artists indicates that the poet is in touch with the latest fashion.

Again, the poet may include references to Greek sculpture in order to furnish information to readers—a purpose not truly poetic, to be sure, but one to which poets have often devoted their abilities. In the "Age of Enlightenment," in particular, poetry was often a substitute for textbooks, of sculpture as well as of other arts and sciences. Learning itself was popularized, and poets lent their aid by versifying the "progress" of the arts in numerous "essays," odes, and epistles. Thomson's *Liberty* (1734–36) and Hayley's *Essay on Sculpture* (written at the very close of the eighteenth century and published in 1800) were two important examples of the "progress-pieces." Poetry with information about the arts continued to appear in the nineteenth century, though it was neither so frequent nor so characteristic an element in the poetry of that century.

When poets in England began to reflect interest in the recovery of ancient statues in Renaissance Italy, their descriptions of antiques were rather slight. For poets in the Elizabethan period and through-out the seventeenth century, Grecian statuary signified little more than the names of a few works and artists. The refinement of taste in England in the seventeenth century—seen in the encouragement of the arts by the Stuarts, the classicizing tendencies of Ben Jonson and Inigo Jones, the collecting of works of art by gentlemen, the increase in travel on the Continent, and, in the last third of the century, the adoption of the theories of the French and Italian Academies by English virtuosos and critics—prepared the way, however, for numer-ous references in poetry to the Antique during the flood of connois-seurship in the next century.

Indeed, the Augustan and Academic poets of the eighteenth cen-tury versified a considerable amount of rather technical and theoretical information concerning the process and history of sculpture, especially in Greece. The least poetic accounts of sculpture in these treatises, perhaps, appeared in Erasmus Darwin's *Botanic Garden* (1789–91) and in Hayley's *Essay on Sculpture,* already mentioned, where one seeks in vain for anything suggesting an imaginative or personal feeling for sculpture. As a matter of fact, the didactic intention of the majority of the poets of the eighteenth century, the desire to impart information, oppressed all but the hardiest of their number. Their descriptive and didactic poetry is tolerable today only in so far as the poets were able to add emotive elements to the information or to associate the arts with larger issues of morality, politics, and aesthetics which were emotive. The poetry came, not from the show of knowledge of ancient artists and works, but from the feeling for the beauty of Greco-Roman statues both as figures of ideal propor-tions and abstract perfection and as high points in the history of hu-man skill in the arts and "sciences."

In the treatise-poetry of the eighteenth century, and particularly in the poems dealing with the progress of the arts, the best writing on the statuary of Greece—by Thomson in *Liberty* and by Akenside in *The Pleasures of the Imagination* (1744)—sprang, moreover, from actual sight of works of art. In England there was a marked increase in the emotional and imaginative response, when early in the eighteenth century Pope and Thomson began to look at genuinely classical representations of divinities and heroes. Earlier, of course, there had inevitably been some emotive elements in the poetry which was in some measure associated with the Antique. Poets like Chaucer and Marlowe, with but small knowledge of classical statues, had sometimes caught the feeling of statuary from literary accounts, both ancient and modern. Yet the poetic use of specific works of Grecian statuary waited upon the widespread acquaintance with the Antique among readers, critics, and poets in the eighteenth century. Then and even more conspicuously in the Romantic period the best poetry served both poet and reader as a kind of substitute for actual sight of statuary.

In attempting to give the equivalent of seeing works of sculpture, the poet may describe the appearance of a statue, relief, or vase; or he may disclose the sensations, emotions, and thoughts aroused in him by the work of sculpture; or he may strive to re-create the work of art in what may be termed "imaginatively sculptured" poetry. The three processes are distinguished with difficulty, and it is unlikely that many poets ever concern themselves with such distinctions. Still, in writing of Greek sculpture the poets discussed in this book were following one or more of the suggested processes.

Most frequently the poet combines the first two processes, mingling descriptive details and the "adventures" of his soul with respect to a masterpiece. Description and soul-adventures are so closely linked, apparently, in the workings of human minds that divorcing them is not easy. Nevertheless, their felicitous union is even more rare, perhaps, since a poet inevitably tends either to stress the external or formal characteristics of a statue (whether presented in a matter-of-fact spirit or with emotive and figurative coloring) or to pour forth his own sensations and, it may be, to embroider the life he imagines to exist in the sculpture.

None the less, when a poet endeavors to show in his poetry the inspiration he has derived from works of art in his own or in another medium (and, it may be added, from the specialized knowledge of any particular craft or field of learning), his ideal should be neither the informational or impressionistic description nor the parade of personal sensations, reflections, and fancies, but the imaginative re-creation of sculpture. In the activity of re-creation—which may also be regarded as the attempt to create sculpture in the medium of poetry—description and soul-adventures will be present in varying degrees. Since the reader must know what a work of sculpture, introduced into a poem, looks like, a certain amount of description is required. In the best poems, however, the details are used less for themselves than for their share in the unity of the complete work.

On the other hand, elaborate fancies about a hypothetical "life" belonging to the subject of a statue, or sentimental confessions as to the poet's sensations as he gazed upon a statue, or revelations of "what the Venus de Medici means to me," aid little in the re-creation of sculpture. Instead, such reverie and exhibitionism almost always draw the poet's energies from the object he is trying to re-create. Ideally, therefore, the finished poetic sculpture, adequately visualized either by description or by suggestion but free from soul-adventures which lead one from the work of art, is allowed to reveal its sculptural qualities. In the most successful Romantic poetry where works of Greek sculpture appear—in the "Ode on a Grecian Urn" and in certain lines and passages in the poetry of Byron, Shelley, Landor, and Hunt as well as in that of Keats—the re-created sculpture speaks for itself. In other words, the poet's "experience," including his criticism, of a work of sculpture is shown in the re-created poetic sculpture as a unified presence or feeling of statuesque or sculpturesque qualities, rather than in lengthy description and irrelevant reveries and fancies.

When a poet experiences sculpture emotionally and then re-creates it imaginatively in poetry, the specific works which stimulated his activity may recede into the background and become somewhat incidental. The "Ode on a Grecian Urn" is probably as close as any Romantic—or, for that matter, any English—poem to the ideal of poetic sculpture; yet even there Keats indulged his fondness for exhibiting his personal sensations in the cadenza-like departure from sculpture of the third stanza. In his envious rehearsal of the imagined "happy, happy love" of the figures on the urn, the poet almost lost sight of the actual object. The reader feels, however, that the cadenza of personal feeling represented an essential element in the sculptural quality which Keats had apprehended in gazing on Grecian urns and statues and, consequently, wished to convey in his poetic and imaginative re-creation.

Quite another kind of emotional response appears in poems where the poet may be said to "take off" almost at once from the sculpture, which is but the means of starting him on a flight of fancy and reflection. Byron presents excellent examples of such operatic arias: in a serious and semi-ecstatic vein in the *Childe Harold* report of the intoxication with beauty which came over him as he beheld the Venus de Medici; in a humorous and satirical spirit in *The Curse of Minerva,* where he pictured English maidens eyeing the heroic anatomies of the Parthenon figures in what he chose to call Lord Elgin's "stone shop."

A twentieth-century example of a similar emotionalizing of Grecian statuary may be cited here for the contrast with both Keats and Byron. In "Canons of Giant Art," written as "a kind of school of my poetical emotions," Sacheverell Sitwell undertook to see what he could do with the Farnese Hercules, the Laocoön, and the Hermes of Praxiteles, despite his "profound horror" for two of those once-admired works.[4] After reading such a confession, one is hardly surprised when Mr. Sitwell's experimental toyings with variations (mainly of horror) on a sculptural theme turn out less successfully than either Byron's presentation of the adventures of Childe Harold's sentimental soul or Keats's re-creation of the Grecian urn.

The use of Greek sculpture in figurative passages is another kind of poetic re-creation to which some attention may be given, since a number of English poets have turned to the Antique as a source of imagery. In an age when a relatively large number of readers, critics, and artists are familiar with ancient art, one may expect poets to draw images from Grecian statuary. In the Augustan age, for ex-

[4] See *The Cyder Feast and Other Poems* (1927), p. 90.

ample, every cultivated gentleman was aware of the grace of the Venus de Medici. Accordingly Thomson could pose his Musidora in *The Seasons* (1730) with the words, "So stands the statue that enchants the world," and feel confident that his readers would visualize the celebrated effort of the goddess to shield her beauties from curious eyes. In *Prometheus Unbound* nearly a century later, Shelley could refer to "Praxitelean shapes" with the expectation that his audience had at least some conception of what differentiated figures by Praxiteles from those by Phidias.

Images from sculpture may be set pieces or purple patches or conceits elaborated for their own sakes, as in the case of Thomson's Venus in *The Seasons* or Byron's picture of Zuleika in *The Bride of Abydos* as "a younger Niobe." Again, they may be carefully woven into the fabric of a poem, as was usually the case with the relief-like figures in Shelley's poetry or with Landor's sculpturesque passages. They frequently appear as extended similes or metaphors, while on occasion they are important in the more general way of aiding poets in the "stationing" of figures or in achieving sculptural qualities. Poets as different as Pope and Shelley, Addison and Keats, Blake and Byron posed or "stationed" figures under the inspiration of the Antique. The work of Addison, Pope, Collins, Keats, Landor, and Shelley presents, at times, a sculptural feeling as well as passages of sculpturesque decoration.

The merit of an image from sculpture depends, moreover, not on the accidental fame of the statue or vase which inspired the poet, but on the context of the figure in the poem. In judging the effectiveness of imagery derived from Greek sculpture, one must analyze the several figurative passages as he analyzes imagery from other realms of experience. The statues inspiring imagery need not be well-known works, since a poet may create an image from an unfamiliar work of sculpture which has made a striking impression upon his imagination and emotions. Unless the poet specifically names, either in letters and journals or in the poetry itself, the works of sculpture which he admires and studies, the precise works which influence him may be difficult to identify. The reader with a fondness for tracking down specific sources finds his task complicated by problems of iconography.

As the Antique became more widely known to cultivated Englishmen during the seventeenth century, critics and writers on matters of taste and culture also recommended sculpture to poets as a source of imagery. As early as 1622 Henry Peacham in *The Compleat Gentleman* pointed out "the uses of statue-craft" to poets as well as to artists and gentlemen. In general, though, English poets waited until theorists of the late seventeenth-century Academies had persuasively maintained the sisterhood of the arts of poetry, painting, and sculpture. The Horatian *Ut pictura poesis,* which had induced poets for at least a century to consider the kinship between poetry and painting, may be said to have been extended to include sculpture.

Dryden reflected the growing interest in sculpture by describing, in the Preface to *Annus Mirabilis* (1667), different kinds of poetic imagery in terms borrowed from sculpture. Addison suggested, in his poetical *Dialogues upon Ancient Medals* (1721), that the study of poetry, painting, and sculpture "may serve as comments on each other." Pope approved Addison's study of the "affinity of coins and poetry" in lines which echoed down the eighteenth century:

> The verse and sculpture bore an equal part,
> And Art reflected images to Art.

Pope's praise of Addison encouraged other poets to store their minds with imagery derived from classical sculpture as well as literature. Thomson explicitly confessed that in Italy he set out to gather material for poetry by studying how the arts "reflect light and images to one another." Within a few years after the death of Milton, his poetry, too, began to remind connoisseurs of the Antique, and a number of critics, both in the eighteenth century and in the Romantic period, expressed a similar appreciation of the statuesque qualities of Milton's poetry. The taste for Grecian simplicity, which supplanted Roman elegance in the middle of the eighteenth century, led poets like Collins to aim at a sculptural simplicity.

In the Romantic period as well, poets and critics often illustrated the poetical process by references to sculpture. Coleridge, Hunt, Hazlitt, and De Quincey sometimes stated their criticism of poetry and drama, both ancient and modern, in the language of the sculptor's art. Among the Romantic poets who looked to sculpture for principles to follow in their poetry, Shelley, Keats, and Landor profited most. Shelley sought to discover in the plastic arts of sculpture and painting (but especially in the former) "the rules according to which, that ideal beauty, of which we have so intense yet so obscure an apprehension, is realized in ideal forms." Under the tutelage of Haydon and Hazlitt, Keats learned from the Elgin Marbles as well as from ancient and modern poets lessons in the "stationing" or "statuary" of poetry in the grand style. Landor strove to achieve sculptural feelings of coldness and grandeur in many of his poems.

Of course, the poets who strove to produce the feeling or presence of sculpture through the means of rhythm and language and imagery undertook no easy labor. Yet a number of English poets have approximated sculpture with considerable success, and they have conveyed in poetry some of the qualities which they felt in ancient marbles—both the more "classical" nobility and repose and simplicity admired by eighteenth-century poets and by Landor, and the more "romantic" activity and energy and emotive richness sought by Shelley, Hunt, Byron, and Keats.

Finally, the attempt to re-create sculpture imaginatively in poetry, though more difficult than the mere description of a work of art or the reporting of soul-adventures, is the better part of poetic wisdom. In part this is true because the factual description and the soul-adventures inspired by a specific statue are likely to lose interest when another type of statuary wins popular esteem. For example, both Hayley's factual descriptions of the Greco-Roman figures in *An Essay on Sculpture* and Byron's soul-adventures as he beheld those Academic favorites in *Childe Harold* receive scant notice today, when archaic and fifth-century sculpture of Greece is in favor.

The poetic or imaginative re-creation of sculpture, however, challenges the attention of readers on poetic grounds alone. Even when one knows more about Greek sculpture than the poets of the early nineteenth century could possibly know, one may still enjoy their poetic re-creations. An imaginative response to sculpture, like that of Keats or Landor or Shelley, which reveals itself in a moving poem, never goes out of date. Nor can their re-creations of sculpture in poetry be discarded merely because certain works have gone out of fashion.

The efforts of such Romantic poets as Keats, Landor, and Shelley to create sculptural feeling in the medium of poetry represent the most subtle and, on properly aesthetic grounds, the most significant influence of Greek sculpture upon English poetry. Yet these poetic and aesthetic considerations fail to take into account other important elements which English poets have found in Grecian marbles. For the sculpture of Greece often meant, as has already been hinted in connection with the treatise-poetry of the eighteenth century, other things than poetic re-creations of statues or sculptural imagery. Indeed, almost as soon as the antique works were known, they collected about themselves a cluster of "ideas" concerning sculpture, its origin and progress, and its place among the arts and sciences. For convenience the "ideas" associated with Greek sculpture may be divided into four groups: "ideas" related to the theory of art, history, morality, and political and social ideals. Though of secondary importance to the critic of poetry today, these "ideas" seem to have interested many poets quite as much as the aesthetic attributes of the ancient statues.

In the first place, many English poets sought to explain the nature of the processes of art by reference to what they conceived to have been the practice of the Greek sculptors. Apparently the ancient statues have always been regarded by some poets at least—in this book from Thomas of Britain to Wordsworth—as counterfeits of nature or breathing stones. Again, poets, particularly in the late seventeenth century and in the eighteenth century, when rules were sought for all the arts, have seen in Grecian statuary the best proportions of art, masterpieces possessing a beauty drawn from many individuals in order to produce a perfection not found in any single model. Moreover, sculpture represented the enduring existence which the sculptors had given to their conceptions: the statue was the concrete manifestation of the idea-in-the-mind; and the sculptor was philosophical to the extent that he had converted marble into thought, or, in other words, had expressed his thoughts in stone. Therefore the poets analyzed the methods and intentions of the sculptors who had endowed significant moments from their experience with lasting life in stone in works of an abstract and mental beauty. Poets often envied both the skill and the medium of the creators of works of art which had survived as long as had the Antique. In general, however, they were loyal to their own art, which they felt was more expressive than sculpture.

Theory led, of course, to the consideration of the history of Greek sculpture so far as it was known: the early beginnings in Egypt and elsewhere; the refinement in "artful" Greece under the guiding spirit of Liberty; the migration to Rome, which in turn departed from the genius of Freedom; the centuries of Gothic darkness; and the recovery of classical statuary and the rebirth of the arts in the Revival of Learning or Renaissance. In this partly philosophical view of history the fostering spirit of the poetical or artistic faculties was Liberty.

Theory and history were related, moreover, to morality in the broadest sense, that is, to general principles of morals and ethics. Through Neo-Platonic "ideas" in particular the English poets often wrote of the moral aspects and values of sculpture and other arts. Beautiful or harmonious forms teach men beauty: there are sermons in sculptured stones. Through an aesthetic morality poets sometimes turned from the exterior form to the harmonious spirit or inner form. As Shaftesbury, who contributed more than any other Englishman to this element in the tradition of interest in Grecian statuary, remarked, "Who can admire the *outward* Beautys, and not recur instantly to the *inward,* which are the most real and essential, the most naturally affecting?" [5]

The poets who were thoroughgoing Platonists felt that a statue leads the beholder from the material object to the higher realm of

[5] *First Characteristicks* (1711), III, 185.

intellectual beauty; as an expression of abstract beauty a statue leads one from physical beauty to the essential or inner harmony and spiritual loveliness. Thus the Grecian sculptors were thought to have been wielders of great moral powers. Particularly in the Romantic period English poets analyzed the intimate connection between the forms and the religious beliefs of ancient Greece. From seeing how the Grecian artists had given life to their gods and heroes—

> not yet dead,
> But in old marbles ever beautiful—

many an English poet felt the desire to emulate the ancient masters. Through creating forms of mental or abstract or spiritual beauty, poet and sculptor could produce works which might resist the ravages of time.

Finally, morality, history, and the theory of art reflected the condition of society as a whole: beautiful forms in art and society make men more beautiful and also better, and vice versa. Greece, where the masterpieces of sculpture had been produced, became for many English poets an ideal state. Sculpture had flourished under the Grecian way of living. It had been encouraged by the free spirit of the political institutions, by the religion which utilized the service of artists in honoring the gods, and by the cult of physical perfection in athletics and festival games. Poets pictured an ideal Greece, where the arts and society had been inseparably linked and where the Greeks had imbibed, as it were, a spirit of beauty from the sculptured forms everywhere about them. Sculpture came to be considered the characteristic art of classical antiquity, and the Greeks a people as heroically beautiful as their statues.

Stated first rather tentatively in the seventeenth century, these "ideas" of theory, morality, history, and society spread in unnumbered ways through the thought of the eighteenth century. Critics and philosophers like Shaftesbury, Winckelmann, and their followers disseminated these "ideas" throughout Europe, while poets converted them into verse. Thus they became the bases of the Hellenism of the early nineteenth century, when Romantic poets, under the influence of the Antique, treated the large body of "ideas" about Greek and its sculpture more imaginatively and poetically than the earlier English poets.

For many reasons, then, Grecian marbles went "for much" among English poets, not only as works of art to be described and re-created and studied for poetic imagery, but also as focal points from which radiated "ideas" concerning the history and theory of sculpture and its relation to morality, religion, and social and political institutions and ideals.

II. THE EARLY POETS

THE TWELFTH CENTURY: DALLIANCE
WITH A DEMON THING

WHEN GREGORY THE GREAT beheld the white bodies and the fair complexions of the young Britons brought to Rome about 587 to be sold in the slave market in the Forum, the Venerable Bede reports him as having exclaimed, " 'Alas! alas! that beings with such bright faces should be slaves of the prince of darkness! that with outward form so lovely the mind should be sick and void of inward grace.' " [1] For one of exceeding piety his response was strangely aesthetic, and his remark suggests the language which many an English poet has used in describing the beauty of statues and images like the figures Gregory himself so avidly destroyed. Deciding that the attractive young pagans with angelic faces "should be co-heirs with the angels in heaven," the churchman shortly sent missionaries to England, where many Angles and Saxons accepted the Christian beliefs.

Today one would give much to know the other side of the story. What, for example, were the thoughts of the lovely but benighted Angles in the Roman city? With what feelings did they behold monuments surviving from classical antiquity? As the years passed, other Northerners went to Italy; and the picture of the visitors from the Gothic North discovering classical remains in Mediterranean countries gives ample scope to the play of the imagination. Among the Northern migrants were chieftains with barbarian tribes, Irish monks on missionary tasks, crusading knights and pilgrims marching to shrines throughout Christendom, kings and churchmen on business of church and state. What, indeed, did these medieval people feel

[1] *Ecclesiastical History of England*, ed. Dudden, Book II, chap. i.

and think when they encountered the Forum, the Pillar of Trajan, and other remains in Greece and Asia Minor?

Such a theme stirred the historically minded poets of the nineteenth century, who liked to tell what the Goths themselves had failed to relate. Felicia Hemans in "Alaric in Italy," and, following her, Matthew Arnold in *Alaric in Rome* went back to the early Middle Ages in order to show the boorish and crude Goths in classic surroundings. The lady-poetaster rose to the occasion with glowing lines:

> Oh! not for them hath genius given
> To Parian stone the fire of heaven,
> Enshrining in the forms he wrought
> A bright eternity of thought.
> In vain the natives of the skies
> In breathing marble round them rise,
> And sculptured nymphs of fount or glade
> People the dark-green laurel shade;
> Cold are the conqueror's heart and eye
> To visions of divinity;
> And rude his hand that dares deface
> The models of immortal grace (ll. 87–98).

Richard Monckton Milnes, Lord Houghton, set the action later in the Middle Ages in "The Northern Knight in Italy," a poem taken from an essay by Heine. In Keatsian lines Milnes wrote of a knight stumbling upon a ruined temple with a "glorious image" of Venus. In the forest at midnight he found her shrine and submitted to this *belle dame sans merci*. Falling asleep, the knight enjoyed visions of old Greece until his northern home and his Christian mother praying for him rose before his eyes. One blow of his sword, and he awoke to find himself alone with the head he had cut from the statue. Northward he hurried to happiness at home.[2]

From such representative nineteenth-century attempts to present

[2] In *Poems, Legendary and Historical* (1844 ed., pp. 18 ff.). Milnes wrote an interesting essay on "The Goddess Venus in the Middle Ages," followed by "The Northern Knight in Italy" and "Venus and the Christian Knight." In the latter he employed a Coleridgean ballad for a free paraphrase of the Tannhäuser legend. For Heine's treatments of this legendary material, see *Elementargeister, Salon III*, in *Sämtliche Werke* (Leipzig, 1910–15), VII, 407 ff.

the medieval reaction to classical sculpture, fortunately one can turn to a few records surviving from the Middle Ages. During two periods, especially, of what used to be termed the Dark Ages—the flowering of humanism in Charlemagne's court at Aachen in the ninth century and the renaissance of the twelfth and thirteenth centuries in western Europe—historians have shown that there was considerable interest in classical matters, even including the arts. In the Carolingian renaissance, for example, Einhard is reputed to have made a collection of works of antique art, an undertaking in which he may have been aided by the learned Alcuin from York. In regard to the indebtedness of Carolingian artists to the ancients, Hinks remarks that "the humanism of antique art is taken over by the medieval artist for its expressive value, not for its power of creating an illusion." [3] In stressing thus the "expressive value" in ancient art, these medieval artists suggest the response of the English Romantic poets, because Carolingian artist and English poet admired the perfect forms of ancient art less for their beauty of appearance than for the meaning they could read in them.

In the renaissance of the twelfth century one comes upon more significant material to compare with the use of Grecian statuary by later poets. The first English writer to give what approaches an adequate reflection of his feelings about works of ancient sculpture was William of Malmesbury, who had a poetic spirit though he was not a poet: Into his Latin *Chronicle of the Kings of England* (*c.*1125) the imaginative monk introduced several pages about Rome and its antiquities. Familiar with the learning of the day, William incorporated into his history a famous poem by one of the best poets of the Middle Ages, an elegy on Rome by Hildebert of Lavardin. Late in the eleventh century the Christian poet mourned the decay of Rome and reflected, in a fashion suggesting Du Bellay, Petrarch, and Spenser in the Renaissance, on the mutability which had changed the splendid buildings of antiquity into the ruins he saw about him. His

[3] See Roger Hinks, *Carolingian Art* (1935), pp. 105 ff., 210, and Christopher Dawson, *The Making of Europe* (1937), pp. 222 ff.; for the later period, see the classic work by Charles H. Haskins, *The Renaissance of the Twelfth Century* (Cambridge, Mass., 1927).

feeling, however, was essentially medieval rather than Renaissance, for he felt no admiration of the ruins as ruins and no desire for their restoration. Rather, in the second part of the elegy he gloried in Christian Rome and looked upon the ancient remains as "specimens of 'Vanity'—signal examples of divine chastisement." [4] Yet Hildebert felt there was nothing like the statues he saw in Rome:

> Here gods themselves their sculptur'd forms admire,
> And only to reflect those forms aspire;
> Nature unable such like gods to form,
> Left them to man's creative genius warm;
> Life breathes within them, and the suppliant falls,
> Not to the God, but statues in the walls.

Suppliants bowing to statues in the walls marked a great change from the time of Constantine, who had showed "the image of heathen deities to excite the contempt of the beholders." [5]

The specific statues which inspired French poet and English chronicler about 1100 with sentiments so unexpected will never be known; yet about this time was written the medieval prototype of a Baedeker for Rome, the *Mirabilia urbis Romae,* which gave information concerning the classical monuments and works of art to be seen in the capital of Christendom. More important in the present study was the description of Rome written late in the twelfth or early in the thirteenth century by one Master Gregory, probably an Englishman. [6] Writing with a kind of hostility toward churchmen like Gregory

---

[4] W. S. Heckscher, "Relics of Pagan Antiquity in Mediaeval Settings," *Journal of Warburg Institute,* I (1938), 208.

[5] *Chronicle of the Kings of England,* ed. J. A. Giles (1911), pp. 367–73. See also B. Haureau, *Les Mélanges poetiques d'Hildebert de Lavardin* (Paris, 1882), pp. 59 ff.; Helen Waddell, *The Wandering Scholars* (1927), p. 99; F. J. E. Raby, *History of Christian Latin Poetry* (1927), pp. 266 ff., and *A History of Secular Latin Poetry* (1934), I, 324; Friedrich von Bezold, *Das Fortleben der antiken Götter im mittelälterlichen Humanismus* (Bonn and Leipzig, 1922), pp. 46–47; and Percy E. Schramm, *Kaiser, Rom, und Renovatio,* "Studien der Bibliothek Warburg," No. 17 (Leipzig and Berlin, 1929), pp. 296 ff.

[6] See M. R. James, "Magister Gregorius de Mirabilibus Urbis Romae," *Eng. Hist. Rev.,* XXXII (1917), 531–54; G. McN. Rushforth, "Magister Gregorius de Mirabilibus Urbis Romae; a New Description of Rome in the Twelfth Century," *Journal of Roman Studies,* IX (1919), pp. 44–58; and Bezold, *Das Fortleben der antiken Götter im mittelälterlichen Humanismus,* pp. 50 ff.

the Great who destroyed statues, Master Gregory admired in particular a statue of Venus appearing—as Beattie, Byron, and Tennyson
were to figure the goddess—"in the shape in which it is said that she
exhibited herself naked to Paris in venturesome rivalry with Juno
and Pallas." Moreover, the statue of Parian marble was fashioned
with such marvelous and inexplicable skill that the Venus seemed a
living person rather than a statue: "for it bears its nudity like a
person blushing, the form suffused with a reddish glow. And to
those observing carefully blood seems to flow in the snowy countenance of the image." No wonder Master Gregory confessed that
he was drawn—"by I know not what magical power"!—to see the
Venus three times, even though his lodging-place was some two
miles away. He was not the last Englishman to be disturbed by the
mysterious attraction of a nude Venus. His account might come from
a letter written by a gentleman or a poet on a grand tour in the
eighteenth or nineteenth century.

Master Gregory had a twelfth-century brother in spirit in the
Anglo-Norman poet Thomas of Britain, whose *Roman de Tristan*
presumably would have pleased him with its descriptions of Tristan's
Hall of Images. Tristan displayed great skill in carving the figure
of Queen Ysolt:

Under the middes of the vault raised they up an image so beautiful of
stature and countenance that no man beholding it might think otherwise
than that life was in all the limbs, and so fair and so well wrought that
in all the world one might not find a fairer image. . . . No man can show
nor tell the subtlety that was in those images that Tristan let arear within
the vault. And now hath he finished all that he intended in his mind.

His admiration of the statue of his goddess of love—a Venus in all
but name—was Renaissance in fervor:

and ever when he came within before the image of Ysolt, he kissed her
as oft as he came and took her in his embrace and put his arms about her
neck as she had been on live, and with many loving words Tristan re-
hearsed afore the image the joys of great love and their teen and dolors
and pains and woes.[7]

    [7] *The Romance of Tristan and Ysolt by Thomas of Britain*, tr. Roger S. Loomis
(New York, 1923), pp. 218, 220–21. See also *Le Roman de Tristan par Thomas*, ed.

Had the carven image come to life, Tristan would have been almost a medieval Pygmalion. These twelfth-century examples of the admiration of the counterfeiting of nature almost foretell the fondness for exact imitation—the pseudo-Aristotelian "mimesis"—which characterized the appreciation of antique statuary by many Elizabethan and later poets.

To the twelfth century, likewise, belongs the first collection of antique sculptures known to have existed in England. Henry of Blois, Bishop of Winchester and brother of King Stephen, gained a lead of several centuries over the rest of his countrymen in his admiration of classical statuary by acquiring some antique statues on a mission to Rome in 1151 and by transporting them to his cathedral. Like many later English poets and gentlemen, statesmen and scholars, Henry acquired his interest in the Antique on Italian soil. Yet even in the twelfth century there were those who made sport of the collecting of antiques. Someone—very likely the narrator of the incident, who was none other than the erudite John of Salisbury—ridiculed the Bishop for buying idols, in the name of common sense as well as piety, quoting Horace (*Sat.,* II, iii, 64): "Damasippus is a madman for purchasing antique statues." The fate of Henry's marbles is unknown, but other persons in Winchester may have shared his enthusiasm for old statuary. Indeed, the lovely figure of a headless woman, dating from the thirteenth century, now in Winchester Cathedral, makes one wonder whether the sculptor had seen the figures brought back by Bishop Henry.[8]

J. Bédier (Paris, 1902), I, 310 ff. In *Arthurian Legends in Medieval Art* (New York, 1938) the Loomises praise Thomas for giving "enough detail to reconstruct and visualize the image of Queen Ysolt in her carved and colored splendor" (p. 26). To their mention of the Romanesque art as inspiration for Thomas should be added, I believe, the knowledge of classical texts and actual antiques in the twelfth century. Some lines in Euripides (*Alcestis,* ll. 349–53), which Thomas certainly could not have known, offer a parallel worth quoting here.

"ADMETUS. Fashioned by craftsmen's cunning hands, thy form
Imaged, shall lie as sleeping on a bed,
Falling whereon, and clasping with mine hands,
Calling thy name, in fancy shall mine arms
Hold my beloved, though I hold her not." (A. S. Way.)

[8] See *Mon. Germ. Hist. Script.,* XX, 542, and *Hist. Pontif.,* ed. R. L. Poole (1927), pp. 81–82. E. F. Jacob ("Some Aspects of Classical Influence in Mediaeval

With Hildebert writing ardently of images of pagan deities to which men might bow in almost Byronic adoration, and with no less a figure than the Bishop of Winchester importing statuary to adorn his cathedral, one is not surprised at the legends concerning ancient statues that sprang up in the later Middle Ages—legends which were to interest poets again in the nineteenth century, when the conflict between Christian and classical or pagan ideals became an insistent problem for the first time since the classical ideals had triumphed in the Renaissance.

William of Malmesbury again occupies the position of honor because he narrated the earliest version of the legend known as "The Ring of Venus." Among the English writers who later treated the popular story are such diverse authors as Robert Burton, Thomas Moore, and William Morris. The *novella* is too long to quote, but briefly the medieval legend was the following. A group of young Romans were playing ball (usually tennis). In order not to damage a valuable ring, one of them placed it upon the finger of a bronze statue of Venus. When he came for his ring at the end of the sport, he found to his dismay that the Venus had closed her finger: the ring was fast. The young man was in a predicament since the ring was for the bride whom he had wed earlier that very day. Misfortune pursued him when Venus came between him and his wife that night and every succeeding night. After several days he went to a priest, Palumbus, who was able to exorcize the spirit and get the ring returned to the young man. Thus religion was able to conquer the magical or demonic powers in the statue.[9]

England," *England und die Antike, Vorträge der Bibliothek Warburg, 1930–31*, X, 14) mentions Henry's sending his treasures abroad to Cluny, where they seem to have disappeared; yet some of the collection may have been left behind. Of the Winchester statue T. D. Atkinson (*Archaeologia*, LXXXV [1936], 161–62) has remarked, "The drapery has been influenced, I think, by some knowledge of classical sculpture, but the anatomy is purely medieval." He does not mention the Bishop's collection of statuary, which might have furnished hints to the superior medieval sculptor who carved the beautiful female figure.

[9] See *Chronicle of the Kings of England*, pp. 232 ff.; R. M. Milnes, *Poems, Legendary and Historical*, pp. 18–30; S. Baring-Gould, *Curious Myths of the Middle Ages* (1876 ed.), pp. 224 ff.; P. F. Baum, "The Young Man Betrothed to a Statue," *PMLA*, XXXIV (1919), 523–79; Graf, *Roma nella memoria e nelle immaginazione*

The statue of the legend was not a work of beauty of the kind which had attracted Hildebert, the Bishop of Winchester, and Master Gregory, but a thing of evil and an object of fear and wonder. As a work of art it excited no interest; its powers belonged to the realm of black magic rather than of aesthetics. With its supernatural powers of speech and motion and with its human attributes of jealousy and malevolence, the Venus statue was associated with the Pygmalion and Don Juan stories, the Tannhäuser-Venusberg legends, and the mythological and folklore accounts of goddesses, vampires, and sorceresses in love with mortals, as in Keats's *Lamia*. But those inviting bypaths of medieval story cannot be followed here.

CHAUCER AND GOWER: QUEYNTE MANER OF FIGURES OF OLDE WERK

England and northern France were the most important centers of the renaissance of the twelfth century, and they were naturally the "focal point" of the late medieval compiling of information concerning ancient mythology to satisfy the growing interest in classical literature. Two mythographers, at least one of whom was a scholarly Englishman, may be mentioned here among the possible sources of Chaucer and Gower, with whose poetry the tradition of interest in ancient statuary traced in this study may be said to begin. Alexander Neckham (d. 1217) is supposed to have compiled "the conclusive compendium of medieval mythography," the work known as *Mythographus tertius*. Boccaccio used this work, along with ancient writings, for his famous *Genealogia deorum,* and Petrarch employed it "for the description of the sculptural representations of classical divinities which were admired by Scipio in the palace of the African king Syphax." Pierre Bersuire (Berchorius) added Christian coloring in the widely read *Ovide moralisé* in Latin (*c.*1340), and by the end of the fourteenth century some scholar, omitting the moralizations, produced an abridged text of Bersuire's work under

---

del medio evo, II, 388 ff.; Bezold, *Das Fortleben der antiken Götter im mittelälter-lichen Humanismus,* 63 ff.; and G. Huet, "La Légende de la statue de Venus," *Revue de l'histoire des religions,* LXVIII (Paris, 1913), 193 ff.

the title *De deorum imaginibus libellus,* which served as a hand-book of mythology for poets and artists.[10]

When Chaucer was in Italy, in the winter of 1372–73 and again in 1378, very few antique statues had been recovered, though various works of different degrees of classical feeling could be seen. Yet when he wanted to describe the "figures" or "portreitures" or "images" in *The House of Fame* (? 1379–80), *The Parliament of Fowls* (*c.*1380), and *The Knight's Tale* (? 1387–92), Chaucer seems to have turned more often to literary accounts of works of art in Latin, French, and Italian poetry and in medieval handbooks of mythology than to the actual statues, tapestries, and wall-paintings he must have seen. In the fourteenth century—as, indeed, until antique statues became a part of the general knowledge of poets and gentlemen late in the seventeenth century—poets depended primarily on textual descriptions of the "portreiture" of gods and goddesses in poetry, ancient and modern, and in medieval commentaries and encyclopedias. Hence Chaucer decorated his temples with statues and mural decorations based mainly on what Ovid and Virgil, Boccaccio and Guillaume de Lorris, or the author of *De deorum imaginibus* had written; while later poets, like Thomson, Byron, and Shelley, described the statues they saw in Italian galleries, and Keats responded to the Elgin Marbles in the British Museum. Even after the Antique became familiar in the eighteenth century, poets sometimes turned to literary or textual sources; and Keats's early study in Lemprière's *Classical Dictionary* and Tooke's *Pantheon* and Landor's versifying of Plutarch and Pliny, for example, may be said to correspond roughly with Chaucer's probable use of *De deorum imaginibus*. Still, the best poetry on the Antique in the eighteenth and nineteenth centuries sprang from a personal and emotional response at the sight of Grecian statuary—an experience all but denied to earlier poets.

Chaucer's use of literary "sculptures" of classical subjects is well

[10] See Erwin Panofsky and Fritz Saxl, "Classical Mythology in Mediaeval Art," *Metropolitan Museum Studies,* IV, Part 2 (New York, 1933), 255, and Hans Liebeschütz, *Fulgentius metaforalis,* "Studien der Bibliothek Warburg," No. 4 (Leipzig and Berlin, 1926). Both the *Mythographus tertius* and *De deorum imaginibus* were sometimes known as "Albricus."

illustrated in *The Knight's Tale*. To adorn the temples of Venus, Mars, and Diana in the noble theater Theseus had built as the setting for the tournament between Palamon and Arcite, he placed figures of the deities in their oratories and gave especial attention to

> The noble kervyng and the portreitures,
> The shap, the contenaunce, and the figures,
> That weren in thise oratories thre (ll. 1915–17).

The writer of *De deorum imaginibus* announced that *Venus, the loveliest girl, was portrayed nude and swimming in the sea . . . and wore a garland of red and white roses . . . with doves flying round about her. Cupido, her blind and winged son,* was with her, bearing *bow and arrow.* Chaucer transferred the scene into poetry thus:

> The statue of Venus, glorious for to se,
> Was naked, fletynge in the large see,
> And fro the navele doun al covered was
> With wawes grene, and brighte as any glas.
> A citole in hir right hand hadde she,
> And on hir heed, ful semely for to se,
> A rose gerland, fressh and wel smellynge;
> Above hir heed hir dowves flikerynge.
> Biforn hire stood hir sone Cupido;
> Upon his shuldres wynges hadde he two,
> And blynd he was, as it is often seene;
> A bowe he bar and arwes brighte and kene (ll. 1955–66).[11]

This unsculptural or astrological posing of the statue of Venus had already appeared "naked fletynge in a see," in the temple of glass Chaucer described in *The House of Fame* among the

[11] For the passage from *De deorum imaginibus,* chap. v, see Van Staveren, *Auctores mythographi Latini* (Leyden, 1742), or Liebeschütz, *Fulgentius metaforalis,* p. 118. For the account of the gods and goddesses in *Mythographus tertius,* see *Scriptores rerum mythicarum Latini tres,* ed. G. H. Bode (Cellis, 1834), pp. 228 ff. See also T. R. Lounsbury, *Studies in Chaucer* (New York, 1892), II, 381; W. W. Skeat, *The Complete Works of Geoffrey Chaucer* (1894), V, 78; and W. W. Curry, *Chaucer and the Mediaeval Sciences* (1926), p. 150. Professor Robinson (in his edition of Chaucer, p. 778) termed "the account of the temple of Venus . . . a condensed version, with a few additions, of *Teseide,* vii, 53 ff." and also cited the *Aeneid,* i, 446 ff. That Cupid is blind proves that Chaucer had used a source later than the *Mythographus tertius,* either the *Ovide moralisé* or *De deorum imaginibus.*

> . . . curiouse portreytures,
> And queynte maner of figures
> Of olde werk (ll. 125 ff.).[12]

The other two temples in *The Knight's Tale* had similar figures of classical divinities.

> The statue of Mars upon a carte stood
> Armed, and looked grym as he were wood;
>
> . . .
>
> A wolf ther stood biforn hym at his feet
> With eyen rede, and of a man he eet;
> With soutil pencel depeynted was this storie
> In redoutynge of Mars and of his glorie (ll. 2041–42, 2047–50).

The statue showed the Mars of astrology and mythography, in *De deorum imaginibus* a *figure like that of an enraged man . . . sitting in a cart* and *armed with cuirass and other offensive and defensive weapons*.[13] Diana received less attention from the poet:

> In gaude grene hir statue clothed was,
> With bowe in honde, and arwes in a cas (ll. 2079–80).

The mythographer said she was *portrayed in the guise of a matron with her hair unbound,* and *she held a bow and arrow.*[14]

Mural decorations like those in *The Knight's Tale*—Gothic "portreitures" of the antique gods and heroes which were hardly statues at all—were a common convention in medieval poetry. After Chaucer, temples, wall-paintings, and other decorative devices became familiar in English visions and poems of the court of love. Yet Chaucer apparently tried his best to vitalize the convention, carefully choosing characteristic qualities for the ancient authors standing on pillars in

---

If, as seems likely, he used the latter, the date of that work may now be given as no later than 1390.

[12] See Robinson, p. 889, and W. O. Sypherd, *Studies in Chaucer's Hous of Fame* (1907), pp. 80 ff.

[13] *De deorum imaginibus,* chap. iii (Liebeschütz, p. 117). Professor Robinson (p. 779) refers also to *Teseide,* vii, 29–37, and *Thebaid,* vii, 34–73.

[14] *De deorum imaginibus,* chap. vii (Liebeschütz, p. 119). Professor Robinson notes (p. 780) that "the temple of Diana is not described by Boccaccio."

The House of Fame and again for the figures in the temple in *The Parliament of Fowls*. In writing of works of art, like the majority of English poets, he treated the figures as though they were alive, and he left no doubt that he sought vitality or life in "images" and "portreitures." Hence it was that he asserted that Nature surpassed the efforts of the painter and the sculptor, letting Nature challenge man to equal the beauty of Virginia in *The Physician's Tale*.

> "Lo! I, Nature,
> Thus kan I forme and peynte a creature,
> Whan that me list; who kan me countrefete?
> Pigmalion noght, though he ay forge and bete,
> Or grave, or peynte; for I dar wel seyn,
> Apelles, Zanzis, sholde werke in veyn
> Outher to grave, or peynte, or forge, or bete,
> If they presumed me to countrefete" (ll. 11–18).

Many a later English poet, especially in the Renaissance, was to use the names of ancient artists to advance a similar argument.

To describe classical figures then, Chaucer, for lack of genuine antique models on which to draw, turned to poetry, astrology, and mythological handbooks. No wonder Thomas Warton in the eighteenth century commented on the "imageries" in the temple of Mars in *The Knight's Tale* as "the effort of a strong imagination, unacquainted with selection and arrangement of images." [15] In the eighteenth century and later, poets saw representations of the ancient deities as the classical sculptors had carved them. Moreover, few, if any, poets could write a description of Venus or Apollo without thinking of the antiques they had seen or, what would have been even more unlikely, without looking at a statue or engraving at least. In other words, classical subject matter and classical "selection and arrangement of images" were united in the ancient works then available to poets. The fourteenth-century poet, however, was dependent on literary sources, often many times removed from the original classical conceptions of the gods. Chaucer's classical "portreitures"

[15] *The History of English Poetry* (1870 ed.), p. 237.

were neither orderless nor artless, but well executed according to the
medieval manner of the "selection and arrangement of images." [16]

John Gower also earns a place in this study with his account of the
Pygmalion story in the *Confessio Amantis* (1393). His aesthetic sense
was slighter, perhaps, than Chaucer's; yet his redaction of the Ovidian
tale was an interesting illustration of the medieval description of the
most famous work of Grecian "statuary" before the Torso Belvedere
became the "school of Michelangelo" or the Laocoön and the Venus
de Medici became the darlings of the later Renaissance Academies.
Gower united with Master Gregory and Thomas of Britain in praising the skill with which some artists have been able to counterfeit
nature.

> Pymaleon
> Which was a lusti man of yowthe:
> The werkes of entaile he cowthe
> Above alle othre men as tho;
>
> . . .
>
> He made an ymage of entaile
> Lich to a womman in semblance
> Of feture and of contienance,
> So fair yit nevere was figure
> Riht as a lyves creature
> Sche semeth,
>
> . . .
>
> For with a goodly lok sche smyleth,
> So that thurgh pure impression
> Of his ymaginacion
> Withal the herte of his corage
> His love upon this faire ymage
> He sette, and hire of love preide. (Book IV, ll. 372 ff.)

[16] For the Gothic "statues" in *The Knight's Tale,* some interesting parallels occur
in the illustrations of a North Italian manuscript (*Cod. Vat. Reg.* 1290) of *De deorum
imaginibus.* When one examines these "portreitures," done some twenty years after
the death of Chaucer in 1400, one finds the same imaginative feeling for mythological figures in unclassical forms as in the "images" drawn by the English poet. See
Liebeschütz, *Fulgentius metaforalis,* Plates XVII, XVIII, XIX, and Panofsky and
Saxl, "Classical Mythology in Mediaeval Art," pp. 257–58.

So the statue went to bed with Pygmalion and proved a "lusty wyf" obedient to his will!

But Gower was really "moral Gower," and later in the *Confessio* he condemned idolatry with the zeal of an iconoclast. Still, he borrowed from Godfrey of Viterbo's list of the gods and goddesses of Greece to swell his own pantheon. He described no images, however, for he was concerned with the folly of human beings who bow to their own handiwork. In writing thus of the spirit of Grecian belief, he mildly suggests Wordsworth, Coleridge, or Byron, though his tone is that of the image-breaker rather than that of the poet or student of mythology.[17] Gower even attempted a history or "progress" of the arts—foreshadowing those of the late seventeenth and eighteenth centuries—in which he maintained that naturalness was the only quality in art worthy of notice.

> Zenzis fond ferst the pourtreture,
> And Prometheüs the Sculpture;
> After what forme that hem thoghte,
> The resemblance anon thei wroghte. (Book IV, ll. 2421–24.)

The medieval suspicion of art reflected in the legend of "The Ring of Venus" was present in Gower's mind, for he reported that Love sometimes made and employed statues for purposes of sorcery (Book VI, ll. 1343 ff.). Yet in his desire for knowledge of the arts and in his vigorous telling of an Ovidian tale, Gower hesitated on the threshold of the Renaissance, a few steps behind Chaucer, whose temples of classical figures came from ancient and modern writers and from mythographers who offered their learning to poets and artists.

THE ELIZABETHANS:
THE LIFE-RESEMBLING PENCIL

To everything classical, poets, artists, and gentlemen in many parts of Europe soon gave reverent scrutiny; by no means least in their

---

[17] Book V, ll. 747–1970, especially 1497–1508 (*The Complete Works of John Gower* [1911], II, 422–56). See G. C. Macaulay's notes (pp. 515 ff.) and below, pp. 124 ff., 143 ff.

attention were the statues, coins, and sculptured monuments and ruins. The figures of ancient and beautiful deities, which had aroused interest in the twelfth century and which had created the legends about the magical powers of statues, were now carefully studied and preserved. From the fifteenth century onward, the recovery of the treasure of statuary with which (thanks to the rapacity and fore-sight of the old Romans) Italy was almost overflowing, kept hu-manist and artist, archaeologist and patron, supplied with excitement. By 1500 travel to Italy had become a requisite to the higher culture. Many a humanist journeyed south, however, from necessity rather than desire; Erasmus, for one, felt compelled to "go to Italy to gain for my poor learning some authority from the celebrity of the place." [18] Lesser Northerners crossed seas and mountains, returning with minds greatly changed, much to the dismay of moralistic scholars like Roger Ascham, who regretted in *The Schoolmaster* (1570) that "the *Siren* songes of *Italie*" could "untwyne" so many Englishmen "from the maste of Gods word." [19]

But the beautiful nudes of Hellenistic and Greco-Roman sculpture must have played a minor role in the demoralization of those visitors, because the English travelers of the sixteenth century displayed small concern and less knowledge about art, classical or otherwise. To the well-known antiques they paid some attention, of course; and travel-ers like Sir Thomas Hoby enumerated the Belvedere sculptures among the mementos of ancient days. The large number of trunks of statues which ruthless collectors had decapitated attracted interest, while some travelers studied ancient coins and inscriptions with en-thusiasm then as in the next two centuries. In general, though, Eng-land, which had been a leader in the twelfth-century renaissance, now lagged far behind in the competition for classical sculpture.

On the other hand, allusions to ancient artists and art became in-creasingly common in Renaissance English literature, as in the writ-ings of John Lyly. Most of the references were stereotyped; moreover, they are to be accounted for not so much by actual travel or by direct

[18] See Clare M. Howard, *English Travellers of the Renaissance* (1914), p. 8.
[19] *English Works of Roger Ascham*, ed. W. A. Wright (1904), p. 226.

knowledge of art as by increased reading in classical texts, especially
Pliny the Elder, Horace, Ovid, Quintilian, Xenophon, Aristotle,
Virgil, Pausanias, and Plutarch. In the writings of the Italian and
French disseminators of the new learning and, to a lesser degree, in
certain earlier English poems, there was considerable information
about the arts. The writer in Renaissance England had, therefore,
a larger body of sources on which to draw than his predecessors. The
tendency toward Alexandrian erudition and learning in the Renaissance found encouragement in late Greek and Roman writers, thereby
further strengthening the literary nature of the references to ancient
art. For many reasons, therefore, knowledge of the arts remained
mostly the names of a few artists, anecdotes like those of Zeuxis and
his grapes or Apelles and the composite beauty of his Helen, or a
number of catch phrases of criticism.

To represent the knowledge-of-a-sort current in the middle of the
sixteenth century, one may select the poem "Concerning Virgils
Eneids" by Nicholas Grimald in Tottel's *Miscellany* of 1557, the year
before Elizabeth ascended the throne.

> By heauens hye gift, in case reuiued were
> Lysip, Apelles, and Homer the great:
> The moste renowmd, and ech of them sance pere,
> In grauyng, paintyng, and the Poets feat:
> Yet could they not, for all their vein diuine,
> In marble, table, paper more, or lesse,
> With cheezil, pencil, or with poyntel fyne,
> So graue, so paynt, or so by style expresse
> (Though they beheld of euery age, and land
> The fayrest books, in euery toung contriued,
> To frame a fourm, and to direct their hand)
> Of noble prince the liuely shape descriued:
> As, in the famous woork, that Eneids hight,
> The naamkouth Virgil hath set forth in sight.

The poet named an artist for each of three arts, but his knowledge
was obviously slight. Still, the poem was a kind of treatment of the
question of the supremacy among the arts—the "paragone" or comparison of Renaissance criticism to determine the order in which the

arts were to be ranked [20]—a problem which was to become a major one again in eighteenth-century and Romantic poetry and criticism. A true-born, if pedestrian, poet, Grimald gave the precedency to his own craft, preferring the "poyntel" and "paper more or less" of poetry to the pencil of painting or the chisel of sculpture, and choosing Roman Virgil rather than Grecian Homer in poetry.

The Renaissance commonplaces—such as the theories that art is "mimesis" or imitation or the counterfeiting of nature; or that poetry and painting are parallel arts, *Ut pictura poesis;* or that poetry is a speaking picture and painting a mute poetry, *Poema pictura loquens, pictura poema silens*—occur in many critical treatises. In *An Apologie for Poetrie,* Sidney, for example, showed his acquaintance with two of them.[21] Again, by using the names of ancient artists an Elizabethan author added tone to his writings. Lyly knew the most about ancient art. He referred to Grecian artists as precedents for the "counterfaite" he drew of his hero in *Euphues; or, The Anatomy of Wyt* and *Euphues and His England,* and he introduced Apelles into his play *Campaspe,* setting several scenes in a studio and versifying Pliny's accounts of the painter's technical skill. Commissioned to paint a picture of Campaspe for Alexander, Apelles fell in love with the model, whose attractions led to a moving soliloquy on his predicament (which, incidentally, echoes the many contemporary discussions of the relative rank of painting and sculpture).

Arte must yeeld to nature, reason to appetite, wisdom to affection. Could *Pigmalion* entreate by prayer to haue his Iuory turned into flesh? and cannot *Apelles* obtaine by plaints to haue the picture of his loue chaunged to life? Is painting so farre inferiour to caruing? or dost thou *Venus,* more delight to be hewed with Chizels, then shadowed with colours? [22]

Turning from profane to pure love, one finds Spenser touching upon the problem of the "paragone" in his remark that not even the

---

[20] For an illuminating account of the "paragone" discussions, see *The Literary Works of Leonardo da Vinci,* ed. J. P. Richter and Irma Richter (2d ed., 1939), I, 14 ff. See also below, pp. 40*n*, 47, 242 ff.

[21] The sources of these commonplaces were Aristotle, Horace, and Plutarch. Sidney used the first and third; see *Elizabethan Critical Essays,* ed. Gregory Smith (1904), I, 158, and notes.

[22] See *The Complete Works of John Lyly,* ed. R. Warwick Bond (1902), I, 179 ff.; II, 336–43; and notes.

"life-resembling pencill . . . all were it *Zeuxis* or *Praxiteles*" possessed sufficient power to describe the excelling beauty of the chastity
which was his theme.[23] Thus, even if a poet or critic had very likely
seen few, if any, antiques or *statuas* of classical subjects, like those
which began to appear in English mansions and gardens, he could
still acquire and display a knowledge-of-a-sort of the ancient arts and
artists.

The derivative nature of the poetry of the English Renaissance
which is associated, even remotely, with the remains of classical antiquity is seen clearly in one of the most important works, Spenser's
translation of Du Bellay's *Antiquitez de Rome*. It was a significant
work because it included two motifs which constantly recur in the
English poetry inspired by antiquity: the general description of the
grandeur of Rome and the complaint over its ruin. As many later
English poets were to show even more exactly, Du Bellay pointed out
that Rome owed a large measure of its impressiveness to the statuary,
painting, and architecture it had taken from Greece.

> All that which *Greece* their temples to embraue,
> After th' Ionicke, Atticke, Doricke guise,
> Or *Corinth* skil'd in curious workes to graue;
>   All that *Lysippus* practike arte could forme,
> *Apelles* wit, or *Phidias* his skill,
> Was wont this auncient Citie to adorne,
> And the heauen it selfe with her wide wonders fill.
>   (Sonnet XXIX, ll. 2–7.)

Likewise literary in inspiration was the writing about sculpture
in the myth of Pygmalion, the Grecian sculptor enamored of his
handiwork. The Renaissance fondness for Ovid almost inevitably
led several English poets to relate the myth, which has been a favorite
of artists and poets. In Tottel's *Miscellany* there was "The Tale of
Pigmalion with Conclusion upon the Beautye of his loue." In Marston's more elaborate *Metamorphosis of Pigmalions Image* (1598),
as in the earlier poem, the description of the statue—

---

[23] *The Faerie Queene*, III, Prologue 2, 2–3. See also Dedicatory Sonnet XVII, 1–4,
where Spenser turned the Venus of Apelles into a pleasing compliment "to all the
gratious and beautifull ladies in the Court."

> So fair an image of a woman's feature,
> That never yet proudest mortality
> Could show so rare and beauteous a creature—(ii, 2–4)

and the skill of the artist were incidental to what the earlier poet termed the "conclusion," namely, the Renaissance delight in the physical beauty of the ivory figure.

> O that my mistress were an image too,
> That I might blameless her perfections view! (xi, 5–6)

cried Marston's Pygmalion; and the interest of the poem shifted to the caressing of the statue and the eventual coming to life of the marvelous work of art. In these Pygmalion poems the standard of appreciating sculpture was the desire for mimicking nature. The statue stood, Marston's argument announced, "as if it had been a breathing creature." Pygmalion had molded a statue so "lifelike" that he was rewarded by having his handiwork come to "life." [24]

The great Elizabethan trio of Spenser, Marlowe, and Shakespeare found "literary" sculptures occasionally useful, even though their acquaintance with the art of statuary was clearly limited. Had they seen some examples of the best antiques—but speculation is idle. Spenser rarely mentioned the art of sculpture, Grecian or otherwise; yet two accounts of ancient statues, drawn from his reading rather than from sight, deserve notice. The figure of Venus in her ornate temple in the style of similar decorations in medieval poetry surpassed the works of the ancients:

> But it in shape and beautie did excell
> All other Idoles, which the heathen adore,
> Farre passing that, which by surpassing skill
> *Phidias* did make in *Paphos* Isle of yore,

---

[24] See *Tottel's Miscellany*, ed. H. E. Rollins (Cambridge, Mass., 1928–29), pp. 125–26, and also p. 259, for mention of a ballad on Pygmalion (1568–69) and a poem by William Fullwood (1568) in which the statue fails to come to life. For a thorough consideration of the question of a satirical motive in Marston's poem, and for correspondences between it and *Hero and Leander* and *Venus and Adonis*, see Douglas Bush, *Mythology and the Renaissance Tradition in English Poetry* (Minneapolis, 1932), pp. 178 ff.

With which that wretched Greeke, that life forlore,
Did fall in loue.[25] (*Faerie Queene,* IV, x, 40, 1–6.)

Again, in the original conclusion to Book III of *The Faerie Queene*
Spenser pictured the embrace of Scudamour and Amoret, after long
separation, as a union of perfect ravishment:

> Had ye them seene, ye would haue surely thought,
> That they had beene that faire *Hermaphrodite,*
> Which that rich *Romane* of white marble wrought,
> And in his costly Bath causd to bee site:
> So seemd those two, as growne together quite (xii, 45, 1–5).

Probably removed from *The Faerie Queene* as too sensual, too Ovidian, these lines were a distant reflection of the story of Salmacis and
Hermaphroditus and the Platonic Idea of a perfect union which lay
behind the fable. Yet Spenser found the account of the statue useful
in this extravagant image.

Marlowe's literary and traditional material about the art of sculpture in connection with classical subjects was more conspicuous. In
Hero and Leander he created the imaginary "sculptures" in the fane
of Venus (I, 133 ff.) where amorous Leander first beheld the lovely
Hero, "Venus' nun."

> There might you see the gods in sundry shapes,
> Committing heady riots, incest, rapes:
> For know, that underneath this radiant floor
> Was Danae's statue in a brazen tower,
> Ioue slily stealing from his sister's bed,
> To dally with Idalian Ganymed,
> And for his love Europa, bellowing loud,
> And tumbling with the Rainbow in a cloud (ll. 143–50).

Yet these "statues" of living passion were not so much sculpture
as "carved" Renaissance tapestries or woodwork, with little reference
to classical representations of mythological figures. More classical
in feeling than Chaucer's "portreitures," these scenes were, at the

[25] Actually the statue was the Venus of Cnidus by Praxiteles, but Spenser was
following Pliny, *Nat. Hist.,* XXXVI, v, 21. For Spenser and sculpture, see Ida Langdon,
Materials for a Study of Spenser's Theory of Fine Art (Ithaca, 1911), p. ix.

same time, more energetic and passionate than in Musaeus or Ovid, the principal ancient sources of the poem. Marlowe caught something of the classical spirit as the Renaissance conceived it, but the "statues" in his "small shrine of Parian sculpture"—as Swinburne doubtfully described *Hero and Leander*—were unsculptural and un-Grecian.[26] The time for the presentation of classical subject matter in the forms of the Antique had not yet come in England. Marlowe vitalized his figures, but the inspiration stemmed from books rather than actual works of art. References to "Pygmalion's ivory girl," Niobe being turned into stone, and the frown of "Jove's marble statue" when Pyrrhus killed Priam reflected his learning without showing much aesthetic feeling. Though as keenly sensitive as any English poet, perhaps, to the beauties of the nude body, Marlowe achieved a sculptural quality in his works only occasionally, as in the statuesque description of Tamburlaine as a kind of Hercules or Atlas:

> So large of limbs, his joints so strongly knit,
> Such breadth of shoulders as might mainly bear
> Old Atlas' burthen; 'twixt his manly pitch.

Midway between Chaucer's Gothic "portreitures" of Lycurgus and Emetrius in *The Knight's Tale* and Milton's more chastely featured Beelzebub in *Paradise Lost,* Tamburlaine suggests Renaissance— especially early Renaissance—woodcuts and engravings of the newly recovered antique statues or of figures based upon them.[27]

The Renaissance liking for statues which counterfeited nature gave rise to the device of the apparent statue that comes alive whenever exigencies of plot demand—a device used in various plays on the Continent. Like every trick of the contemporary stage, it found its way into a play by Shakespeare. In *The Winter's Tale* (1611) the Third Gentleman ascribed the apparent statue of Hermione to a "rare Italian master, Julio Romano," whom he termed the most perfect "ape" of nature; for the statue was "so near to Hermione . . . that they say one would speak to her and stand in hope of answer."

[26] For criticism of Swinburne and the fashion he set in judging *Hero and Leander,* see Bush, *Mythology and the Renaissance Tradition in English Poetry,* pp. 129 ff.

[27] See *Tamburlaine the Great,* Part I, Act II, scene i, ll. 7 ff., Part II, Act I, scene iii, l. 38, and *The Tragedy of Dido,* II, i, 3–5, 14–16, 255 ff.

Apparently Shakespeare presented the statue in the tradition of literary "sculptures" mimicking nature and of the native English colored
works, with no thought of the Antique. Among the "singularities"
in Paulina's gallery may have been ancient works, but in the play
Leontes was interested in the statue of Hermione:

> Her natural posture!
> Chide me, dear stone, that I may say indeed
> Thou art Hermione;
>
> . . .
>
> O, thus she stood,
> Even with such life of majesty (warm life,
> As now it coldly stands), when first I woo'd her!
>
> . . .
>
> O royal piece,
> There's magic in thy majesty (V, iii, 20 ff.).

Here indeed was a breathing statue: "The very life seems warm
upon her lip." She was the perfect counterfeit of nature admired by
medieval and Renaissance poets and also by Ovid, to whose story of
Pygmalion A. H. R. Fairchild has indicated the plausible indebtedness of Shakespeare.[28] For the mimetic theory of the arts, especially
painting and sculpture, was the one which the Renaissance poets
found in the classical poets and critics first known to them and in
which they most often read.

Similarly the chimney piece in Imogen's chamber in *Cymbeline*
(? 1610) was a carving of "chaste Dian bathing" of a most exacting
literalness. After praising "the true life" of the tapestry of Cleopatra
meeting Antony at Cydnus, Iachimo described the relief or woodwork with a typically Renaissance appreciation of sculpture:

> Never saw I figures
> So likely to report themselves. The cutter
> Was as another nature, dumb; outwent her,
> Motion and breath left out (II, iv, 82–85).

[28] See *Shakespeare and the Arts of Design,* "University of Missouri Studies," No. 12
(1937), pp. 71 ff., for Fairchild's development of Henry Green's suggestion of the
Pygmalion story in *Shakespeare and the Emblem Writers* (1870), p. 109n. For the
mimetic theory of sculpture among classical writers, see Frank P. Chambers, *Cycles
of Taste* (Cambridge, Mass., 1928), pp. 11–14.

In writing of sculpture Shakespeare always praised the lifelike or living quality he found in works of art. The skill of the sculptor called forth praise, but the important thing was the life given to the artifact. Because sculpture and painting seemed to address the senses alone in the attempt to approximate the external appearances of things and persons, the addition of the significant living (emotional or mental) qualities was difficult to achieve. Like many later poets, therefore, Shakespeare several times condemned the coldness and inactivity of statuary. Sculpture contributed to the unfavorable description of Octavia in *Antony and Cleopatra* (III, iii, 20–21):

> She shows a body rather than a life,
> A statue than a breather.[29]

Even more conspicuous were the lines in *Venus and Adonis* where Venus, upbraiding the coldness of Adonis to her appeals, labeled him a

> liveless picture, cold and senseless stone,
> Well-painted idol, image dull and dead,
> Statue contenting but the eye alone (ll. 211–13).

Adonis had a sculptural beauty—even classical perhaps—a perfect form; but he lacked life, activity, the vital breath of passion. For Shakespeare breathing nature was always superior to a statue. The Hermione-statue wanted only breath and motion to be alive; Dian bathing all but breathed; the wanton pictures in the Induction to *The Taming of the Shrew* (ii, 51 ff.) were very much alive. The stones which moved Shakespeare were those that breathed. Breath, the sign or symbol of life, was the key to all his descriptions of statues and paintings:

> what fine chisel
> Could ever yet cut breath?[30]

---

[29] See also *Richard III*, III, vii, 25; *Henry VIII*, I, ii, 88; *Titus Andronicus*, III, i, 258. Sometimes, as in *Troilus and Cressida*, V, x, 17 ff., this sort of reference is mythological and literary, stemming from Ovid and Marlowe. For some cogent remarks on the "ear-mindedness" of Shakespeare, see Margaret F. Thorp (*PMLA*, XLVI [1931], 689).

[30] *The Winter's Tale*, V, iii, 78–79. See also Bush, *Mythology and the Renaissance Tradition in English Poetry*, p. 180. Yet one notices that in the brief dialogue between

On at least one occasion Shakespeare may have described a statue on the basis of an actual figure he had seen, without doubt not an antique but a new statue of classical subject and, perhaps, partly ancient in design. When Rosalind in *As You Like It* (IV, i, 147) exclaimed, "I will weep for nothing, like Diana in the fountain," Shakespeare was very likely thinking, as Mr. Fairchild suggests, of one of the Diana-fountains popular in Elizabethan times. Drayton also wrote in the "Epistle of Rosamond to Henry II":

> Here in the garden, wrought by curious hands,
> Naked Diana in the fountain stands.[31]

The references of the Elizabethan poets to statues of classical subjects were based, then, almost entirely on literary sources; and their own imaginary "sculptures" reflected the taste of the English poets before imitation gave way to invention late in the seventeenth century. To them, to paraphrase Shakespeare's Timon of Athens, the statue was almost the natural man; but that qualifying word "almost" made a vast difference in their estimation of sculpture. The nudity or "naturalness" in many classical statues helped attract the Renaissance poets, but they found more vitality and life and expressiveness

---

the Poet and the Painter in *Timon of Athens* (? 1606), the latter had the better of the argument:

> "[His painting] tutors nature; artificial strife
> Lives in these touches, livelier than life" (I, i, 37–38).

He asserted his superiority thus:

> "A thousand moral paintings I can show
> That shall demonstrate these quick blows of Fortune's
> More pregnantly than words" (ll. 90–92).

While the incident is not characteristic of Shakespeare, one need not follow C. H. Herford ("Shakespeare and the Arts," *Bulletin of John Rylands Library,* Manchester, XI [1927], 280), who found in it "something un-Shakespearean." Questions of authorship aside, Shakespeare may have heard similar discussions of the arts in the halls of Elizabethan patrons like Timon, or again he may have been responding to the new taste for the arts under the Stuarts; see pp. 34*n*, 47 ff., and Anthony Blunt, "An Echo of the *Paragone* in Shakespeare," *Warburg Institute Journal,* II (1939), 260 ff.

[31] Fairchild, *Shakespeare and the Arts of Design,* p. 69. Fairchild discusses the statues running with blood in *Julius Caesar,* II, ii, 76, and III, ii, 192, in relation to Elizabethan conduits. But the use of the statues of Caesar and Pompey in Plutarch was of little significance, as was Lucio's jocular allusion to "Pygmalion's images" in *Measure for Measure,* III, ii, 49, borrowed from Lyly; see *Works,* ed. Bond, I, 174, 188, and 330.

in their own art of poetry than in painting and sculpture. Statues contented but the eye alone; poetry pleased the understanding and the affections. Picture and statuary showed a body rather than a life, a static form rather than a living soul or spirit.

But a refinement of taste, by which the plastic arts became the equals—and often the superiors—of poetry, had already carried the day in Italy. Indebted to the remarks of Cicero and Quintilian concerning the relation of gesture and aspect to emotion and, even more strongly, to the Neo-Platonic theory that "the body is the expression of the soul," the great Italian artists maintained, in the words of Leonardo, that "the soul is composed of harmony, and the harmonious proportions of a work of art are reflections of this harmony." [32] Thus the artist was lifted above the poet; and, in his use of sight, "the most spiritual of the senses," the artist was thought to achieve effects more immediate than those of the poet, who necessarily depended on a succession of impressions.

But since England lacked a group of artists as brilliant and as aggressive as the Italians, these ideas appeared in England only occasionally—as in the Painter's argument in *Timon of Athens*—and they became naturalized very slowly in the seventeenth century. Painting was dignified before sculpture, of course, but gradually the Grecian statuary then known became increasingly familiar to the critics and poets and gentlemen who created the Neo-Classical taste by which the Antique became a more fruitful subject for poetry than it had been in the Elizabethan age.

[32] "Paragone," *Works* (Richter), I, 66. See also the illuminating discussion of the theories of "expression" in the Renaissance in Rensselaer Lee's exhaustive study *"Ut Pictura Poesis;* the Humanistic Theory of Painting," *Art Bulletin,* XXII, No. 4 (Dec., 1940), 219 and notes.

III. THE SEVENTEENTH CENTURY

PRE-RESTORATION: THE USES
OF STATUE-CRAFT

WITH THE COMING of the Stuarts there was a conscious movement to encourage the fine arts in England. The desire for the refinement of taste called forth in 1622 Henry Peacham's *Compleat Gentleman,* a work written to educate the nobility of the seventeenth century. Ancient statues were recommended to poets, painters, architects, and gentlemen, and Peacham's advice to the first and last of those groups may be noticed here. Poets were to study the antique statues "for the presentation of Comedies, Tragedies, Maskes, Shewes, or any learned scene whatsoever; the properties whereof can neither be appointed nor judged of, but by such as are well seene in statue-craft." Peacham probably had in mind the "learned scenes" of Inigo Jones, who brought the Italian style of stage ornamentation to England.

In his own account of *Hymenaei* (1606) Ben Jonson mentioned costumes "taken from the antique Greek statues." [1] This turning to the Antique was appropriate in Jonson—a galleon built far higher in learning than the man-of-war Shakespeare. Jonson's classical tragedies were correct in scholarship and archaeology, while Shakespeare was more concerned to show the spirit—the breathing life—rather than the form of the ancient world. Jonson's attempts to show a past age as it actually appeared set him apart from most of his contemporaries; and Peacham's advice to the poets was somewhat premature. Yet statuary was becoming an accessory of the

---

[1] See *Designs by Inigo Jones for Masques & Plays at Court,* ed. Percy Simpson and C. F. Bell (1924), p. 28, and *Inigo Jones and Ben Jonson,* ed. David Laning, "Shakespeare Society Publications," No. 39 (1848), p. 95. Charlotte Porter (*MLN,* XXXI [1916], 281–87) suggested that actual statues were used in productions of *Julius Caesar.*

theater in the early seventeenth century even as it had begun to be the handmaiden of architecture earlier in the Renaissance.

The Antique, said Peacham, ought to be familiar to gentlemen, "the onely men that imploy Poets, Painters, and Architects, if they be not all these themselves. And if they bee not able to iudge of their workes, they well deserve to be couzened." [2] Acquaintance with the ancient masterpieces and interest in the fine arts was clearly becoming an essential part of an English gentleman's liberal education. Statues of classical subjects, if not always classical in feeling and design, were now indispensable in a gentleman's mansion and garden in England as elsewhere in Europe. In the essay *Of Building* Bacon recommended "some fair work of statua's" to adorn the inner court of a model house.

Travel to Italy and France was important, of course, in refining English taste; yet the travelers of the seventeenth century were mostly concerned, like the Elizabethans, with the size and cost of works of art and with their ingenuity and ornateness. The "hydroptique immoderate desire of humane learning" of the seventeenth century was best satisfied perhaps by the private museums which dotted Italy— the collections of oddities of a sort to delight Bacon and Sir Thomas Browne and Evelyn—museums "where pictures and statues and coins lay cheek by jowl with objects of scientific interest." Akenside a century later described just such a curio cabinet of an English collector:

> There gums and amber found below the line,
> The beak of Ibis here, and there an Antonine.[3]

From travel likewise English interest in the Antique received an important stimulus when Thomas Howard, Earl of Arundel and

[2] To avoid the "couzening," one was to follow rules that may be of interest to students: look for the signs, such as the club of Hercules, the apples of Pomona, and so forth; check the profiles of statues and busts with the "half-faces" on coins; study the books picturing the statues at Rome; and look at statues with those who already know what and who the works of art are!

[3] *The Virtuoso,* stanza vii, ll. 8–9. See Lacy Collison-Morley, *Italy after the Renaissance* (1930), p. 25. In *The Anatomy of Melancholy* (Part II, sec. 2, mem. iv) Burton mentioned princes' cabinets to cure melancholy; for a scholarly study of this aspect of seventeenth-century culture, see Julius von Schlosser, *Die Kunst und Wunderkammern der Spätrenaissance* (Leipzig, 1908).

Marshal of England, began the tradition of collecting ancient marbles, a tradition which was followed by many of his countrymen in the next two centuries. To be sure, Henry, Bishop of Winchester, had brought statues to England some four hundred and fifty years before, and someone had adorned Nonesuch Palace with "so many statues that seem to breathe, so many miracles of consummate art, so many casts that rival even the perfection of Roman antiquity" that the German traveler Hentzner in 1598 had felt that the statuary justified the name of the royal palace.[4] But Howard visited Italy and sent his agents to Mediterranean countries with the express intention of seeing and collecting art treasures. His acquisitions became, therefore, the first collection of classical sculpture in England. To Howard, Peacham reported,

this angle of the world oweth the first sight of Greeke and Romane Statues, with whose admired presence he began to honour the Gardens and Galleries of Arundel-House about twentie yeeres agoe [1610], and hath ever since continued to transplant old Greece into *England*.[5]

The transplanting of old Greece soon took place at the Royal houses; for King Charles I was also reported to have collected "a whole army of old forraine Emperours, Captaines, and Senators . . . to attend him in his palaces of *Saint Iames* and Sommerset-House." The first Duke of Buckingham, the fourth Earl of Pembroke, and Sir Kenelm Digby were other founders of famous and large collections. Indeed, collecting became so fashionable that as early as 1628 the antiquary with classical interests appeared in satire as a "character" in Earle's *Micro-cosmographie:* "He is of our Religion, because wee say that it is most ancient; and yet a broken Statue would almost make him an Idolater. . . . His estate consists much in shekels, and Roman Coynes, and hee hath more Pictures of Caesar, then *Iames* and *Elizabeth*."

As far as the tradition traced in this study is concerned, the new

---

[4] See J. Alfred Gotch, *Early Renaissance Architecture in England* (1901), pp. 33–34.
[5] See also Adolf T. F. Michaelis, *Ancient Marbles in Great Britain* (1882), pp. 22 ff., and Warner G. Rice, *Early English Travellers to Greece and the Levant*, "University of Michigan Studies in English and Comparative Literature" No. 10 (1933), pp. 233 and 247 ff.

court taste manifested itself first in a reaction against the coloring of statuary in favor of the white which was thought to have been characteristic of the Antique. Shakespeare's statues in *The Winter's Tale* and *Cymbeline* were in the native tradition of colored figures and the literary tradition of "counterfeits of nature"; but Jonson lent his support to the classicizing tendency in *The Magnetick Lady* (1632) in lines satirizing the City or bourgeois (that is, non-Court) taste:

> RUTLAND. I'ld have her statue cut, now, in white marble.
> INTEREST. And have it painted in most orient colours.
> RUTLAND. That's right! all Citie statues must be painted:
> Else, they be worth nought i' their subtile judgements.
>   (V, vii, 90 ff.)

Sir Henry Wotton, according to Izaak Walton, a "most dear Lover, and a most excellent Judge" of all the manual arts, termed "the Fashion of *colouring,* even *Regal Statues* . . . an *English Barbarism.*" [6]

Yet the fashionable taste for the Antique appeared but seldom in English poetry. To be sure, poets wrote of "Parian stones" or "white marble brows" or "rigid" and "cold marble melting," and the like. "Carving in marble" was a favorite image. The inspiration for the conceits of this nature in amatory poetry came, however, from older poets, classical and Renaissance, rather than from the Grecian statues newly transplanted into England. A few lines from Thomas Randolph's "Pastorall Courtship" will indicate this sort of writing sufficiently, with the following beauties from the anatomical description of the loved one:

> . . . to the touch the Ivory thighes
> Veil gently, and again doe rise,
> As pliable to impression,
> As Virgins waxe, or *Parian* stone

---

[6] Peter Whalley, who edited Jonson in 1756, pointed out that Jonson's remark "was probably designed to ridicule the taste, which at that time prevailed with the connoisseurs in the fine arts, who directed the elegance and judgment of the city. Gaudy and profuse ornaments are objects of admiration, with those who have no relish for the decent simplicity of nature" (IV, 462). See also Wotton, *The Elements of Architecture* (1624), in *Reliquiae Wottonianae* (1685 ed.), p. 53.

> Dissolv'd to softnesse, plump and full,
> More white and soft then *Cotsall wooll*.[7]

Occasionally a poet wrote of a Venus, a Diana, or a weeping statue—for example, William Drummond of Hawthornden's "On a Statue of Venus Sleeping"; but there were fewer attempts to describe "statues" or "portreitures" of classical subjects than among the Elizabethans. Grecian statuary was still too little known to have touched the emotions of the lyrical poets, whether pastoral, religious, or metaphysical. Among the subjects for poetry in the "argument" of Herrick's *Hesperides* (1648), which may stand here for the lyrical poetry before the Restoration, there was no place for the Antique. More numerous were the poetic references to colored effigies of English polychrome sculpture and to funerary urns and star-ypointing pyramids. From Donne's superb image in *The Extasie,*

> And whil'st our soules negotiate there,
> Wee like sepulchrall statues lay;
> All day, the same our postures were,
> And wee said nothing, all the day.

to the vague accounts of "animated busts" and "storied urns" in elegies and memorial verses, one finds in seventeenth-century poetry the story of English rather than Grecian sculpture.[8]

Among the critics and gentlemen of the early seventeenth century, moreover, the fine arts were still admired for their imitation. *"Poetry* and *Picture* are Arts of a like nature, and both are busie about imitation," wrote Jonson, and sculpture was included under picture. The belief that art was the "aping" of nature led to the theory that, while pictures and statuary addressed the senses by showing the external appearances of things and persons, poetry spoke to the mind by presenting ("imitating") emotions and thoughts. For that reason, in the

[7] *Poems,* ed. G. Thorn-Drury (1929), pp. 111–12. See also "De Magnete; ex Claudiano" (pp. 46–47) for statues of Venus and Mars that "seem'd to move"; "An Apology . . ." (pp. 67–69) for a Parian statue of Alcides in Charing Cross converted into a Venus.

[8] See unsigned article, "English Sculpture in English Literature," *TLS,* July 18, 1929, pp. 565–66.

words of Jonson, "the Pen is more noble then the Pencill; For that can speake to the Understanding, the other but to the Sense." Because literature addressed the mental and intellectual powers of men, it was superior to painting and sculpture; not only was it more "noble" but it also surpassed the pencil or the chisel in showing the mental and spiritual activities of mankind. "What figure of a Body was *Lysippus* ever able to forme with his Graver, or *Apelles* to paint with his Pencill, as the Comedy to life expresseth so many and various affections of the minde?" [9] A man of letters, Jonson spoke, of course, as a defender of the supremacy of literature among the arts. The ancient authorities with whom he was familiar encouraged his position, while he very likely knew little of the views of the Italian artists and critics who, we have seen, had awarded the prize for expressiveness to painting. Not until the Neo-Classical critics at the end of the seventeenth century granted sculpture and painting places among the mental or noble activities, as distinguished from the sensual or mechanic, were those two arts considered, in England, worthy to rank with poetry and philosophy.

Despite the onus of inferiority to literature, the history of ancient sculpture began to draw the attention of a number of English writers in the first half of the seventeenth century. Every branch of human activity was being investigated, and the growing interest in antiquities, reflected both in the taste of the Court and in the travel on the Continent, naturally created a desire for information concerning the history of the arts. Bacon was justly the first Englishman to project a "History of Painting, Sculpture, Modelling, etc." [10] That "History" was never written, however, so that the honor of giving a historical account or "progress" of sculpture—a view of the art which was to become increasingly important in the English tradition of interest

[9] See "Poesis et Pictura" in *Timber; or, Discoveries,* ed. Felix E. Schelling (Boston, 1892), p. 49, and Joel E. Spingarn, *Critical Essays of the Seventeenth Century* (1908), I, 29 and notes. Yet Jonson, like Shakespeare, once allowed the supremacy of painting in the language of Quintilian: "It doth so enter and penetrate the inmost affection (being done by an excellent Artificer) as sometimes it orecomes the power of speech and oratory." See above, p. 34; *Institutio oratoria,* XI, 3, 67; and Lee, in *Art Bulletin* (Dec., 1940), pp. 197–98n, 204n, and 254.

[10] See *Works,* ed. J. Spedding, R. L. Ellis, and D. D. Heath (1859–70), VIII, 378.

in Grecian sculpture—fell to an appropriate heir, Jonson. Because the first "progress" was brief, it can be quoted in full:

The Art Plasticke was moulding in clay or potters earth anciently. This is the Parent of *Statuary,* sculpture, *Graving,* and *Picture;* cutting in brasse and marble all serve under her. *Socrates* taught *Parrhasius* and *Clito,* two noble Statuaries, first to *expresse manners by their looks in Imagery.*[11]

In other words, the history or "progress" of art was from verisimilitude to the expression of "manners" in outward forms and attitudes. Peacham implied the same theory when he felt that statues must be the most venerable antiquities, since "it was more obvious and easier for man to figure and represent his outward body than his inward minde." [12]

The basis of Jonson's remarks was Xenophon's reporting in *Memorabilia* (III, x, 1-8) that Socrates had told the artists that mental states and qualities are reflected in the face and the attitudes of the body and that the sculptor must "represent in his figures the activities of the soul." Jonson had hit upon the ancient authority most frequently cited in the eighteenth century, when the interest in the Antique passed from the Renaissance concern with the perfection of the imitation to the Neo-Classical stress on invention, the showing of the inner feelings in form and attitude. When the study of the Antique later became frozen into the Academic rules—a set of canons of form and a code of imagery; a body rather than a life—the more sensitive poets would again feel the necessity for discovering the activities of the soul in the highly praised forms of Grecian sculpture.

From other authorities came the information in the most famous and most bulky handbook of ancient art produced in the seventeenth century, the *De pictura veterum* (in Latin, Amsterdam, 1637; in English, London, 1638) compiled by the celebrated Dutch scholar Franciscus Junius, librarian to Lord Arundel, known now not for his classical lore but for his saving of the "Caedmon" manuscript bearing his name. His learnedly dull tome became the *vade mecum* of critic and artist, remaining an easily plundered storehouse of wisdom

---

[11] "De progressu Picturae," *Timber,* pp. 50–51. Italics in the last phrase added.
[12] *The Compleat Gentleman,* 1906 ed., p. 106.

until well into the eighteenth century when Lessing used it and Reynolds quoted from it, apparently at first hand.

Along with the collecting of antiques and the cultural concern of Peacham for antiquities and the arts, and along with the historical and theoretical discussion of ancient art in *Timber* and *De pictura,* several more general interests drew attention to ancient statuary. First, there was the attraction of antiquity itself. "Next men and manners," Peacham opined, "there is nothing fairely more delightfull, nothing worthier observation, than these Copies, and memorials of men and matters of elder times; whose lively presence is able to perswade a man, that he now seeth two thousand yeeres agoe." [13]

Secondly, ancient statuary showed that the Greek and Roman custom of honoring heroes, athletes, and philosophers with statues had stimulated noble actions. For this reason the galleries of the House of Salomon, an institute of learning in Bacon's *New Atlantis,* were to be adorned with "Statua's of all Principall Inventers." Cowley's College for the Advancement of Experimental Philosophy, modeled on Bacon's in 1661, was to have "Pictures or Statues of all the Inventers of any thing useful to Human Life," including America.

Again, some persons found a therapeutic value in the study of Grecian statuary. Among the recreations "fit & proper to expell Idleness and Melancholy," the incomparable Burton listed sculpture:

What so full of content, as to read, walke, and see Mappes, Pictures, Statues, Jewels, marbles, which some so magnifie, as those that *Phidias* made of old so exquisite and pleasing to be beheld, that as Chrysostome thinketh, *if any man be sickly, troubled in minde, or that cannot sleep for griefe, and shall but stand over against one of Phidias Images, he will forget all care, or whatsoever else may molest him in an instant?* (*Anatomy,* Part II, sec. 2, mem. iv [1638 ed.], p. 275.)

Finally, the ancient statues, like all antiquities, offered a perpetual preachment on mortality. From seeing the changes wrought by the whirligig of time, James Howell felt that one might ponder the destiny of man.

Nor are the observations of the Eye anything profitable, unless the Mind draw something from the Externe object to enrich the Soule withall, to

13 *Ibid.,* p. 105.

informe, to build up and unbeguile the Inward man, that by the sight of so various objects of Art and Nature, that by the perlustration of such famous Cities, Castles, Amphitheaters, and Palaces; some glorious and new, some mouldred away, and eaten by the Iron-teeth of Time, he come to discerne, the best of earthly things to bee but frayle and transitory.[14]

In ancient stones as in everything else the seventeenth century was able to find sermons on a text which has attracted English poets from Spenser to Shelley and Landor. Indeed, the mutability theme seems indigenous in English genius, since it occurs in such early documents as *Beowulf,* "The Wanderer," and "The Ruin." In "The Ruin," in particular, the poet's melancholy sprang from seeing architectural ruins of the sort which induced Howell's reflections concerning "the Iron-teeth of Time."

VIRTUOSO (EVELYN) AND CRITIC (DRYDEN): MODELS OF SUPERIOR BEAUTIES

In the Restoration a gentleman needed no urging to cultivate an acquaintance with the masterpieces of painting and sculpture, since *noblesse oblige* almost demanded that he be something of a virtuoso. Even a person of noble rank could dabble in the fine arts, now that they were esteemed intellectual rather than servile activities. As an amusement for aristocrats, however, sculpture, then as always, lagged behind the other arts; for the physical labor required by the art made it seem less gentlemanly and less liberal. Still, owing to the diffusion of the history and theory of the arts, the knowledge of sculpture was increasing to such an extent that a writer could feel sure that allusions to Grecian statues would be understood by cultivated readers.

Even as the Elizabethan antiquary had been ridiculed, so the virtuoso, interested in all knowledge including the arts and antiquities, became a target for satirists, as in Shadwell's play, *The Virtuoso* (1676). Isaac Newton, though the friend of virtuosos, had no use for ancient statuary, and he referred contemptuously to the eighth Earl of Pembroke, who added to the collection of antiques begun by his grandfather at Wilton House, as "a lover of stone

---

[14] *Instructions for Forreine Travell* (1642), ed. Arber (1868), pp. 69–70.

dolls." [15] From John of Salisbury to Byron, many an Englishman agreed with Newton; yet the anti-virtuoso and the satirist were powerless to stop the collecting, study, and imitation of ancient works of art, nor could they lessen the poets' admiration for the "stone dolls."

During the latter part of the seventeenth century the many discussions of the merits of the Ancients and the Moderns also helped to popularize the history and theory of the arts. Through this controversy, therefore, a considerable body of information about the fine arts began to appear in criticism and in poetry. In the case of sculpture, painting, and architecture, supremacy was conceded to the Ancients without much hesitation. An ardent champion of the Ancients, Sir William Temple discovered in their arts "unparallel'd and inimitable excellencies," which were still "undisput'd." William Wotton, protagonist for the Moderns, was none the less forced to grant the superiority of the Ancients in the arts. What could poor Wotton do, when the greatest Moderns in sculpture, Michelangelo and Bernini, themselves declared that "their best Pieces were exceeded by some of the ancient Statues still to be seen at *Rome*"? [16]

But the interest of the Baconian virtuosos in the ancient arts found its best expression two years after the founding of the Royal Society, when in 1662 John Evelyn published *Sculptura; or, The History and Art of Chalcography*. Having collected all he could find concerning *sculptura* in Greek and Roman critics, in the Church Fathers, and in modern writers such as Junius, Salmasius, Vasari, Sir Henry Wotton, and Leon Battista Alberti, Evelyn produced a strange hodgepodge of sound theory and erudite nonsense about the arts. The first English book to consider sculpture as a branch of learning and philosophy at much length, *Sculptura* gave the story of the "original" and "progress" of the art which Bacon had projected and Jonson had briefly sketched—the historical account of art which the eighteenth-century poets were soon to make so familiar that it survived

[15] See Sir David Brewster, *Memoirs of the Life, Writings, and Discoveries of Sir Isaac Newton* (Edinburgh, 1855), II, 411.

[16] See Temple, *An Essay upon the Ancient and Modern Learning*, 1690 (Spingarn, *Critical Essays of the Seventeenth Century*, III, 38 ff., particularly pp. 50 and 60), and Wotton, *Reflections upon Ancient and Modern Learning*, 1694 (Spingarn, III, 201 ff.).

into Romantic poetry. In its mixture of scholarship, science, antiquities, and history of art, this curious treatise admirably displayed the nature and scope of the knowledge of the arts among the virtuosos of the Royal Society. If Abraham Cowley reflected the views of these learned gentlemen-philosophers, the members of the Royal Society entertained a view of art close to that of the Elizabethans.

> Who to the Life an exact Piece would make,
>
> . . .
>
>   before his Sight must place
> The natural and living Face;
> The real Object must command
> Each Judgment of his Eye, and Motion of his Hand.[17]

Vigorous as is Cowley's injunction to keep the eye on the object, the verisimilitude he recommended was soon to be replaced by the Ideal Beauty of the Academies.

The last third of the seventeenth century saw, as a matter of fact, the English virtuoso's native or Baconian interest in antiquities augmented by influences from across the Channel. From France came ideas to transform English taste, theories of art, and poetry. Poet, artist, gentleman-philosopher—to whom was now added the connoisseur—looked from the barbarous North toward the Mediterranean. Mentally, at least, they made the pilgrimage of culture, eagerly accepting the theories of art and literature stated by the French critics, behind whom stood Italy and the classical works discovered in the Renaissance. In short, the English gentlemen-philosophers or virtuosos followed the theories of the French Academies: they became Neo-Classical, and imitation gave way to invention, in theory at least.

What these Neo-Classical theories meant in practice is best seen, perhaps, in the work of Nicolas Poussin, whose genius epitomized the artistic ideals of the age. Valuing form or design above color, Poussin stressed the mental or intellectual or analytical elements in painting, and he made his art into a kind of double of sculpture or of litera-

---

[17] "To the Royal Society," ll. 79, 85–88. Hazlitt took this passage as his text for an attack on Ideal Beauty.

ture,[18] presenting epic or historical scenes with suggestions of statuary. Frequently, too, he placed his figures in attitudes reminiscent of antique statues and clothed them in classical tunics and togas. Something of a Neo-Platonic philosopher, the painter presented what he termed "the imitation of human actions" in perfect forms derived, though not copied, from ancient sculptures and the paintings of Raphael. Unlike the Flemish and Dutch painters, who were thought to be mere artisans ignorant of Academic theory, copying individual and particular forms rather than the generalized or composite beauty of ideal forms, and unaware of beauty other than that of the flesh, Poussin worked with his mind. Like Winckelmann, he found his spiritual homeland in the classical scenes of Rome.

Such, in briefest outline, were some of the leading ideas in the aesthetics of art adopted by Englishmen of taste in the cultural awakening announced by Dryden's *Astraea Redux* (1660). Rapid was the enlightenment, and they quickly shook off the Gothic inelegances of their rude forefathers. One sign of the refinement was the increase in the number of references in poetry to the polite arts; in the works of Waller and Dryden, for example, mentions of painting were numerous. In slighting sculpture, the English poets were, as usual, behind the critics who had admitted it into the sisterhood of the arts. Thus it happened that sculpture, before many years to enter poetry as a companion to painting (which it sometimes supplanted in interest), was infrequently used before the Augustan poets for whom an audience was being prepared by the virtuosos and the theorists of the Academies of the late seventeenth century. Had Mistress Anne Killigrew, "excellent," we learn from Dryden's ode, "in the two sister-arts of poesie and painting," been accomplished also in the third art of sculpture, the story of course would have been different. As it was, classical statuary often inspired her work:

---

[18] Louis Hourticq, *De Poussin à Watteau* (Paris, 1921), p. 78. See also Esther Sutro, *Nicolas Poussin* (1923). Professor Erwin Panofsky has remarked, "curiously enough, fewer direct 'borrowings' from the antique are to be found in the work of this so-called classicist than in the works of Rubens; Rubens often paints seemingly realistic figures, which upon analysis prove faithfully classical in pose, while Poussin paints apparently classical figures which, in reality, are free inventions, or rather reincarnations of a classical entity." ("Et in Arcadia Ego," *Philosophy and History,* ed. R. Klibansky and H. J. Paton [1936], p. 244.)

The Ruines too of some Majestick Piece,
Boasting the Pow'r of ancient Rome or Greece,
Whose Statues, Freezes, Columns, broken lie,
And tho' defac'd, the Wonder of the Eye (ll. 119-22).[19]

Both in such passages and in versifying portions of the information
disseminated by Baconian virtuoso and French Academician, the
poets were helping to create the taste which was to lead the Augustans to the poetic use of Grecian sculpture. In "The Progress of
Learning" (1668) John Denham outlined the story of the arts without treating them individually. Dryden's "To Sir Godfrey Kneller"
(1694), though undistinguished as poetry, has some weight as perhaps the first English poem to relate the history of a specific art,
namely, painting. While Denham began his account with God, Dryden was more "classical" in making Prometheus the molder of Adam!
The principal facts in the "progress" of the arts—their "shadow"
origin; the technical advances in Greece; Rome's preservation of the
arts until the Goths arrived; their revival from centuries of "iron
sleep" [20]—were the facts which the poets, critics, and connoisseurs
in the eighteenth and nineteenth centuries were to elaborate and
moralize and associate with the religion and polity of the ancient
Greeks. Waller stated a theme which English poets were to descant
upon for many years:

> The British monarch shall the glory have,
> That famous Greece remains no longer slave;
> That source of art and cultivated thought!
> Which they to Rome and Romans hither brought.
> The banished Muses shall no longer mourn,
> But may with liberty to Greece return.[21]

[19] John Dyer borrowed these lines in the *Epistle to a Famous Painter* (1726), a
poem that "gathers together the ideals of that age for landscape painting" (Elizabeth
W. Manwaring, *Italian Landscape in Eighteenth Century England* [1925], p. 107).

[20] See "To Kneller," ll. 21-110. Evelyn's *Sculptura* (p. 106) had a similar historical account, and he was inclined to accept the "shadow" origin of the arts.
Denham's poem reflected both the Christian background of the seventeenth century
and its Baconian interest in all knowledge in its inclusion of the Hebrew, Chaldean,
and Egyptian portions of the history of learning—sections which some writers in the
eighteenth century were inclined to drop out or to slight.

[21] "A Presage of the Ruin of the Turkish Empire," (? 1684), ll. 37-42. See also
"Of the Invasion and Defeat of the Turks, in the Year 1683," ll. 69-70. (*The Poems
of Edmund Waller*, ed. G. Thorn-Drury, "Muses' Library" [1893], pp. 232, 230.)

Nor was Dryden's work free from the jargon of the arts, phrases like the "animated canvas or bust," the "speaking marble," or the "mimic strife with nature"—phrases prominent in the cant of criticism for more than a century.

Yet Dryden's very important place in the tradition of English interest in sculpture—and this meant, of course, ancient, especially Hellenistic and Greco-Roman, sculpture—comes through his criticism rather than his poetry. For he gave the connoisseurs and poets of the eighteenth century perhaps their most important as well as most convenient source of ideas about antique sculpture in his translation (1695) of Du Fresnoy's *De arte graphica,* which had become a handbook for the Academies on its appearance in 1665. To the treatise of the French critic Dryden prefixed *A Parallel of Poetry and Painting,* and in both works sculpture had a conspicuous place. Since the ideas of Du Fresnoy, Dryden, and similar critics turned up in poetry as well as in criticism throughout the eighteenth century, certain of their Neo-Classical theories about Grecian sculpture which were to be particularly common in poetry, even occasionally in that of the Romantic period, may be noticed here.[22]

First of all, the art-process was primarily mental or intellectual: the idea, the design, the cerebration must be supreme in directing the hand of the artist, who must not neglect to give a nobler beauty than a mere resemblance to nature. For the pleasure derived from the fine arts is not so much the apelike or literal imitation which had

[22] *De arte graphica* was to be translated three times in the eighteenth century at intervals arranged almost as if by plan, in 1728, 1754, and 1781. The last, by William Mason, had notes by Reynolds, and it might be called the Academic successor to Dryden's Neo-Classical translation. Though Dryden felt "not sufficiently vers'd in the *Terms of Art,*" he turned out the "tolerable translation" he wished. In his critical writings the arts assumed a role more important than the casual reference or hoary commonplace of Renaissance treatises. Indeed, Dryden gave more attention to the arts than they were to receive from any general literary critic until Coleridge. Though primarily concerned with the principles of poetry, each of these great poet-critics made clear his views on art in connection with the art most discussed in his day. Therefore, appropriating ideas from the foreign writers most congenial as well as most accessible to them, Dryden drew from Academic critics in France and Italy in his writing on pictorial art, and Coleridge borrowed from German propounders of the Romantic aesthetics in connection with the plastic art. In the case of each critic the material derived from foreign sources, however, was not so much a discovery of new theories as a corroboration of principles already held.

been admired so greatly among Renaissance theorists, even when they were aware of Aristotle's theory of ideal imitation, as a delight in "images more perfect than the life in any individual . . . the pleasure to see all the scattered beauties of Nature united by a happy chemistry, without its deformities or faults." Nature stands corrected in the light of a more perfect abstract or composite beauty, a "second" nature freed from the imperfections of actual nature. The artist reveals the idea-in-the-mind: "the artful painter and the sculptor, imitating the Divine Maker, form . . . a model of the superior beauties." [23] This was characteristic Neo-Classical theorizing in its combination of Aristotle's ideas concerning the universality of art and the Neo-Platonic idealism.

The ancient statues, it goes almost without saying, were thought to express Ideal Beauty and also to show how sculptors had been able to reveal their "ideas" in stone. Superior to human figures, their forms were models of the highest sort of beauty: "upon this account, the noblest poets and the best orators, when they desired to celebrate any extraordinary beauty, are forced to have recourse to statues and pictures." Thus, critics, artists, and poets could base the canons of proportion and beauty which guided their work and theory upon the ancient statues.[24]

In applying these ideas to poetry—and the ripples from his reluctant plunge into aesthetics in *A Parallel of Poetry and Painting* are more interesting than the treatise—Dryden made it clear that, after working with Neo-Classical criticism, he considered the highest type of poetry to be the epic, a poetry corresponding to the grand or sculptural style of such a painter as Poussin. The idea of a perfect nature was

[23] *A Parallel of Poetry and Painting, Essays of John Dryden,* ed. W. P. Ker (1900), II, 118, 137. Dryden quoted the "idea of a Painter" from Bellori's *Vite de' pittori, scultori ed architetti moderni* (1672). After a characteristically English warning against the "pompous expressions" of the critics, he added that Bellori's account "cannot be unpleasing, at least to such as are conversant in the philosophy of Plato." See Erwin Panofsky, *'Idea'; ein Beitrag zur Begriffsgeschichte der älteren Kunsttheorie,* "Studien der Bibliothek Warburg," No. 5 (Leipzig and Berlin, 1924); René Bray, *La Formation de la doctrine classique en France* (Paris, 1927), p. 171; Lee, in *Art Bulletin* (Dec., 1940), p. 204; and, of course, Ker's notes.

[24] *A Parallel,* p. 121. See also William G. Howard, "Ut Pictura Poesis," *PMLA,* XXIV (1909), 40 ff.

suitable to the heroes of the epic though not to the figures in tragedy, who must always have their tragic flaws or imperfections, or to the portraits of comedy. The epic alone, he wrote in the Dedication of *The Aeneis* (1697), could show men as they ought to be rather than as they are:

> where a character of perfect virtue is set before us, it is more lovely; for there the whole hero is to be imitated. This is the Aeneas of our author; this is that idea of perfection in an epic poem which painters and statuaries have only in their minds, and which no hands are able to express. These are the beauties of a god in a human body.

To Dryden as to many poets after him, the Antique showed, apparently, the beauties of gods in human bodies—the perfect, ideal, or heroic forms appropriate to lofty epics and high romances.

Yet Dryden himself did not always prefer, in theory any more than in practice, the severe or ideal or epic style of poetry. Through a theory of "kinds" of poetry he was able to defend his liking for comedy and satire as well as for epic and, significantly, for the less severe and stern epics. He first stated this theory of "kinds" in justifying the richly figurative language of his first important poem *Annus Mirabilis* (1666) by pointing out in the Preface a difference in the quality of the imagery in two ancient writers. The poet was to be like the sculptor, sometimes showing noble heroes "like those of Juvenal, *stantes in curribus Aemiliani* heroes drawn in their triumphal chariots, and in their full proportion," and sometimes showing softer figures "like those of Virgil, *spirantis mollius aera*." Similar sentiments appeared again in *An Essay of Dramatic Poesy* (1668) where Neander, the character who voiced the views of the author, criticized French poetry as rather too lifeless and perfect: "they are indeed the beauties of a statue, but not of a man, because not animated with the soul of Poesy, which is imitation of humour and passions." [25] To express the passions by outward signs—"to expresse manners by their looks in Imagery"—was the difficult problem for dramatic poet as well as for painter and sculptor.

Apparently Dryden was somewhat unhappy as an "academic"

[25] See also above, pp. 47 ff.

theorist; and at the close of *A Parallel of Poetry and Painting* he chose Virgil, who stressed expression or color—*operum colores*—in preference to Homer, whose superiority lay in design. In poetry, Dryden explicitly stated, "the expression is that which charms the reader, and beautifies the design, which is only the outlines of the fable." Design alone was merely so many "naked lines" or outlines. In the period of greatest interest in Greek sculpture, in the eighteenth century, those simple and barren lines and unadorned contours received high praise and were honored as "Grecian outlines." In the closing years of the seventeenth century, when Dryden wrote *A Parallel of Poetry and Painting,* however, the more strict standards being introduced by the theorists of the Academies gained partial acceptance only. In England the Neo-Classical idols remained Rome, elocution, elegance, color, painting, Raphael, Virgil, though in a few years poets were to transfer their esteem to the standards of Greece, invention, simplicity, design, sculpture, Michelangelo, Homer.

Evelyn the virtuoso and Dryden the Neo-Classical critic were similar, then, in showing that at the end of the seventeenth century critics, gentlemen, and poets looked to the Antique for precepts concerning literature and the arts. The more general praise of the Ancients by the men of the early Renaissance had given way to the study of particular statues and literary works as models. Rules of technique, canons of beauty and proportion, and principles of theory were now being deduced from the Antique. The medieval and Renaissance stress on imitation had been turned into a theory of invention in which one "imitated" the idea-in-the-mind. Dignified thus by an ideal and mental beauty, sculpture became the study for gentlemen, poets, and philosophers. At the close of the seventeenth century sculpture took its place as a sister of painting and poetry: all three were arts of design or invention; all expressed the idea-in-the-mind of the creator.

Since the English poets before the eighteenth century had but limited knowledge of the art of sculpture and of the Antique, they wrote little poetry on such themes, and most of what they did write stemmed from literary sources rather than statues. None the less, their marveling at the skill of workers in another art and their pleasure in seeing nature counterfeited prophesied the greater admiration of the forms of the Antique in the eighteenth century. Only occasionally, moreover, did they versify the theories disseminated by ancient works like those of Pliny and Plutarch or by such modern writings as Jonson's *Timber,* Junius's *De pictura,* Evelyn's *Sculptura,* or Dryden's *Parallel of Poetry and Painting.* Yet these treatises stressed Grecian statuary and helped spread information of and interest in the art, an interest that led to the more frequent appearance of the sculpture of the Greeks in the didactic and descriptive poetry of the eighteenth century.

MILTON THE "GRECIAN"

Since John Milton stood somewhat apart from his contemporaries in the grandeur of his poetry as in many other respects, he belongs in this study on the threshold of the century for which he was the "Grecian" Milton. His earlier and shorter pieces were Renaissance in feeling and manner, and they come to mind often in reading the later poems. But in general the longer masterpieces were written in what Matthew Arnold later labeled "the grand style severe." That grand severity was recognized immediately. Even as Byron woke up to find himself famous after having written *Childe Harold,* so Milton with as much justice might have said he became an Ancient almost overnight. For he was hardly in his grave when critics began to associate him with the masters of classical antiquity. Dryden, most readers probably feel now, was rather too generous in saying that Milton outdid even the Ancients.

In any case, Atterbury, writing before Addison's papers on *Paradise Lost* in the *Spectator,* "was chiefly susceptible to his Greek beauty and simplicity." [26] Connoisseurs thought of the plastic or sculptural quality of such grand figures as Beelzebub,

> Majestic, though in ruin. Sage he stood,
> With Atlantean shoulders,

[26] See Laura Wylie, *Studies in the Evolution of English Criticism* (Boston, 1894), p. 67.

and referred to the Antique. In his important edition of *Paradise Lost* in 1734, Jonathan Richardson, Senior, friend of Pope and inspirer of Reynolds, boldly proclaimed: "Milton . . . writes like an Antient, a *Greek,* and it gives a Noble Beauty to his Works. . . . Milton is Alwaies Antique. . . . All his Images are Pure Antique." [27] Milton possessed, in fact, the "certain Grace, Majesty, and Simplicity" which connoisseurs felt to be the distinguishing trait of the Antique "to a Degree beyond what We have ever found in Any Modern Painter or Sculptor, not Excepting *Rafaelle* Himself." Richardson's most interesting claim was his most extravagant. To form anything like an adequate conception of the physical loveliness of Adam and Eve, the reader must refer to the Antique as well as to painting:

Their Complexions cannot be well Conceiv'd but with *Pittoresque* eyes; Neither can their Forms by one who is not Acquainted with Antique Sculpture, nor by Him that is Intirely; the *Apollo* of the *Belvedere,* the *Antinoüs,* the *Meleager,* the *Venus* of *Medicis,* with the Body, and part of the Thighs of a more Ancient, and more Exquisite Statue of that goddess (judg'd to be of *Phidias*) in the Collection of the Great Duke, &c. These will help our Imagination as to their Limbs, and their Harmony One with Another, but let us still Imagine the First of the Human Race were not only of more Excellent Forms than any Since, but more Excellent than any of their Descendants, even the Best of the *Greek* Sculptors, were able to Represent; tho' the Utmost of Humane Wit and Skill was professedly Employ'd to produce the Most Exalted Forms, that could be Conceiv'd to be in a Humane, in a Divine Body. Or if they could give us the Lifeless Figures in Brass or Marble, the Animated Beauty, and That which arises from the Constant Variety of Attitudes, Lights, Shadows, and Reflections are utterly Inexpressible (p. 156).

Grecian statuary aided one in realizing the form and shape of Milton's figures, but their life and breathing vitality—their "animated beauty" —was beyond the reach of the sculptors of the antique masterpieces. Richardson was likewise with the poets in remarking that Milton did not copy or imitate the Ancients but wrote of matters of expressive

[27] Pp. cxlviii, 49, 251. This is the earliest *OED* citation of "antique" as referring to "the manner of the Greeks and Romans." But the word had had this meaning in Evelyn's *Sculptura* (1662), and probably may be found even earlier.

value in his own day with "the Self-same Poetical Genius" as that of Homer.[28]

Fifty years later the climax of this sort of comparison of Milton's work with the Antique came when Horace Walpole wrote in a letter to John Pinkerton (June 26, 1785), "Milton had such superior merit, that I will only say, that if his angels, his Satan, and his Adam have as much dignity as the Apollo Belvidere, his Eve has all the delicacy and graces of the Venus of Medicis." It was atrocious criticism, yet in the 1780's Milton had received the highest compliment a connoisseur could offer a poet! Artists, including Blake, gave classical forms to the "Grecian" figures of the great Puritan poet in their illustrations for his works in the late eighteenth and early nineteenth centuries.

Though he was praised for possessing the qualities of the Antique, the rarity of Milton's own allusions to the fine arts was strange, especially in the light of both his visit to Italy when still an impressionable young poet and his virtuoso-like acquaintance with many fields of human learning. Jonathan Richardson was apparently the first to comment on the silence that has puzzled many readers of Milton.[29] There were but two considerable mentions of sculpture and architecture in his poetry, and in each case the sculpture was part of the architectural design rather than statuary used for its own sake. The palace of Satan where the fallen angels gathered in *Paradise Lost* (Book I, l. 716) did not want "Cornice or frieze, with bossy sculptures graven." Chief among the glories with which Satan tempted Christ in his panorama of classical lands in *Paradise Regained* (Book IV, ll. 58–59) were noble edifices at Rome with

> Carved work, the hand of famed artificers
> In cedar, marble, ivory, or gold.

In these two instances Milton may have drawn on his memories of buildings and ruins in Italy, responding in the fashion of the men

---

[28] *Ibid.*, p. cxlix. None the less, Richardson advanced the opinion that Milton pictured a beardless Adam because the Grecian statues of gods and men were without beards, as were the figures in Raphael; see pp. 158–59.

[29] *Ibid.*, p. xv; Ida Langdon, *Milton's Theory of Poetry and Fine Art* (New Haven, 1924), p. 33; Coleridge, *Table Talk*, August 7, 1832; and Hazlitt, "On Milton's Versification" and *Lectures on the English Poets* (*Works*, ed. Howe, IV, 38 ff.; V, 60 ff.).

of the early seventeenth century to the ingenuity and magnificent splendor of the classical works. The "gold-and-glitter" of his lines was in keeping, too, with similar descriptions of temples and statues in the earlier Greek writers like Homer, Hesiod, Pindar, or Herodotus. He was actually more "antique" in such descriptions than one usually thinks, for they helped make him, in Richardson's phrase, "more a Greek than a Roman." [30]

The same early Greek and English Renaissance lack of aesthetic feeling for statuary appears in the newly discovered prose work, "Of Statues and Antiquities," printed by the editors of the Columbia *Milton* as "perhaps by John Milton." The writer of the fragment was concerned with the value and location of Grecian statues and with the practical instructions for obtaining them, such as the proper approach to a Turk, the presentation of a letter of credit, the necessary equipment of saws and cranes, and the removal of the rarities of carved work to warehouses and finally to ships. If Milton was the composer of the notes, he had a mercenary rather than aesthetic partiality for the nude: "The things to be sought for are these following: Statues clothed & naked, but the naked ones are of greatest value." Virtuosos were willing to pay well to possess a "nudity."

Though writing so scantily of the Antique,[31] in the eighteenth century Milton had a great influence in developing the interest of English poets in Greek sculpture. To begin with, vague as his descriptions of classical buildings were, they came into the minds of later poets, Addison and Pope for example, when describing similar objects. But through his moral and political ideas Milton exerted an influence greater than that of any other English poet upon the non-artistic aspects of the tradition of interest in Grecian statuary. From his beliefs and personality as well as from his poetry in the vein of

[30] See F. P. Chambers, *Cycles of Taste*, pp. 3 ff.

[31] From the large body of Milton's prose Miss Langdon (pp. 37, 50) cited but two passages concerned with sculpture: *Prose Works,* ed. St. John (1870–73), II, 469, and III, 154. They were learned references out of his reading, the latter based on Aristotle, *Ethics* X, 9 (1181a). Miss Langdon's conclusion that Milton's "indifference to much of the builder's and the sculptor's work . . . is of course his by right of birth and calling. As Englishman and as poet, he may be expected to turn elsewhere for aesthetic enjoyment" was obviously too sweeping. After the Antique became known, sculpture was the favorite art with many Englishmen, especially poets.

the Ancients stemmed in large measure the Grecianizing of English taste which was to bear such splendid results in the poetry of the Romantic period.

For the poets of the eighteenth century, as for those of the Romantic period, Milton the "Grecian" stood as the great advocate of liberty and the great humanist. In his work they found an insistence on the idea (classical in origin, but Ciceronian and Ovidian rather than early Greek) that eloquence and morality go hand in hand: freedom and the arts rise and fall together.[32] For more than a century similar sentiments were to be on almost every English poet's lips. Milton specifically acknowledged the debt of English poetry and learning to "the old and elegant humanity of Greece." Only "the civil commotions in England," which broke out while he was in Italy, could draw him from his plan "to pass over into Sicily and Greece."[33] In a spirit prophetic of Byron, Shelley, and other English poets he wrote in a letter to the Athenian Leonard Philaras (January, 1652),

Did I possess their [the ancient writers'] command of language and their force of persuasion, I should feel the highest satisfaction in employing them to excite our armies and our fleets to deliver Greece, the parent of eloquence, from the despotism of the Turks. . . . And what did formerly men of the greatest courage and eloquence deem more noble, or more glorious, than by their courage and their valour to assert the liberty and independence of the Greeks.

Literature remained first in the knowledge and affection of the poets, of course, but Grecian sculpture was already becoming a second symbol of perfection, so that the unsurpassed achievement of the Greeks in art was to be often in the minds of poets. As critic and gentleman, artist and poet, increased their knowledge of the Antique, the Grecian statues became favorite examples of beautiful figures revealing the activities of the soul by their attitudes and shapes—lessons which English poets found first of all in the works of their

[32] See *Prolusio* VII, in *Prose Works*, I, 241; Langdon, *Milton's Theory of Poetry and Fine Art*, pp. 287 ff.; and Spingarn, *Critical Essays of the Seventeenth Century*, I, ci; III, 210-11, and notes.

[33] *Areopagitica* and *Second Defense*, respectively, in *Prose Works*, I, 256; III, 52.

greatest "Grecian," John Milton. Against the background of the ideas which were beginning to cluster about the poetry of Milton, one may study the use of Grecian statuary by representative poets of the eighteenth century from Addison to Darwin and Hayley.

IV. THE EIGHTEENTH CENTURY

ADDISON AND POPE: THE MANNERS
AND THE MIND

FOR ADDISON, as for Milton, a tyrannical state spelled the end of the liberal arts. In *A Letter from Italy* (written in 1701) and later works, he frequently contrasted the Italy of the age of Cato with the wretched state through which he had traveled. Taking his cue from Milton and Waller, Addison regretted, too, that Greece languished under the Turks. The new land of liberty was England, and London had become the Athens of the West. Proclaiming his faith in the renaissance taking place in that ideal England of the Augustans, Addison announced a sentiment which included several fundamental ideas of the eighteenth century: "Riches and plenty are the natural fruit of liberty, and where these abound, learning and all the liberal arts will immediately lift up their heads and flourish" (*Spectator,* No. 287).

Anxious not to neglect anything which dignifies mankind, Addison disseminated a certain amount of information about the arts and enrolled himself among the aesthetic critics. Moreover, he was the first English poet in whose work the art of sculpture was of more importance than painting. He had visited Italy where ancient "pillars rough with sculpture pierce the skies"; and, like poets from Hildebert to Shelley, he had been stimulated most by the statuary, reporting that "no part of the antiquities of Rome pleased me so much as the ancient statues." [1] Perhaps the preference of statuary was inevitable when one viewed Italy, as Dr. Johnson remarked of Addison, "with the eyes of

---

[1] *A Letter from Italy*, p. 77, and "Remarks on Italy," *Works,* ed. Hurd (1870), I, 33, 459. In *Topographical Poetry in XVIII-Century England* (New York, 1936), pp. 242–44, Robert A. Aubin places Addison's poem in the "seriously descriptive" group of journey-poems: "Addison conscientiously packs in historical reflections and notices of statues and paintings."

a poet." Still, his interest in the antiquities was chiefly historical and archaeological; his feeling for sculpture was that of the seventeenth-century poets and critics, instead of the more personal and emotional response of Shaftesbury and Thomson and other heralds of the "romantic" views of the Antique.

The beauty Addison found in the ancient statues described in *A Letter from Italy* and later in books was the skill of the mimicry of life admired by earlier poets:

> Still to new scenes my wandering muse retires,
> And the dumb show of breathing rocks admires;
> Where the smooth chisel all its force has shown,
> And softened into flesh the rugged stone.
> In solemn silence, a majestic band,
> Heroes, and gods, and Roman consuls stand;
> Stern tyrants, whom their cruelties renown,
> And Emperors in Parian marble frown (ll. 83–90).

The poetic level of those lines was higher than the sensitivity of a poet who could refer to statues as breathing "rocks." The burden of all his remarks about sculpture was that "a man would wonder how it were possible for so much life to enter into marble"; he never tired of asserting that statues "live." [2]

In a poetic eulogy addressed to Sir Godfrey Kneller, Painter to His Majesty, Addison devoted one-third of the lines to some elaborate "sculptures," praising thus the painter who immortalized George I after having portrayed all the monarchs from Charles II, thereby following "the wise Phidias" who advanced through a series of sculptures of the lesser deities to Jove himself. The sculptures attributed to Phidias were vignettes out of mythology and contemporary politics rather than actual statues; yet the poet took pains to pose the figures in characteristic attitudes.

Above all, Addison valued ancient statuary for the pleasure gained from the passages of Latin poetry it called to mind; his approach to the Greco-Roman sculptures was mainly that of the literary critic. In the *Dialogues upon Ancient Medals* (1721) Eugenius expressed the

[2] See "Remarks on Italy," *Works*, I, 376, 459, 461. Addison even added the statement of "life" to descriptions of statuary by Propertius.

opinion of the critic himself when he remarked, "Poetry being in some respects an art of designing as well as painting or sculpture, they may serve as comments on each other." The statement reflected the feeling of English men of taste, and Pope singled it out for special praise in a poem commending Addison for the *Dialogues*.

> Nor blush, these studies thy regard engage;
> These pleased the fathers of poetic rage:
> The verse and sculpture bore an equal part,
> And Art reflected images to Art.[3]

Pope's phrases, especially the last two lines, echoed down the highroad of eighteenth-century taste, and the use of sculpture to "explain" literature became a commonplace in aesthetics. Joseph Spence, in particular, elaborated Addison's ideas in the famous *Polymetis* (1747), adding what amounted to an *Ut sculptura poesis* to the universally accepted Horatian parallel of painting and poetry. Owing to the influence of Addison and Pope as well as Spence and other critics, writers in England were still repeating the cant about the arts mutually assisting one another and "reflecting images from art to art" when Lessing broke the strangle hold of such ambiguous phrases and, in the words of Goethe, "made clear the difference between the plastic and literary art." [4]

Addison's remarks indicated that in the early eighteenth century sculpture had become a true sister-art of poetry and painting; an acquaintance with the art of the sculptor was now expected of poet and critic as well as of artist and connoisseur. To maintain a ready supply of images, the poet must study the works of painter and sculptor, and the artist must regard those of the poet. Everyone who aspired to write "should be very well versed," said Addison, "in everything that is noble and stately in the productions of art, whether it appear in painting or statuary" (*Spectator,* No. 417). A cultivated Augustan, Addison foretold the course of a considerable body of English poetry

---

[3] See *Works,* I, 270, and pp. 267 and 320 for "the affinity between coins and poetry" and Pope, Epistle VII, "To Mr. Addison Occasioned by His Dialogues on Medals," pp. 51–52.

[4] See *Dichtung und Wahrheit,* ed. Smith and Breul (1913), II, 282, and Spingarn, *Critical Essays of the Seventeenth Century,* III, 301.

and, despite his limited appreciation of sculpture, helped to direct his countrymen to the Antique.

Alexander Pope, in the opinion of commentators like Warburton, always displayed "real science" in his many references to the fine arts; no Augustan poet was more "deep in pictures, statues, or architecture." [5] In the fashion of many English gentlemen of the time, he gathered information about the arts and cultivated the friendship of artists. He dabbled in painting and studied landscape gardening; he prepared treatises on Italian antiquities and collected objects of virtu for his grotto. To Richard Boyle, Earl of Burlington, whose editions of the *Designs of Inigo Jones* and the *Antiquities of Rome* by Palladio were important "art-events," Pope addressed Epistle IV, "Of Taste," of the *Moral Essays*. Sir Godfrey Kneller made some adornments for Pope's house at Twickenham, and the poet thanked him with the fulsome quatrain "On Drawings of the Statues of Apollo, Venus, and Hercules."

Early in his career Pope reflected the growing familiarity of English writers with sculpture. In the translation of *The First Book of Statius's Thebais* (1703) he wrote of an age when

> No laboured columns in long order placed,
> No Grecian stone the pompous arches graced (ll. 202-3).

In *The Temple of Fame* (written in 1711) Pope contrived some literary "sculptures" corresponding to Addison's "Phidian" figures. The younger poet was more clearly in the tradition of literary descriptions of statuary, with the "hint" for his poem "taken from Chaucer's *House of Fame,*" as he explained, and with various details derived from temples and mural decorations in Virgil, Milton, and Dryden. Despite the setting reminiscent of the landscapes of Claude Lorrain, the Temple of Fame was utterly unlike the chastely classical buildings of the painter. Designed to include all the architectural and statuary art of the world—classical architrave and sculptures; luxurious and vague Assyrian figures; Egyptian statues, obelisks, and hieroglyphics;

[5] See *An Essay on Criticism . . . with Notes by Mr. Warburton* (1749), p. 64, and Spence's *Anecdotes, Observations, and Characters, of Books and Men,* ed. Singer (1820), p. 210, where Pope remarked that Bolingbroke "was not deep in pictures, statues, or architecture."

and Gothic "colosses" and runic inscriptions—the edifice was just
what the poet chose to term it: a "stupendous pile!" The temple was
"Gothick," partly because it was inspired by a medieval poet and
partly because it mingled various kinds of art.

While the inspiration was mainly literary, Pope was better
acquainted with "the selection and arrangement of images" than
Chaucer had been; hence many of the figures on the four faces of
the temple were really sculptures.

> Here fabled chiefs in darker ages born,
> Or worthies old, whom arms or arts adorn,
> Who cities raised, or tamed a monstrous race,
> The walls in venerable order grace.
> Heroes in animated marble frown,
> And legislators seem to think in stone (ll. 69–74).

He was partial, of course, to the westward or classical front, to which
he gave the Doric style "peculiarly sacred to heroes," and some of
the finest poetry in the work.

> A sumptuous frontispiece appeared,
> On Doric pillars of white marble reared,
> Crown'd with an architrave of antique mold,
> And sculpture rising on the roughen'd gold.
> In shaggy spoils here Theseus was beheld,
> And Perseus dreadful with Minerva's shield:
> There great Alcides stopping with his toil,
> Rests on his club, and holds th' Hesperian spoil.
> Here Orpheus sings; trees moving to the sound
> Start from their roots, and form a shade around:
> Amphion there the loud-creating lyre
> Strikes, and beholds a sudden Thebes aspire!
> Cithaeron's echoes answer to his call,
> And half the mountain rolls into a wall (ll. 75–88).

Of these sculptures giving definite form to the suggestions of the
"Doric pillars overlaid with golden architrave" and the "bossy sculptures" in *Paradise Lost,* the most interesting was that of Hercules.
Pope had stationed the statue, he told his readers in a footnote, "with
an eye to the position of the famous statue of Farnese." Whether he

had seen a cast of great Alcides resting on his club or merely an engraving of the figure, he had his eye on the object. This seems to have been the first time that an English poet "drew" a figure after looking at a specific antique representation of a classical subject. Other statues on the exterior of the temple were in older and different traditions, the "posture" of the Egyptian priest on the "southern" front being suggested by a passage in Herodotus, and the Orpheus and the Amphion described as imaginary "sculptures." [6] They were all presented as though they were alive, but whenever the poet followed actual models, they held his fancy in check.

Enjoying the chance to portray decorative effects and to show his learning, young Pope constructed the interior of the marvelous Temple of Fame in the ornate style of Milton's Pandaemonium. Within the vast hall, arranged as in Chaucer's temple or as in galleries in noble mansions, stood many literary and imaginary "sculptures." Along with the inevitable warrior-emperors, Alexander and Caesar, Pope placed the favorite Augustan heroes: servants of the common weal like Epaminondas, Timoleon, Scipio, and Aurelius; "fair Virtue's silent train" of Socrates, Aristides, Phocion, Agis, Cato, and Brutus; and, standing even closer to the shrine of Fame, seven of the greatest ancient writers, Homer, Virgil, Pindar, Horace, Ovid, Aristotle, and Cicero. His ingenuity, however, was not equal to the task of conceiving such an ambitious number of statues. Only in the group of authors was there an approach to sculptural feeling or effect; the figure of Cicero may indeed have been taken from a statue. In presenting the authors Pope tried to be sculptural to the extent of seizing one significant or characteristic scene for each figure. Mounted on "pompous" columns which, according to the plan announced in the notes, were to be "adorned with sculptures, taken from the most striking subjects of their works, which sculpture bears a resemblance, in its manner and character, to the manner and character of their writings,"

[6] John Dennis criticized the lines describing the last two figures: "Trees starting from their roots, a mountain rolling into a wall, and a town rising like an exhalation are things that are not to be shown in sculpture" (*Works,* I, 207). It was an early attempt to distinguish between the subjects suitable to poetry and those suitable to sculpture.

the writers of antiquity dominated the hall. The "bold" actions of
the Trojan war flamed on Homer's pillar, while Virgil's showed

> In living sculpture . . .
> The Latian wars, and haughty Turnus dead;
> Eliza stretched upon the fun'ral pyre,
> Aeneas bending with his aged sire (ll. 204–7).

In the decoration of Pindar's column Pope's verse was nearest the
sculptural effect he wished; here he looked ahead to Thomson, Akenside, Keats, Shelley, and Landor in his description of scenes not unlike those on an Athenian frieze.

> The figured games of Greece the column grace,
> Neptune and Jove survey the rapid race.
> The youths hang o'er their chariots as they run;
> The fiery steeds seem starting from the stone;
> The champions in distorted postures threat (ll. 216–20).[7]

After the ambitious *Temple of Fame* Pope referred only infrequently to sculpture. That his acquaintance with the contemporary
ideas about the Antique was not small, however, is suggested not
only by the Lucius Verus, "large profile," and the Antinous of "Mr.
Pope's drawing"—a parallel worthy of note both to Collins's designs
for medallions *à l'antique* and to Keats's tracing of the Sosibios vase
—and the drawings of the Apollo, Venus, and Hercules at Twickenham, but also by the ease with which he incorporated portions of his
learning into the poetry.[8] In the *Dunciad* one finds the partly Ovidian
allusion to Niobe:

> Fast by, like Niobe (her children gone)
> Sits Mother Osborne, stupefy'd to stone (Book II, ll. 311–12),

while the reign of dullness foretold strange metamorphoses of the
works of ancient art:

> 'See the Cirque falls, th' unpillar'd Temple nods,
> Streets pav'd with Heroes, Tiber chok'd with Gods:

[7] For Pope's own note and for Warton's suggestion of a statue in the Pomfret
collection presented to Oxford, see *Works* (ed. Elwin and Courthope, 1871 ff.), I, 214.

[8] Spence (*Anecdotes*, p. 336) reported the Lucius Verus and the Antinous, apparently copies of prints of statuary, among Pope's paintings. See also George Sherburn,
The Early Career of Alexander Pope (1934), p. 103.

'Till Peter's keys some christ'ned Jove adorn,
And Pan to Moses lends his pagan horn;
See, graceless Venus to a Virgin turn'd,
Or Phidias broken, and Apelles burn'd.' (Book III, ll. 107-12.)

A passage in Epistle VII, "To Mr. Addison, Occasioned by His Dialogues on Medals," pictured the ruins of Rome and partly explained the fate of classical statuary before the Renaissance; among the "imperial wonders" were

> Fanes, which admiring Gods with pride survey,
> Statues of men, scarce less alive than they!
> Some felt the silent stroke of mouldering age,
> Some hostile fury, some religious rage.
> Barbarian blindness, Christian zeal conspire,
> And Papal piety, and Gothic fire (ll. 9-14).

The theories of the Academies and the catchwords of the connoisseurs found their way into the poetry of Pope. Since no poet could neglect to associate the condition of the arts with the condition of the body politic, he also expressed the Augustan faith in liberty, though less passionately than Addison and Thomson. Like Dryden, he had more interest in the history and theory of the arts than in their moral and political aspects. *An Essay on Criticism* was Pope's history of art, an abbreviated "progress" because he failed to take the story back to Greece, concentrating on "Leo's golden days" when sculpture led the recovery of the ancient genius.

> Then sculpture and her sister-arts revive;
> Stones leaped to form, and rocks began to live;
> With sweeter notes each rising temple rung;
> A Raphael painted, and a Vida sung (ll. 701-4).

Pope expressed these common ideas so well that his phrases were much imitated. Epistle VIII, "To Mr. Jervas," included many commonplaces of criticism, learned both from the artist himself and from "Mr. Dryden's Translation of Fresnoy's Art of Painting" given to the painter along with the poem. More interesting, however, was the poet's imaginary flight to Italy where the "well-studied marbles" of Jervas rose among "Rome's pompous glories." [9]

[9] See 11, 24 ff., 42-43, and 75 (*Works*, II, 212 ff.).

In satire, as one might expect, Pope used the fashionable interest in the Antique to better advantage than in his theorizing or in all but one or two "stationings" in *The Temple of Fame*. Too widespread to escape his scrutiny, the follies and affectations engendered by the virtuoso-passion invited the shafts of his wit. In ridiculing the collectors, antiquarians, and connoisseurs, Pope pointed out a field for satire which attracted many later poets, among them Akenside, Edward Young, Thomas Warton, Goldsmith, Cowper, and, in the Romantic period, Byron and Hunt. With Pope satire became a definite and recurrent though minor element in the poetry dealing with Grecian statuary.

The principal object of Pope's satiric thrusts was vulgar and lavish display, the false taste of Timon's villa where the formalized style of topiary art and the excessive use of statuary, he believed, offended reason and good sense.

> The suffering eye inverted Nature sees,
> Trees cut to statues, statues thick as trees;
>
> . . .
>
> Here Amphitrite sails through myrtle bowers;
> There gladiators fight, or die, in flowers.[10]

The eighth Earl of Pembroke was singled out for ridicule for his collection of "statues, dirty gods, and coins," while Bufo, the vain patron in *The Epistle to Dr. Arbuthnot,* was satirized as receiving would-be wits in a

> library (where busts of poets dead
> And a true Pindar stood without a head).

Such expressions of Pope's indifference to objects of virtu were clearly something of a pose in the light of his pride in his own taste; nevertheless, the position of the mature poet was best stated perhaps in the following Horatian lines:

---

[10] *Moral Essays,* Epistle IV, ll. 119 ff. (*Works,* III, 180). A note identified the gladiators as "the two statues of Gladiator pugnans, and Gladiator moriens." See also Pope's essay in the *Guardian,* No. 173, Sept. 29, 1713 (*Prose Works,* ed. Norman Ault [1936], I, 149), for the satirical suggestion that "the World stands much in need of a Virtuoso Gardiner who has a turn to Sculpture, and is thereby capable of improving upon the Ancients of his Profession in the Imagery of Evergreens."

> Gold, silver, ivory, vases sculptured high,
> Paint, marble, gems, and robes of Persian dye,
> There are who have not—and thank Heaven there are,
> Who, if they have not, think not worth their care.[11]

Even had Pope traveled in the realms of classical art, he would doubtless have continued to assert

> Not with such majesty, such bold relief,
> The forms august of king, or conquering chief,
> E'er swelled on marble, as in verse have shined
> (In polished verse) the manners and the mind.[12]

In poetry, the poets have maintained, "the manners and the mind" may best be seen. Statues show majestic or graceful forms and "reflect images" to the poet, but they cannot equal poetry in presenting the mental activities of the living man.

THOMSON AND AKENSIDE: A WARM DISPLAY OF MORAL BEAUTY

In James Thomson the feeling for landscape and the spirit of Platonism prevailed over connoisseurship and a mild sense of humor. Through his interest in the spirit operating within the forms of nature and of art—in short, the aesthetics of Shaftesbury—Thomson came to write passages about Grecian statuary quite different from those of Pope. To the "Grecian" poetry of Milton, Shaftesbury added for the eighteenth century a "Grecian" philosophy; and not even Milton had so direct an influence in nourishing the spreading tree of ideas whose fruit was the Hellenism of the Romantic poets, as had Anthony Ashley Cooper, third Earl of Shaftesbury, whom Herder called "the virtuoso of humanity." [13]

---

[11] *Imitations of Horace,* Book II, Epistle II, ll. 264–67; see also Book I, Epistle VI, ll. 30–31 (*Works,* III, 392, 320).

[12] *Ibid.,* Book II, Epistle I, ll. 390–93 (*Works,* III, 372).

[13] Modestly sprinkled through the moral philosophy of his famous *First Characteristicks* (1711), Shaftesbury's opinions on art were to have made a series of four treatises entitled "Second Characters; or the Language of Forms." The "great part" of that work, the "Plastics; or, The Original Progress and Power of the Designatory Art," was first printed in *Second Characters,* ed. Benjamin Rand (Cambridge, Mass., 1914). Shaftesbury's passage on the "Judgment of Hercules," however, had considerable influence on the Continent as well as in England; among other things it

A thinker of Platonic and Puritan coloring, Shaftesbury was concerned with beauty and harmony or proportion as moral agents and social ideals. His trust in liberty as the condition essential to the flourishing of the arts and in beauty attained not so much by following the "rules" as by Pythian enthusiasm was an ideal associated with the arts of the Ancients, especially sculpture, which was to become one of the greatest inspirations for many poets of the Romantic period. Simplicity, he believed, had characterized the Greek state; and sculpture, the eldest of the plastic arts as the art of design, had thrived there, encouraged by the religion and the "social publick and *free* spirit" of the Greeks.[14] Sculptors perfected their art in the schools of anatomy available in the athletic life and festival games. In reading ancient writers and modern critics and in studying the Antique in Italy, Shaftesbury found, like Winckelmann, the explanation of the glory of Greek sculpture in the life and institutions of Greece, an explanation which found poetic expression in the eighteenth century and among the Romantic poets. Shaftesbury might have written Winckelmann's chapter introductory to Greek art entitled, "Grounds and Causes of the Progress and Superiority of Greek Art beyond that of other Nations."

Shaftesbury knew the theories of the Academies, and the Grecian statues were the norms of beauty studied by artists "as esteeming them a better Rule, than the perfectest human Bodys cou'd afford." [15] But with poets from Jonson to Shelley and Wordsworth, Shaftesbury emphasized the inward beauty as the important thing: "Who can admire the *outward* Beautys, and not recur instantly to the *inward,* which are the most real and essential, the most naturally affecting . . . ?" [16] Among the English poets of the first half of the eighteenth century, Thomson and Akenside in particular responded

---

included "the fullest treatment of the 'fruitful moment' before Lessing." (See William G. Howard's memorable edition of the *Laokoon* [New York, 1910], p. lxxvii.)

[14] See *Characteristicks* (1723 ed.), III, 138 ff., and "Plastics," *Second Characters,* pp. 117, 124 ff., etc. He noted tersely (p. 123): "To insist beautiful forms beautify: polite, polish. On the contrary, gothic gothicize, barbarous barbarize." Had he been aware of his influence on eighteenth-century taste, he might have added, "Grecian forms Grecianize."

[15] *Characteristicks,* I, 145.   [16] *Ibid.,* III, 185.

to many of Shaftesbury's ideas, indicating in their verse several strands of interest in Grecian sculpture which they shared with later poets.

The first description of a specific antique statue in Thomson's poetry, however, was concerned with outward beauty, not the inner beauty of Shaftesbury's theory. In *The Seasons* he used the painter's effects for the most part; yet to do justice to the physical loveliness of the heroine of one of the narrative vignettes, he turned as a man of taste to the darling of the connoisseurs, the Venus de Medici. In a mildly Ovidian episode Musidora chanced to select for her bathing place the retreat of her lovelorn Damon. With the "naturalness" of eighteenth-century mythological poetry and painting, Damon was compared to Paris at the judgment on Mount Ida as he watched the nymph disrobe and enter the stream. He fled before long, but not until he had penned a note promising to guard his bathing lover from "each licentious eye." Her posture and behavior at the sight of "the alarming paper" demanded the Venus de Medici:

> With wild surprise,
> As if to marble struck, devoid of sense,
> A stupid moment motionless she stood:
> So stands the statue that enchants the world;
> So, bending, tries to veil the matchless boast,
> The mingled beauties of exulting Greece.[17]
> ("Summer," ll. 1344–49.)

Terror departed, though, on the sight of "her Damon's well-known hand," and soon she carved upon a tree: "The time may come you need not fly." Thomson had outdone Pope in "stationing" a figure in an image borrowed from an antique statue. Musidora-Venus trying to "veil the matchless boast" of Greece led a popular life; Thomson's simile remained the most famous description of a specific Grecian statue in English poetry until *Childe Harold*.

[17] The later version (1744) is quoted, since that was the one referred to by the Romantic poets and others. In the first appearance of the episode in the 1730 *Seasons*, the lines on the statue came earlier, at the account of Musidora's disrobing. They were more effectively presented in 1730, I believe, without the unnecessary turning to marble. On the other hand, the original lines were somewhat weaker:

> "So stands the statue that enchants the world,
> Her full proportions such, and bashful so
> Bends ineffectual from the roving eye."

Having shown in *The Seasons* how a poet might utilize a work of sculpture, when in Italy in 1731 Thomson naturally looked, as he wrote in letters describing his activities, upon the remains of ancient art "in regard that the sisters [the fine arts] reflect light and images to one another." Yet he had none of Addison's archaeological zeal: he had "no taste for smelling to an old musty stone." Nor did he visit the learned Academies, as Milton had done. He was less excited by the scenery than Gray was to be a few years later. A tutor-companion, he probably carried few funds with which to collect antiquities, though he took home a number of engravings of classical statuary. Travel soon palled, and only the antique statues, "where several of the fair ideas of Greece are fixed for ever in marble," and paintings remained "enchanting." [18] The end of travel, he felt, was the impulse to creative work or lofty endeavor. Wed to genius, study of the Antique was to produce noble works of art in England:

The nature of the great painter, architect, and statuary, is the same as ever she was; and is no doubt as profuse of beauty, proportion, lovely forms, and real genius, as formerly she was to the sunny realms of Greece, did we but study the one and exert the other.

Liberty (published between 1734 and 1736) was both the fruit of Thomson's travel and the proof of his learning. It was the "poetical landscape of countries, mixed with moral observations on their government and people," planned when he set foot on the Continent, according to a letter to Bubb Dodington (December 27, 1730). His ideas gathered on classic ground were intended to encourage the muses in England, and the essay on morality predominated over the "poetical landscape" which might otherwise have become another *Seasons*. *Liberty* rose to its highest flight of poetry in the account of antique statues (Part IV, ll. 141 ff.). Reflecting not only a Neo-Classical interest in fine models and in history and theory but a more emotional response to Grecian statuary, Thomson gave in this treatise the poetic equivalent of Shaftesbury's prose on Greece and its art.

[18] Letters to Bubb Dodington, Oct. 24, 1731 and Nov. 28, 1731. See "Memoir" by Sir Harris Nicolas, *The Poetical Works* (1847), I, lvi–lix. For the influence of Thomson's travel on his poetry, see Manwaring, *Italian Landscape in Eighteenth Century England*, pp. 104 ff.

The framework of *Liberty* was the sketch of the ages of freedom —Greece, Rome, Renaissance Italy, Augustan England, with the assertion that wherever there had been an era of liberty, the arts had flourished. The technical "progress" of the arts was the one then accepted:

> First, elder Sculpture taught her sister art
> Correct design; where great ideas shone,
> And in the secret trace expression spoke.
> (Part II, ll. 324–27.)

To Thomson the outline of history was no commonplace; rather the role of sculpture in leading the procession of the arts, in Greece and in the Renaissance, was eloquent testimony to the power of the plastic spirit which had molded "great ideas" and still guided men and nations in the shaping of new forms. In lines suggestive of Wordsworth and Shelley as well as of Shaftesbury and Winckelmann he showed that the forms of art may teach men virtue: Painting (he was thinking as much perhaps of her elder sister Sculpture)

> Caught from the heavenly Muse a nobler aim,
> And scorning the soft trade of mere delight,
> O'er all thy [Greece's] temples, porticos, and schools,
> Heroic deeds she traced, and warm displayed
> Each moral beauty to the ravished eye.
> There, as the imagined presence of the god
> Aroused the mind, or vacant hours induced
> Calm contemplation, or assembled youth
> Burned in ambitious circle round the sage,
> The living lesson stole into the heart,
> With more prevailing force than dwells in words.[19]
> (Part II, ll. 339–49.)

In the account of the statues Thomson had his eye on the actual works, describing them both from memory and from prints by Castelli. The poetry was in the manner of Pope's Hercules in *The Temple of Fame* and his own Venus in *The Seasons*, but here the poet tried to give a complete and technical account of each statue.

[19] The passage as a whole suggests Wordsworth's *Excursion*, Book IV, ll. 720 ff., while the last two lines present the argument of the Painter in *Timon of Athens* (I, i, 92–94); see above, p. 40*n*, and below, pp. 124–27.

Where an appreciation of the sculptor's art was added, Thomson was adding a new element to the poetry on Grecian statuary. The earlier critics had asserted that the sculptor must express "the manners by looks in imagery," and Thomson now showed how the makers of the favorite statues of the Neo-Classical theorists were thought to have applied that theory. He read the activities of the soul from the posture and "air" of the statue; the form was expressive of the emotions and passions, in short, "the manners and the mind." As the types for many eighteenth-century and Romantic descriptions of sculpture, the visionary parade of the finest examples of the Antique may be quoted here.

1. The Farnese Hercules: expanded from Pope into the most technical account.

> In leaning site, respiring from his toils,
> The well known Hero, who delivered Greece,
> His ample chest, all tempested with force,
> Unconquerable reared. She [Sculpture] saw the head,
> Breathing the hero, small, of Grecian size,
> Scarce more extensive than the sinewy neck
> The spreading shoulders, muscular, and broad;
> The whole a mass of swelling sinews, touched
> Into harmonious shape;

2. The Meleager: slightly noticed but showing that the Grecian artists expressed "ideas."

> The yellow hunter, Meleager, raised
> His beauteous front, and through the finished whole
> Shows what ideas smiled of old in Greece.

3. The Fighting Gladiator: rhetoric increases in this and the companion figure.

> Of raging aspect, rushed impetuous forth
> The Gladiator: pitiless his look,
> And each keen sinew braced, the storm of war,
> Ruffling, o'er all his nervous body frowns.

4. The Dying Gladiator.

> The dying other from the gloom she drew:
> Supported on his shortened arm he leans,

Prone, agonizing; with incumbent fate,
Heavy declines his head; yet dark beneath
The suffering feature sullen vengeance lours,
Shame, indignation, unaccomplished rage
And still the cheated eye expects his fall.

5. The Apollo Belvedere: Byronic in style but expressing Shelleyan feeling for graceful, youthful, "softened form."

All conquest-flushed, from prostrate Python, came
The quivered God. In graceful act he stands,
His arm extended with the slackened bow:
Light flows his easy robe, and fair displays
A manly softened form. The bloom of gods
Seems youthful o'er the beardless cheek to wave:
His features yet heroic ardour warms;
And sweet subsiding to a native smile,
Mixed with the joy elating conquest gives,
A scattered frown exalts his matchless air.

6. The Flora: welcome in her brevity.

On Flora moved; her full proportioned limbs
Rise through the mantle fluttering in the breeze.

7. The Venus de Medici: possessing all the ambiguities of eighteenth-century sentiment and verse concerning the Queen of Love and of Sculpture.

The Queen of Love arose, as from the deep
She sprung in all the melting pomp of charms.
Bashful she bends, her well taught look aside
Turns in enchanting guise, where dubious mix
Vain conscious beauty, a dissembled sense
Of modest shame, and slippery looks of love.
The gazer grows enamoured, and the stone,
As if exulting in its conquest, smiles.
So turned each limb, so swelled with softening art,
That the deluded eye the marble doubts.

8. The Laocoön: Thomson's Neo-Classical choice for "the best proportions" of Greece, in verse unlightened by the spirit of Virgil.

At last her utmost masterpiece she found
That Maro fired; the miserable sire,

Wrapt with his sons in fate's severest grasp;
The serpents, twisting round, their stringent folds
Inextricable tie. Such passion here,
Such agonies, such bitterness of pain,
Seem so to tremble through the tortured stone,
That the touched heart engrosses all the view.
Almost unmarked the best proportions pass
That ever Greece beheld; and, seen alone,
On the rapt eye the imperious passions seize:
The father's double pangs, both for himself
And sons convulsed; to Heaven his rueful look,
Imploring aid, and half accusing, cast;
His fell despair with indignation mixed,
As the strong curling monsters from his side
His full extended fury cannot tear.
More tender touched, with varied art, his sons
All the soft rage of younger passions show.
In a boy's helpless fate one sinks oppressed;
While, yet unpierced, the frighted other tries
His foot to steal out of the horrid twine.[20]

Despite the tendency toward excessive rhetoric, Thomson had "experienced" the statues; accordingly, he made a sincere effort to capture the emotional and poetic value of each figure. Interpretation was more interesting than mere description; after Thomson had shown the way, his procedure characterized the best poetry on the Antique. Yet no eighteenth-century poet made better use of the language of the studio and of the connoisseurs than did the author of *Liberty*.

Mark Akenside was more explicit than Thomson in recommending the emotional approach to works of art. Impatient with the rules, he announced that the man of innate taste should look at Grecian statuary with the definite intention of seeking its sensuous qualities, its "beauty."

Suppose a statue modelled according to [the canon of Polycletus]: a man of mere natural taste, upon looking at it, without entering into its pro-

---

[20] Of the statues described, only the Flora was not among the engravings bought in Italy. The two statues in prints which Thomson failed to include were the Antinous and the Perseus and Andromeda. (See Léon Morel, *James Thomson, sa vie et ses œuvres* [Paris, 1895], p. 113.) The number of lines apportioned to a statue indicates rather well its relative esteem at the time, while the order of mention was intended to suggest the order of discovery in the Renaissance.

portions, confesses and admires its beauty; whereas a professor of art applies his measure to the head, the neck, or the hand, and, without attending to its beauty, pronounces the workmanship to be just and true.

Those "beauties" were also portions of truth and goodness; for the remark was a commentary on the lines (similar to the more famous ones of Keats, who was in part in debt to Akenside) on beauty:

> The lovely ministress of Truth and Good
> In this dark world; for Truth and Good are one,
> And Beauty dwells in them, and they in her,
> With like participation.[21]
> (*Pleasures of the Imagination*, Book I, ll. 373–76.)

Such sentiments prepared the way for what has become known as "impressionistic" criticism, the "adventures of a soul among masterpieces."

Akenside chose to show the beauties of art by versifying theory rather than by presenting a catalogue of admired statues like Thomson's. In vaguely Platonic terms he attempted to set forth the spirit of high workmanship, the plastic power in the sister-arts. All artists gave concrete expression to their "ideas" or "fair conceptions," with the poet enjoying a superiority over the painter and the sculptor.

> Others, mean time
> The rugged mass of metal, wood, or stone,
> Patiently taming; or with easier hand
> Describing lines, and with more ample scope
> Uniting colours; can to the general sight
> Produce those permanent and perfect forms,
> Those characters of heroes and of gods,
> Which from the crude materials of the world,
> Their own high minds created. But the chief
> Are poets.[22] (Book IV, ll. 93–102.)

Though the aesthetics of Shaftesbury seems always to have been congenial to Akenside, he could write satirically in regard to the fashionable taste for the Antique. In the amusing Spenserian stanzas

[21] The ancestry of the ideas was apparent in the references to Xenophon (*Memorabilia*, III, 8), Shaftesbury, "the noble restorer of ancient philosophy," and Hutcheson.

[22] Added in 1770. See also Book I, ll. 473 ff., and Book III, ll. 361, 584. Wordsworth's *Recluse* is suggested; see below, pp. 127–28.

of *The Virtuoso* he gave one of the best English satires on the tribe
of gentlemen-philosophers and connoisseurs.

> A curious medallist, I wot, he was,
>   And boasted many a course of ancient coin;
> Well as his wife's he knewen every face,
>   From Julius Caesar down to Constantine:
> For some rare sculpture he would oft ypine,
>   (As green-sick damosels for husbands do;)
> And when obtained, with enraptur'd eyne,
>   He'd run it o'er and o'er with greedy view,
>   And look, and look again, as he would look it through.
>   (Stanza iv, ll. 1–9.)

Still, Akenside loudly praised the genius of old Greece in its liberty
and arts, encouraging his countrymen to "chastise" their "English
fancy's eager flame . . . to Grecian purity." [23] In his praise of the
Grecian state and morality, in versifying the plastic spirit of artistic
activity in the manner of a "frozen" Shelley, and in his emphasis
on emotion and feeling, Akenside was prophetic, along with Thomson and their master Shaftesbury, of many elements in the poetry
and criticism of the Romantic period.

THE "GRECIAN GUSTO": GRACE IN EVERYTHING

The various nonclassical aspects of eighteenth-century taste, such
as landscape, Ossian, ballads, Gothic art, and *chinoiserie,* were not so
much the reflections of a revolt from the classical as the symptoms
and companions of a different interpretation of the antique world
itself in which the favor went to Greece rather than to Rome. The
earlier years of the eighteenth century had been Roman rather than
Grecian in taste. With imperial Rome many Englishmen, then as
later, felt great kinship. In a fit of chauvinism Addison paraphrased
Virgil to show that the fine arts belonged outside the manifest destiny
of an empire modeled on Rome:

[23] *Odes,* Book I, Ode xvi, ll. 3–4. See also Book I, Ode vii, and *The Pleasures of the
Imagination,* Book I, ll. 567 ff., and Book II, l. 23.

Others with towering piles may please the sight,
And in their proud, aspiring domes delight;
A nicer touch to the stretched canvass give,
Or teach their animated rocks to live:
'Tis Britain's care to watch o'er Europe's fate,
And hold in balance each contending state.[24]
(*A Letter from Italy,* ll. 141–46.)

Yet even in the Augustan period, when Englishmen felt themselves like the antique Romans, Greece stood as the land of arts and culture in contrast to the empire and commerce of Rome. Poet and virtuoso, artist and connoisseur, always associated Greece with liberty and the arts, with Milton's "old and elegant humanity of Greece." In the choruses of *The Tragedy of Brutus* (altered from Shakespeare in 1722 by the Duke of Buckingham) Pope hymned Britain as "Athens rising near the pole!" The distinction between the ideas of Rome and Greece in the first half of the eighteenth century is seen in the toast of the Society of Dilettanti, founded in 1732 for conviviality and the study of antiquities by noblemen who were also "graduates" of the Grand Tour: these gentlemen with a preference for the classical drank "To Grecian Taste and Roman Spirit."

By the middle of the century the "Grecian gusto" or "taste" was held to be simplicity, that is, "beautiful nature, without affectation or extraneous ornament." [25] The "beautiful nature" in the minds of artists, poets, and gentlemen was most often one or more of three things: scenery, especially of the wilder sort, when untouched by the hand of man; human nature in the free, uncomplex, uncitified stages of society, particularly in the state depicted by Homer, bard of the childhood of mankind; or the great achievements in the arts of Greece (and through her, of Rome). Many a man of taste discovered simplicity most easily, no doubt, in the Antique. William Collins as-

---

[24] John Dyer wrote similarly in *The Ruins of Rome,* 1740 (1761 ed., pp. 26–30), "May others . . . to sculptur'd stone give with superior skill the living look," etc. On the lines of Virgil (*Aeneid,* VI, 848 ff.) imitated by these poets, Blake later based his attack on Rome as the destroyer of the arts.

[25] A writer in the *British Magazine,* perhaps Goldsmith; see "Introduction to the Study of Belles Lettres," *Works,* ed. Peter Cunningham (New York and London, 1900), VI, 48.

sociated mountain liberty, naïve human beings, and the "just designs of Greece" with simplicity in his *Odes* in 1746.

A conscious Grecian, Collins felt the inspiration of ancient sculpture more keenly than any other mid-century poet. On the appearance of the *Odes,* Thomas Gray pointed out, in a letter to Wharton (December 27, 1746), Collins's use of "a fine fancy, modelled on the antique," an element in his work which many subsequent readers have also noticed. Collins was apparently familiar with ancient art, since he sketched at least one design for a medallion of "two elegant Heads *à l'antique*." [26] Though he neither mentioned nor described any specific antique statues in his poems, a sculptural feeling dominated many of them.

Occasionally the figures were statuesque, now in a rather Blakeian manner in the "Ode to Fear,"

> Danger, whose Limbs of Giant Mold
> What mortal Eye can fix'd behold?

and again suggesting Keats and Shelley in the "Ode on the Death of Colonel Ross,"

> lo where, sunk in deep Despair,
> Her Garments torn, her Bosom bare,
> Impatient Freedom lies!
> Her matted Tresses madly spread,
> To ev'ry Sod, which wraps the Dead,
> She turns her joyless Eyes.

His longest account of a statue presented an imaginary figure of Rome, now fallen but with fragments remaining to hint of former perfection:

> Rome, before thy [Liberty's] weeping Face,
> With heaviest Sound, a Giant-statue, fell,
> Push'd by a wild and artless Race,
> From off its wide ambitious Base,

[26] Letter to John Gilbert Cooper, Nov. 10, 1747 (*The Poems of William Collins,* ed. Edmund Blunden [1929], pp. 17–18). For other sculptural emblems and drawings by Collins, see Blunden, p. 14, and *Poetical Works,* ed. Alexander Dyce [1827], pp. 39–40. The chapter on "Collins and the Arts" in *Poor Collins* by Edward G. Ainsworth (Ithaca, 1937) should also be consulted.

When Time his Northern Sons of Spoil awoke,
   And all the blended Work of Strength and Grace,
    With many a rude repeated Stroke,
And many a barb'rous Yell, to thousand Fragments broke.[27]
              ("Ode to Liberty," ll. 18–25.)

The odes of Collins, in their simple precision and polished severity, ordinarily suggest reliefs rather than statues. The poet seems almost to have approached his work in the spirit of a sculptor of reliefs, carefully molding his poetic marble into sculpturesque scenes and figures. The "Ode to Evening" is a sculptured poem; the "Ode to Pity," the "Ode to Fear," and "The Passions" present many sculptural "attitudes" and posings or "stationings."

Collins likewise inherited Thomson's interest in the history of civilization and in the relationship between the arts and the morality and institutions of the body politic. What had been a lengthy treatise in Thomson's *Liberty* became a neatly sculptured outline of the "progress" of the arts in his "Ode to Liberty." Few English poets have made finer poetry out of the advance of mind. With Akenside, he urged his countrymen to "tune to Attic themes the British lyre." Reverently he invoked Simplicity,

              a decent Maid
       In Attic Robe array'd.[28]

In England the tide of "Grecian gusto" swelled perceptibly upon the publication by Stuart and Revett in 1762 of the first volume of *The Antiquities of Athens,* the fountainhead of the Greek revival in architecture. The Society of Dilettanti played an important role in the Grecianizing movement, since it sent artists to Mediterranean lands and helped finance publications concerning the antiquities. The discoveries at Herculaneum and Pompeii were other streams of classical influence. In the sixties Josiah Wedgwood, inspired in part by Thomson's *Liberty,* turned from merely making fine pottery to educating his countrymen with mementos of antiquity in the classical scenes on pottery and with cameos and medallions of the ancient

[27] See Ainsworth, *Poor Collins,* pp. 41–42, 194.
[28] "Ode to Simplicity," stanza ii, ll. 4–5. Mrs. Barbauld, who edited Collins in 1797, has "Simplicity in Attic vest" in her own "Hymn to Content."

illustrious. The Grand Tour also contributed to the spread of classical tastes. The procedure of the average traveler on the Grand Tour, guidebook in hand, is suggested in George Keate's *Ancient and Modern Rome* (1760):

> here the Eye
> Finds rapturous Delight, while it beholds,
> The mimic Stone so cunningly assume
> The Property of Being, that it seems
> As Art could rival Nature.

The conscientious imitation of classical (especially what were regarded as "Grecian") models constituted the prevailing force upon artists throughout Europe, whether or not they were formally associated with the Academies.

Neglecting in a cavalier fashion the growing body of archaeological information, Walpole set Greece on a pedestal above other nations. With sentiments doubtless congenial to many gentlemen and connoisseurs, he remarked in a letter to John Pinkerton (June 26, 1785), "The Grecians had grace in everything." In writing to the Countess of Upper Ossory (July 9, 1785) he became even more specific:

The one nation worth studying was the Greeks. In the compass of two or three centuries half a dozen little towns, or rather one town, scarce bigger than Brentford, discovered the standard of poetry, eloquence, statuary, architecture, and perhaps of painting and music; and then *the learned* have the impertinence to tell one that the Grecians borrowed from the Egyptians, Tartars, Indians, &c. That is, they stole the genuine principles of all beauty and all taste from every idea of deformity and absurdity! The Apollo and the Venus from mummies and idols with four heads, more hands, and two legs, as immovable as oaks in an avenue!

As always, of course, the satirists ridiculed the affectations engendered by the virtuoso-passion. In *Newmarket* Thomas Warton pictured a man of taste:

> In headless statues rich, and useless urns,
> Marmoreo from the classic tour returns (ll. 13–14);

while in *The Progress of Error* William Cowper described a connoisseur displaying his knowledge thus,

Some headless hero, or some Caesar shows—
Defective only in his Roman nose;
Exhibits elevations, drawings, plans,
Models of Herculanean pots and pans (ll. 395–98).

None the less, the taste of gentlemen and poets was constantly directed to the Antique. Classical, especially Grecian, forms were admired as never before, at the same time that the "pre-romantic" interests also flourished. Simplicity was a favorite catchword of the later eighteenth century. In its name Reynolds attacked the "ostentation" of Bernini and late Renaissance art, even as Dr. Johnson condemned the conceits of the metaphysical poets of the seventeenth century or as Blake damned the elegance and "colours" of Rubens and the Venetian painters. Worshiping the same chaste goddess of antique simplicity, Rousseau and other moralists denounced the luxury and decadence of modern civilization and dreamed of savages who were "noble, nude, and antique." The pendulum of taste in literature and the fine arts had swung from the elegant and refined Virgil to Homer the naïve and bold Grecian; from Raphael the master of elocution to Michelangelo, great in sublime ideas and design; from color to outline and form; from painting with its "picturesque" and dramatic contrasts to sculpture with the reposeful forms of Grecian simplicity. The stage was set for statues and paintings of contemporary subjects in classical costumes, as well as for the Lake Poets.

REYNOLDS AND THE ACADEMIC POETS: IN ANCIENT SCULPTURE'S CONSECRATED GROVE

The *Discourses* delivered at the Royal Academy between 1769 and 1790 by Sir Joshua Reynolds contain the most important expression of the English tradition of interest in the Antique, especially as it is related to the works of critics, writers, and artists during the last third of the eighteenth century. Yet Reynolds, unlike Shaftesbury and many poets throughout the century and in the Romantic period, stated none of the ideas about the influence of the political order upon the arts and the necessity for liberty commonly associated with the enthusiasm for the "Grecian gusto." Moreover, he manifested almost no interest in the "origin and progress" of the arts, even in the classical periods. As far as sculpture is concerned, Reynolds seems woefully inadequate, particularly since numerous critics and scholars in France, Germany, and Italy had been thoroughly studying Egyptian, Phoenician, and Etruscan as well as Greek and Roman sculpture. Some thirty years after Reynolds's lecture on sculpture (Discourse X, December 11, 1780), Fuseli and Flaxman displayed a more comprehensive and historical spirit in their remarks before the Academy; but the first president, neither an archaeologist nor a historian, concerned himself almost entirely with the plastic art of the Antique and the *antico moderno:* in short, with the Grand Style of the classical and Renaissance sculptors. The clearest English statement of the Neo-Classical theories of sculpture, the tenth Discourse, includes both careful analysis and eloquent praise of a classical simplicity and an intellectual or abstract beauty which attracted poets then and in the Romantic period.

A gentleman of taste, his head filled with the Antique, Reynolds argued that sculpture is characterized by gravity and by austerity and formality of design. He paralleled to a large extent Winckelmann's famous description of ancient statuary as expressive of "noble simplicity and quiet grandeur"; yet he nowhere mentioned the German theorist by name. His silence, of course, is not conclusive proof of his ignorance of Winckelmann's ideas. It is unlikely that he did not at some time read Henry Fuseli's translation of the *Reflections on the Painting and Sculpture of the Greeks* (1765), since the Swiss painter was a protégé of Burke and himself. Largely through their encouragement, Fuseli traveled to Italy in 1770 with John Armstrong, the poetical physician and author of *The Art of Preserving Health,* on the journey "descanting on ancient sculpture and modern poetry." Nevertheless, the distinctive ideas of Winckelmann about the influence of Grecian climate, social life, and religion upon ancient sculpture do not appear in Reynolds's lectures or notes.[29]

[29] For the relationship between Fuseli and Reynolds, see *The Life and Writings of Fuseli,* ed. J. Knowles (1831), pp. 42 ff., and Allan Cunningham, *Lives of the Most Eminent British Painters, Sculptors, and Architects* (1829–33). Throughout the

Like Winckelmann, Reynolds esteemed sculpture as an ideal art embodying the qualities he most admired: the simplicity of dignified and noble forms, correct and grand. Correctness and perfection of form, together with the grace and dignity of "appropriated expression" (that is, the characteristic or typical qualities of the subject of the statue)—these were the literary, artistic, and social ideals exhibited by the Antique. In Grecian sculpture the president of the Royal Academy saw united Ideal Beauty and simplicity. The Grecian sculptors had achieved the perfect simplicity: in his own words, "the exact medium between too little and too much." [30] Sculpture is not an art of deception; it does not strive with nature; it is not imitation but invention. In the infancy of an art imitation may be permissible, but in its more advanced stages the sculptor employs the representation of the thing itself; but still as a means to a higher end—as a gradual ascent always advancing toward faultless form and perfect beauty (Discourse X). By addressing the mind, the artist gives dignity to his art, which is thereby entitled to a sisterhood with poetry.

Such language had been frequently on the lips of earlier connoisseurs and artists. Reynolds, however, made the mental dignity of art into a theory of pure or abstract form. Yet, mere form would not satisfy him any more than his predecessors. The expressiveness, not the technical or physical perfection, counted most in the end:

there is a nobleness of conception, which goes beyond anything in the mere exhibition even of perfect form; there is an art of animating and dignifying the figures with intellectual grandeur, of impressing the appearance of philosophic wisdom, or heroic virtue. (Discourse III.)

In the pursuit of such conceptions the artist was to draw on his store of imagery collected from the great artists and poets.

All the elements in the position of Reynolds regarding the Antique

seventies and eighties, notes and communications about Winckelmann's ideas and discoveries constantly appeared in magazines and journals in England. What Cunningham terms "the first literary work of the Royal Academy"—James Barry's *Inquiry into the Real and Imaginary Obstructions to the Acquisition of the Arts in England* (1774)—included a passionate defense of British genius against the slurs of Winckelmann. Fuseli had displayed courage in acknowledging the translation. (See Cunningham, *Lives* [2d ed., 1830], II, 101, 276.)

[30] See James Northcote, *Memoirs of Sir Joshua Reynolds* (1817), p. 197.

appeared in the verse of the last third of the eighteenth century. William Mason, to whose translation (1781) of Du Fresnoy's *De arte
graphica* Reynolds contributed notes, gave perhaps the finest statement of the Ideal Beauty of the Academies in *The English Garden*
(1772–81). The account of Raphael's theft of

> ideal grace
> And dignity supernal from that store
> Of Attic sculpture, which the ruthless Goth
> Spar'd in his headless fury (Book I, ll. 286–89),

illustrated the need for ancient models. Mason versified all the ideas
associated with Grecian sculpture by the eighteenth century, including the political and moral values slighted by Reynolds. Still, the
most important thing was the correctness of the designs derived from
the Antique; for the poet remarked in a "Sonnet to a Very Young
Painter,"

> Chastely to paint, correctly to design,
> Deem but one art, and let that art be thine.

Painting poets had long been in fashion, but Mason went them one
better: he modeled "antique" vases! He sang in particular to young
Englishmen of taste possessing

> that vestal purity of soul
> Whence genuine taste proceeds.
>
> . . .
>
> whether in academic groves
> Studious ye rove; or, fraught with learning's stores,
> Visit the Latian plain, fond to transplant
> Those arts which Greece did, with her Liberty,
> Resign to Rome.[31] (*The English Garden,* Book I, ll. 53 ff.)

In Erasmus Darwin's once-famous *Botanic Garden* (1789–91) one
finds an unexpected reflection of English interest in the Antique. In
the elaborate account of the making of the world in Part I, "The
Economy of Vegetation," Darwin took the opportunity of describ-

---

[31] See John W. Draper, *William Mason; a Study in Eighteenth-Century Culture*
(New York, 1924), p. 306. With Mason's work may be mentioned the lines on
sculpture in "The Progress of Liberty" in *The Poetical Works of the Late Mrs. Mary
Robinson* (1806), pp. 37–38.

ing the best antique and modern statues, carefully tracing the chemical formation of marble through various stages until he found the famous statues awaiting the chisel of the sculptor "in white beds congealing rocks beneath."

> Hence wearied HERCULES in marble rears
> His languid limbs, and rests a thousand years;
> Still, as he leans, shall young ANTINOUS please
> With careless grace, and unaffected ease;
> Onward with loftier step APOLLO spring,
> And launch the unerring arrow from the string;
> In Beauty's bashful form, the veil unfurl'd,
> Ideal VENUS win the gazing world.[32] (Canto II, ll. 99–106.)

In *The Progress of Civil Society* (1796), by Richard Payne Knight, sculpture appeared under a heading close to Darwin's, namely, "Of Agriculture." Apparently sculptors were cultivators of the ground! The "mimic art," sculpture,

> In earthly moulds the soul's conceptions drew;
> And raised immortal shapes to mortal view (Part III, ll. 311–12)—

the shapes of Jove, Minerva, Apollo, Hercules, and Venus. In the part entitled "Of Arts, Manufactures, and Commerce" Knight showed the affinity of poetry and sculpture in a way which had been popular for nearly a century:

> Alike the poet sung and sculptor wrought,—
> Each sound breathed sentiment, each figure thought;
> Beauty, and grace, and easy motion shone,
> In forms of ductile brass or fragile stone;
> And each expressive feature learn'd to impart,
> Back to the eye, the impressions of the heart.[33]
>   (Part IV, ll. 407–12.)

[32] See Darwin's notes and also sec. 4, ll. 271 ff., for the lines on the works of the Wedgwoods where "the bold Cameo speaks, the soft Intaglio thinks." The Portland Vase drew a lengthy and learned description. In Part II, "The Loves of the Plants," Canto III, ll. 335 ff., Darwin described the Laocoön episode with the statue in mind.

[33] The description of the Torso Belvedere may be compared with the accounts given by Reynolds and Blake (see below, p. 113n).
> "Stout Hercules' vast limbs and spacious chest,
> Pure abstract strength personified express'd."

In *A Poetical Tour, in the Years 1784, 1785, and 1786,* William Parsons of the Arcadian Society at Rome doubtless spoke for innumerable English travelers of the eighteenth century in his "Ode to the Venus of Medicis" and "Elegy on Visiting the Coliseo, or Amphitheatre, by Moonlight"—poems which also look ahead to Byron and Shelley. Parsons found pleasure in sculpture only in "the simple graces" of the Greek works, and these delighted him so much that he could almost believe Pliny's story,

> How Sculpture's art could so prevail,
> That once a youth, in manner heinous,
> Dar'd to assault the Gnidian Venus! [34]

In "Rome at the Close of the Eighteenth Century" (1799) Henry Tresham, R.A., stressed the power of sculpture as a rival of painting:

> A rival sister, borne on Syren plumes,
> Each mystic path with Attic light illumes:
> Spell-bound by SCULPTURE, in her Parian grove,
> Festive with Pan, to rural strains we move;
>
> . . .
>
> Celestial forms display primeval grace,
> Expressive pathos moulds the meaning face (p. 9).

At the very end of the eighteenth century William Hayley (almost as though conscious that this book would sometime be written!) put into verse the sum of information concerning sculpture then available in *An Essay on Sculpture; in a Series of Epistles to John Flaxman, Esq. R.A. with Notes* (1800). Writing in the spirit which had animated many poets throughout the century, Hayley announced in the foreword that "to encourage a general delight in the ingenious Arts, and to extend the reputation of their most successful professors, has ever appeared to me one of the most desirable purposes that Poetry can pursue." His poem, in part an elegy on his son who had studied sculpture with Flaxman and in part a paean to Flaxman and the Antique, summarized all the "progress-pieces" which touched upon the history of sculpture, "the first and simplest of the arts."

---

[34] See *A Poetical Tour . . .* (1787), pp. 51 ff., 103 ff., 122 ff. The poems also appeared in *Travelling Recreations* (1807), I, 107 ff.; II, 1 ff., 20 ff.

In Greece, of course, the art of sculpture had flourished, "Offspring of Freedom and Feeling." Hayley related the story of the art, listing and describing the most famous artists and works:

> Her [Greece's] time-spared miracles I trace—
> Marbles of highest note, strength, beauty, grace.
>
> (Epistle III, ll. 568 ff.)

To the Venus went the warmest praise:

> Hail, Medicean Venus! matchless form!
> As Nature modest, yet as Fancy warm!
> Thy beauty, mov'd by virtuous instinct, tries
> To screen retiring charms from rash surprise:
> Thy hands are eloquent; they both attest
> The coy emotion of thy feeling breast;
> And prove, by delicacy's dear control,
> Her quick sensations are of grace the soul.
>   Thou darling idol of the Pagan earth.
>
>   . . .
>
> To thee, sweet pride of Nature and of Art!
> Be endless homage from the manly heart
> Which bends, obedient to a law divine,
> In guiltless worship to such charms as thine! [35]

Hayley's last Epistle was an astounding performance; for he ran through the bibliography of critical and historical works on sculpture, briefly indicating their contents. Clearly the literary and critical approach was more important than sight of actual works. Though he was acquainted with the writings of modern critics, Hayley was pleased by such Ancients as Pliny and Pausanias; indeed, the older writers alone almost sufficed as guides to the Antique!

> Taste, by thy guidance, still has power to rove
> Through ancient Sculpture's consecrated grove. [36]

[35] The Torso, as with Reynolds and Blake, was considered the work of highest art, since Michelangelo.
>   "Fed, on this wreck, the passion of his heart
>   For the recondite charms of purest art!" (Epistle III, ll. 542–43.)

[36] Epistle V, ll. 433–34; said of Pausanias. Winckelmann was "fervid" and the "bold enthusiast of a heart benign." Hayley seems not to have known of Fuseli's translation of Reflections on the Painting and Sculpture of the Greeks. Yet he had picked

Still, Hayley was not entirely at ease in worshiping the Venus and other classical works, and he felt that Christianity could surpass paganism as a moral basis for the arts.

> Yes there is room, and Christian subjects yield
> For Art's sublimest aims a happier field.

Even more prophetic of the position taken by many poets in the Romantic period and the later nineteenth century was the outspoken pronouncement in the notes: "Christianity is as much superior to Paganism, for the favourable guidance of art, as it confessedly is for the moral conduct of life." [37] Flaxman was to achieve for "dear England"

> as much
> As ever Grecian hand for Greece achiev'd,
> When hands gave life to all the soul conceiv'd . . .

while the poet hoped to show the value of modern art in another poem, a "Sketch of Modern Sculpture."

That projected "rise and progress" of modern art remained unwritten, however, largely because few people read his ambitious but pedestrian *Essay on Sculpture*. John Johnson, who wrote the memoirs of Hayley, believed that the poem failed to achieve popularity because "the art of which it treats, had not been sufficiently naturalized in England." [38] A more likely explanation, however, is that the poem was too dull, factual, and prosaic in regard to sculpture. In 1800 acquaintance with the Antique was widespread, and within a few years the Romantic poets were to write many fine passages under the inspiration of Grecian statuary. The author of the *Essay on Sculpture* was a poor poet; his didactic verse was entirely Academic.

---

up, probably from Barry, Winckelmann's attacks on British genius and violently criticized the German critic.

[37] Epistle III, p. 295n, ll. 596–97. Hayley's feeling had been foreshadowed by at least one artist, Ozias Humphry, who discovered vicious qualities in the divinities of the Ancients: "their Venus [de Medici] speaks the harlot at first view" and "their Antinous is an effeminate beauty of the carnal sort." Humphry concluded in phrases suggestive of Coleridge: "Innocence, meekness, cleanness of heart, justice of the interior, compassion, etc., I have never found among the ancient works of art." See William T. Whitley, *Artists and Their Friends in England 1700–1799* (London and Boston, 1928), p. 129, and below, pp. 146–47.

[38] See *Memoirs of the Life and Writings of William Hayley* (1823), II, 14.

Almost every poet of the eighteenth century treated some aspect of the tradition of English interest in Grecian sculpture. The historical, moral, theoretical, and political "ideas" associated with the Antique definitely gained a place in English poetry after Dryden. Information derived from French theorists, English critics, and philosophers was versified throughout the century. Moreover, with Addison, Pope, and Thomson actual works of antique sculpture entered this story, showing that the quickening spirit of the ancient works had been felt. However, the tyranny of Renaissance learning and of the theories of the Academies was oppressive in the informational accounts of sculpture, even in the verse of poets as forward-looking as Thomson and Akenside. Knowledge overwhelmed whatever instincts toward poetry Mason, Darwin, and Hayley may have possessed. It was not strange, however, that the poets of the eighteenth century concerned themselves for the most part with theory, history, and morality—that is, with the "ideas" about Greek sculpture which can be treated most easily in didactic poetry.

After the middle of the eighteenth century the "Grecian gusto" was in fashion. Many English poets, painters, sculptors, architects, and interior decorators—not to mention statesmen and political theorists —viewed the ancient forms as models of beauty to be studied conscientiously and to be imitated with painstaking care. Late in the eighteenth century there was almost universal agreement that nowhere was the simplicity which all men of taste admired more apparent than in Grecian statuary—statuary displaying, as Joubert expressed it (*Des Beaux-Arts,* Section XXVIII), "the ravishing beauty of a body, 'the host of a beautiful soul!' to employ . . . an expression which seems to have been born at the foot of some antique statue." Or, as Reynolds, thinking of the Antique, once defined the province of sculpture, "correctness of form, and energy of character."

With Reynolds and the Academic poets "correctness of form" outweighed "energy of character"; yet their emphasis upon the mental or intellectual, the abstract or ideal, beauties in an art beyond nature included the germ of the "romantic" evaluations of the Antique. They were closer than they realized, perhaps, to the "romantic" concern with the "energy" operating within the "correct" forms of Greek sculpture. Hence, "romantic" poets followed in the steps of such predecessors as Thomson and Akenside and Collins who had sought to discover the aesthetic quality of Greek statuary. Their poetry on the sculpture of Greece sprang in large measure from a concern—similar to that of Shaftesbury, Winckelmann, and Thomson—with the general spirit or significance of the Antique and also with the relationship between the achievement of the Grecian artists and the Grecian way of life.

The work of William Blake in the last quarter of the eighteenth century and in the first quarter of the nineteenth offers splendid illustration of the way in which the Neo-Classical and Academic theories of art, which dominated the eighteenth century, were transformed into the "romantic" aesthetics prevailing in the early nineteenth century. One can almost see the change taking place, when Blake writes and paints his Visions.

V. BLAKE

HEROIC ART AND "GRECIAN" WORKMANSHIP

AT ONE of their rare encounters, Sir Joshua Reynolds is reported
to have warned William Blake against extravagance.[1] Apparently the younger artist was to strive for simplicity, the
summum bonum of the Academic scheme of things, the "exact medium between too much and too little."

When one discovers that, at the time, Blake was probably engaged
upon the *Songs of Innocence* and *Songs of Experience,* the advice
seems rather presumptuous, even though the Academician was doubtless unaware of the poetry in which the artist was achieving a lyric
simplicity beyond all but a few poets. Besides, Blake was then working in a manner of art more "simple" than Reynolds's own. Such
pictures as "The Ordeal of Queen Emma" and "The Penance of
Jane Shore" (*c.*1778) leave no doubt that the artist had learned the
Neo-Classical and Academic lingoes of simplicity. In those paintings
English men and women, garbed in classical costume, pose in simple
and linear designs suggested by ancient sculptures and bas-reliefs and
by Renaissance imitations of the Antique. They were examples of the
historical or heroic art admired by connoisseurs and patriots in the
late-eighteenth century.

While still a child Blake formed what was to be a lifelong attachment to the "historic" in art, to the same sculptural or Michelangelesque or grand style which received its most persuasive apologia in
the *Discourses* of Reynolds. Very early he began the serious study of
art, working first from casts of ancient statues both at the school of
Mr. Pars (who had been in Greece in connection with Stuart and
Revett's *Antiquities of Athens*) and at home with the "plaster casts

---

[1] See Alexander Gilchrist, *The Life of William Blake,* "*Pictor Ignotus*" (1863),
I, 267.

of the Gladiator, the Hercules, the Venus of Medici, and models of heads, hands, and feet" bought by his father to aid the youngster.[2] One thinks of the boy Goethe similarly inspired by engravings of classical subjects and by the small collection of marbles brought from Italy by his father. Blake haunted the auction galleries, buying only "historic" prints and thereby winning the nickname of "little connoisseur." The ridicule with which the students at the establishment of Pars greeted his praise of Michelangelo and Raphael (they said his taste was "mechanical") served only to fasten him more tenaciously to the historical or heroic as distinguished from the portrait sort of art. Indeed, the infant William Blake may very well have dreamed of Michelangelesque heroes and of outlines borrowed from Grecian reliefs.

Next the student served an apprenticeship of seven years under Basire (who had also done engraving for "Athenian" Stuart), copying Gothic monuments in Westminster Abbey. Yet the forms of Michelangelo lingered in his mind; he was able to find a Michelangelesque quality even in the Gothic. Therefore one is not surprised that Blake went from Westminster to the Antique School of the Academy, where he could study more seriously the works which had influenced the Florentine master. His stay was brief, but evidences of this period of study, together with his earlier devotion to the Antique and to the "historic" in art, were constantly appearing in his work.

Though he finally set the Bible, the "Original Source," above the Antique, Blake drew on ancient art throughout his life. There were, first, the works of classical subject matter, paintings like "The Judgment of Paris," long a favorite with poets and artists, and drawings like "Hector and Andromache," "Apollo and Daphne," and "Torsos." Blake's illustrations of *Pilgrim's Progress* include a "classical" Giant Despair in the form of the Farnese Hercules leaning dejectedly on his club. On three occasions Blake engraved the Laocoön group, the last time (1820) surrounding the famous figures with the additional coils of his own philosophizing. In selecting an incident from classical story

2 Benjamin Heath Malkin, *A Father's Memoirs of His Child* (1806), pp. xviii–xix.

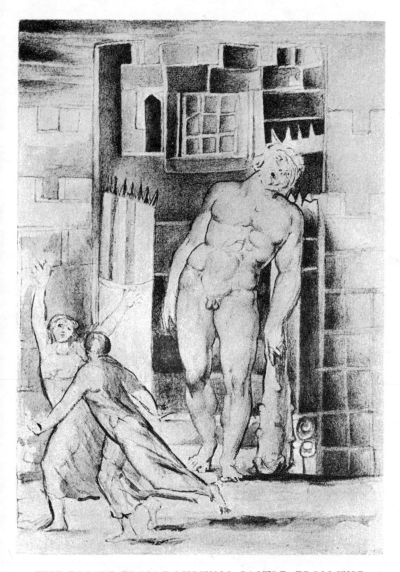

THE ESCAPE FROM DOUBTING CASTLE, FROM THE
DRAWING BY WILLIAM BLAKE

Copyright The Frick Collection, New York

and art as the vehicle for his scheme of a very personal mythology, he suggested the way in which Keats and Shelley and Byron read their own feelings, problems, or philosophies into Grecian statuary.

Equally interesting were Blake's references to and praise of the ancient masters, especially the sculptors, to whom he looked for justification of his own practices. Approving Reynolds's recommendation that the artist should "learn to think originally" by studying the spirit and thoughts of the masters, ancient and modern, he asserted that he was working in the spirit of the Grecian masters. More precisely, he believed that, like the creators of the Venus and the Apollo, he made "representations of spiritual existences," giving tangible and sensible form to supersensory realities.[3] At approximately the same time Wordsworth was similarly describing the work of the Grecian artists in *The Excursion*. Michelangelo, Raphael, and the Antique always found places in Blake's catalogues of the supreme art of all time. Partly to fortify himself and partly to show his admiration, he resorted to the Antique, as have many artists at various periods in history.

In his critical writings, moreover, the Grecian sculptures appeared several times, as, for example, in the critique written in connection with his engraving of "Chaucer's Canterbury Pilgrims" (1809). The core of his remarks was that Chaucer's pilgrims were not individualized portraits but composite or typical figures: "Chaucer makes every one of his characters perfect in his kind; every one is an Antique Statue; the image of a class, and not of an imperfect individual" ("Descriptive Catalogue," p. 787). Insufficient as that comment is in the hard light of modern Chaucer scholarship, Blake's criticism represented the opinion of the eighteenth century concerning the Antique. He agreed with critics from Shaftesbury to Reynolds and Winckelmann in considering the Grecian statues the expression of the typical, the abstract, the generalized—the "characteristic"; and that view of the Antique was not wholly abandoned on the arrival of the Elgin Marbles.

[3] "Annotations to Reynolds's Discourses," *Poetry and Prose of William Blake*, ed. Geoffrey Keynes (London and New York, 1935), pp. 974–75 and "Descriptive Catalogue," pp. 794-95. See also below, pp. 124 ff.

One feels that Blake ought to have welcomed the Elgin sculptures. He should have been in the forefront of battle with Haydon, the more so on account of the Blakeian violence with which the painter attacked their common enemies in the camps of the connoisseurs and the Academicians. Yet he clung, rather in the fashion of Byron among the poets, to the familiar antiques, if we can accept the statement of Samuel Palmer, the best known of his pupils.

He thought with Fuseli and Flaxman that the Elgin Theseus, however full of antique savor, could not, as ideal form, rank with the very finest relics of antiquity. . . . When he approached . . . the Torso Belvidere, and some of the inventions preserved in the Antique Gems, all his powers were concentrated in admiration.[4]

In short, Blake belonged with the eighteenth-century critics and poets in his attention to the old favorites of the Academies; these were the statues he first studied and the ones on which he formulated his ideal of historical and sculptural art early in his career.

More important, however, than either his works on classical subjects or his references to the Antique were the traces of his Academic ideals and training which appear in his work. Several critics have called attention to these classical echoes and motifs in the works of Blake—what Samuel Palmer termed his "stores of classic imagery." Palmer suggested that Ovid had been most favored by Blake, who was also a mythologist, though with a difference. Elizabeth Cary observed, "The long-limbed, deep-chested youths and maidens of his illustrations to *Paradise Lost,* with their small heads and noble gesture, bring us hints of Greek marbles." [5] Robert Ross, who thought of Blake as "ostro-gothic," felt forced to admit that in "Adam Naming the Beasts"

[4] See Gilchrist, *The Life of William Blake, "Pictor Ignotus,"* p. 302. Palmer cited Blake's view of the Theseus as an example of his being at variance with popular opinion. But more important here is the fact that Blake belonged with both Byron and Coleridge in finding the "older" antiques superior to the Theseus as ideal form. The agitation over the Elgin Marbles coincided with the beginning of the so-called "obscure" years in Blake's life. But in 1815 he was at the Antique School of the Academy where he could hardly have missed the studio chatter about the "new" sculptures. Fuseli is not likely to have kept silent about the works from the Parthenon.

[5] *The Art of William Blake* (New York, 1907), p. 19. See also p. 23.

"the type of head faintly recalls some cast of the antique." [6] But in general the emphasis on the Gothic in Blake has led many to under-value his fondness for the sculptural or grand style of the Academic critics, so that Foster Damon could even assert that Blake "detested" classical art.[7] On the contrary, Alan Clutton-Brock was nearer the truth in stating that Blake, "with his passion for pure outline, for. 'the hard and wiry lines of rectitude,' and with his vigorous hostility to the chaotic vegetable universe, was inevitably attracted to . . . the rigidly schematic and abstract style of the late eighteenth century." [8] That attraction left its mark on all Blake's works and theory, for he never swerved from his devotion to outline as he found it in the Greeks and the Renaissance artists.

An interesting commentary on Blake's interest in classical art is the fact that he knew most of the leading figures in the classical revival of art in England. His theories were already formed when at the age of twenty-three he met John Flaxman; but their friendship was one of mutual stimulation and influence of a sort suggesting the association of Wordsworth and Coleridge.[9] Flaxman, the greatest English sculptor among the classicistic artists of the time, became his closest friend and associate; during their forty years of friendship, Blake engraved a number of works for "this happy son of the immortal Phidias," among them illustrations for Hesiod and for Homer's *Odyssey*. The designs for the *Odyssey* were said to have been lost during Flaxman's return from Italy in 1797.

Henry Fuseli, first English translator of Winckelmann's epochal *Reflections on the Painting and Sculpture of the Greeks* in 1765, also became Blake's close friend in 1780. Since Blake is known to have had a copy of the Fuseli translation during his apprenticeship with

[6] "The Place of William Blake in English Art," *Burlington Magazine*, IX (1906), 67.

[7] See *William Blake; His Philosophy and Symbolism* (Boston, 1924), pp. 291 ff.: "Classical art just then was becoming popular, and Blake detested it, even though one of his best friends, Flaxman, was quite given over to it." It is difficult to see what "just then" means, while "detested" is too strong a word for a man who considered the Antique one of the imperishable creations of the imaginative principle.

[8] *Blake*, "Great Lives" series (1933), pp. 91–92.

[9] See Darrell Figgis, *The Paintings of William Blake* (1925), p. 13.

Basire (1771–78),[10] one may picture the young artist returning from Westminster Abbey to read the great German classicist's rhapsodies on the Antique. Though the direct influence of Winckelmann seems to have been slight, one suspects that a puckish Fate made Blake, sometimes called the "Goth," the first English poet of consequence to be in touch with the ideas of Winckelmann.

In 1791 Blake felt honored in being commissioned to engrave some designs for the third volume of Stuart and Revett's *Antiquities of Athens,* the chief begetter of the Greek revival in architecture in the late eighteenth and early nineteenth centuries. Five years later he was engaged upon designs for George Cumberland's *Thoughts on Outline* (1796), a curious book proclaiming (somewhat belatedly after Hogarth) that the secret of the Antique was "the flowing line." These outlines—several times removed from the ancient works— moved Blake to believe that Cumberland and he were to revive "the lost art of the Greeks." [11] Notwithstanding such excessive enthusiasm, he was sincerely interested in the outlines executed by Cumberland, and by Flaxman as well, since they fitted many of his long-held theories.

In a letter to Cumberland (July 2, 1800) praising Flaxman as "more and more of a Grecian," he hailed the "immense flood of Grecian light & glory which is coming on Europe" and approved the English "emulation of Grecian manners." Then, too, the sculptor introduced Blake to William Hayley, whose *Essay on Sculpture; in a Series of Epistles to John Flaxman* had appeared that year. The recorded utterances of Blake in praise of Grecian styles were never more ecstatic than at this time of association with Flaxman and Hayley, the versifier of Pliny, Plutarch, Junius, Winckelmann, Caylus, and so forth. By no means the "new Grecian" which Hayley termed him, Blake began to study the language.[12]

Among his classicistic friends was James Barry, without doubt the most zealous English advocate of classical art. Barry, who railed at

[10] See Geoffrey Keynes, *A Bibliography of William Blake* (New York, 1921), p. 417.
[11] Letter to Rev. Dr. Trusler, Aug. 16, 1799 (*Works*, p. 1037). See also p. 1041.
[12] See Gilchrist, *The Life of William Blake,* "Pictor Ignotus," p. 167.

even the "Gothic" or modern invention of shoes, served Blake as the subject of an epic. In his opinion Barry was the martyr of historical painting, starving to death while Reynolds, the Academician elegantly praising the grand style, battened on the portraits of his noble patrons.

> 'Tis the trading English Venetian cant
> To speak Michael Angelo & Act Rembrandt.[13]
> ("Florentine Ingratitude," ll. 13–14.)

Finally, in 1817 Blake was helping Flaxman in designs for the Wedgwoods, perhaps the greatest English popularizers of the classical.

Throughout his life, then, Blake was often close to the leading spirits in the various classicistic movements. Owing partly to their example and encouragement and partly to his early training and tastes, Blake clung tenaciously to the heroic or "historic"—the poetic, philosophical, and imaginative—style of art as distinguished from portraiture, genre, and landscape. Yet the devotion to the heroic style produced different results in his work from those of Hayley, Flaxman, Fuseli, or Barry. In his case one finds an illuminating illustration of the way in which the ideas and beliefs of the Neo-Classical and Academic theories of art and poetry became transformed into those of the Romantic period. Because Blake clearly indicated what Grecian sculpture was to mean to many Romantic poets, his theories and works must be analyzed at some length. Practice and theory were closely related to his general philosophy; hence, his views on politics and morality have a place in any consideration of his poetry and art. Almost before our eyes, the tenets of the Neo-Classical critics become the bases of the "romantic" views of artistic activity.

NEO-CLASSICAL INTO "ROMANTIC"

The transformation of Neo-Classical into "romantic" can be seen best, perhaps, in relation to three elements which Blake derived from his predecessors: an emphasis on the "mental" in art; a stress on outline or form, with a consequent subordination of color; and an

---

[13] For Wordsworth's comments of the same tenor on Reynolds, see letters to Sir George Beaumont, July 20 and Aug. 31, 1804 (*The Early Letters of William and Dorothy Wordsworth*, ed. E. de Selincourt [1935], pp. 402–3, 409–10).

opposition to the widespread concept of imitation as the counterfeiting of nature.

Madman, or only mystic, Blake·gave a more important role in art to mind than all but a few artists and theorists. With an earnestness surpassed only in his cry that the blessings of life spring from acceptance rather than denial, from enjoyment rather than abstinence, from fulfillment rather than repression—"Everything that lives is Holy!"—Blake expounded this fundamental tenet in the "romantic" faith. Less revolutionary and less obviously modern than his Rousseau-like faith in man and in man's innate tendency toward goodness, his praise of mind reflected his most treasured beliefs. As the intellect or reason, mind had been the god of Cartesian and rationalist; and Blake, like Shelley, sometimes worshiped at that shrine. When he referred to the "mental" element in art, however, he was usually thinking, not of the rational power—what Shelley termed "the calculating faculty" and Wordsworth "the meddling intellect"—but of the imagination. By imagination he meant neither fancy nor caprice but insight or intuitive perception—approximately Coleridge's "esemplastic power."

Yet Blake could announce the importance of mind in art in the very terms of the Neo-Classical critics: "I obstinately adhere to the true Style of Art such as Michael Angelo, Rafael, Jul[io] Rom[ano], Alb. Durer left it, the Art of Invention, not of Imitation" ("Public Address," pp. 819–20). Invention had become one of the key words in the aesthetics of the seventeenth-century Academies, when the "invention" by which the artist discovered and then portrayed the Ideal Beauty supplanted the earlier notions of an imitation which was a counterfeiting of nature. Blake employed the term of his predecessors, however, to mean something quite different from what they had intended. He had in mind neither the design which some critics like to describe in terms drawn from architecture, nor the Neo-Platonic idea-in-the-mind, although his remarks imply those two ideas. He was certainly not accepting Reynolds's identification of invention with a skill in recombining the images which one had stored away in the warehouse of his memory, even though that was what invention sometimes came to in his own practice.

Blake was thinking, rather, of the ability to perceive visions: intellectual or spiritual visions. The sentence following the one in which he stated that "the true Style of Art" is "the Art of Invention" reads, "Imagination is My World." Thus, invention seems practically synonymous with imagination. To leave no doubt, Blake once stated that invention and vision were the same. To Cumberland, compiler of a book of "flowing" outlines, he wrote (August 26, 1799):

Pray let me intreat you to persevere in your Designing; it is the only source of Pleasure. All your other pleasures depend upon it. It is the Tree; your Pleasures are the Fruit. Your Inventions of Intellectual Visions are the Stamina of every thing you value. . . . Do not throw aside for any long time the honour intended you by Nature to revive the Greek workmanship.

Blake seems to have derived his theory of invention as the perception of intellectual visions from his own experience. He often "saw" in sculptures and outlines. His visions were sculpture-like; they appeared in "Grecian" forms. They were usually linear or relief-like, for his eye had been trained on prints and engravings. His own testimony follows:

The other evening, taking a walk, I came to a meadow, and at the farther corner of it I saw a fold of lambs. Coming nearer, the ground blushed with flowers; and the wattled cote and its woolly tenants were of an exquisite pastoral beauty. But I looked again, and it proved to be no living flock, but beautiful sculpture.[14]

Another time he described his sight of the vague but grandiose cherubim; and here a definite feeling of sculpture in the round appeared with outlines and paintings.

Those wonderful originals [of the Grecian statues] seen in my visions, were some of them one hundred feet in height; some were painted as pictures, and some carved as basso relievos, and some as groupes of statues, all containing mythological and recondite meaning, where more is meant than meets the eye. ("Descriptive Catalogue," p. 781.)

In this account of his visionary experiences Blake gave one of the clearest expressions of the sort of conceptions which lay behind both

---

[14] Told to Flaxman, Lawrence, and other artists and reported by Henry Crabb Robinson; see Gilchrist, *The Life of William Blake,* "Pictor Ignotus," pp. 337–38.

poetry and art. In words as well as in color and line sometimes he painted his mighty symbols, while at other times he carved them in reliefs or grouped them as statues. Frequently the illustrations accompanying the poetry suggest the pictures and sculptures in his mind more clearly than the verse; still, lines like the following from *Milton* indicate the nature of his grandiose conceptions—Michelangelesque figures or Grecian shapes or Gothic sepulchral effigies:

> First Milton saw Albion upon the Rock of Ages,
> Deadly pale outstretch'd and snowy cold, storm cover'd,
> A Giant form of perfect beauty outstretch'd on the rock
> In solemn death. (Book I, Part 17, ll. 36–39.)

In an important passage in *Jerusalem* Blake identified the Divine imagination with the cosmic memory found in some form in every mystical system. In his version the eternal ideas were sculptural reliefs.

> All things acted on Earth are seen in the bright Sculptures of
> Los's Halls, & every Age renews its powers from these Works
> With every pathetic story possible to happen from Hate or
> Wayward Love; & every sorrow & distress is carved here,
> Every Affinity of Parents, Marriages & Friendships are here
> In all their various combinations wrought with wondrous Art,
> All that can happen to Man in his pilgrimage of seventy years.
> (Book I, Part 16, ll. 61–67.)

Blake has translated the Platonic Ideas into the terms of an artist, transferring to Los, the eternal poet, his own experience of sculpture-like dreams. Believing with Shelley that through dream or vision the artist participates in the One, he gave a splendid tribute to the arts which record the enduring ideas of men: the visions of the Divine Mind have the clarity and the permanence of sculpture. Blake would not have described his visions thus, had he not felt that the Antique was of great beauty, and had he not also been influenced by the "Grecian simplicity" of reliefs and uncolored outlines praised by the critics of the eighteenth century.

The second theory of the writers of the Academies which Blake continued resulted directly from the emphasis on mind. A statue, for example, was to him the concrete manifestation of the "idea" in the artist's mind even as "Greek statues are all of them representations of spiritual existences, of Gods immortal, to the mortal perishing organ of sight; and yet they are embodied and organized in solid marble" ("Descriptive Catalogue," p. 794). The form—outline, drawing, or molding—revealed the sharpness of the perception and, accordingly, the value of the invention.

The great and golden rule of art, as well as of life, is this: That the more distinct, sharp, and wiry the bounding line, the more perfect the work of art, and the less keen and sharp, the greater is the evidence of weak imitation, plagiarism, and bungling. Great inventors, in all ages, knew this. . . . The want of this determinate and bounding form evidences the want of idea in the artist's mind. . . . Leave out this line, and you leave out life itself; all is chaos again. ("Descriptive Catalogue," pp. 805–6.)

On the basis of that profound remark Blake could have condemned a great deal of his own work in poetry and in art. But many great artists and thinkers can be quoted against themselves and censured in their own words.

Art was, for Blake, the endowing of matter with the determinate line, and he poetized the plastic process thus in *Milton:*

> Some Sons of Los
>
> . . .
>
> Giving to airy nothing a name and a habitation
> Delightful, with bounds to the Infinite putting off the Indefinite
> Into most holy forms of Thought;
>
> . . .
>
> Antamon takes them into his beautiful flexible hands:
> As the Sower takes the seed or as the Artist his clay
> Or fine wax, to mould artful a model for golden ornaments.
> The soft hands of Antamon draw the indelible line,
> Form immortal with golden pen, such as the Spectre admiring
> Puts on the sweet form.[15] (Book I, Part 30, ll. 3–5, 13–18.)

[15] Blake's passion for precision and rectitude of line led him to admire the antique gems, almost as though he were a connoisseur. At least he asserted that "the Greek Gems are in the Same Style as the Greek Statues" ("Annotations," p. 994). Again, he described classical gems thus: "What we call Antique Gems are the Gems of Aaron's Breast Plate" (["Laocoön group,"] p. 766). That was a strange judgment, yet in Blake's opinion he had attributed great beauty to the gems because of that Hebraic or Christian origin. See also above, p. 102.

Moreover, Blake gave his theory of form a definitely Platonic cast. Notwithstanding his many criticisms of Reynolds, he agreed essentially with the president of the Academy that the sublime is the abstract or the generalized, and that it is therefore removed from the accidental and the particular. "The Beauty proper for sublime art," he wrote, "is lineaments, or forms and features that are capable of being the receptacles of intellect" ("Descriptive Catalogue," p. 799). Indeed, the reality is the perfect form residing in the mind, the abstract or imaginative form. Whereas Reynolds arrived at the ideal form by refining nature—in Platonic language, by mounting through successive steps from the beauty of earth to the true beauty—Blake believed, as did Shelley, in a direct or immediate revelation. Discarding the intermediary stages by which one mounts from the forms of nature to the abstract reality, he maintained in his "Annotations" to the *Discourses* of Reynolds (p. 989), "All Forms are Perfect in the Poet's Mind, but these are not abstracted nor compounded from Nature, but are from Imagination [intellectual or spiritual vision]." Those forms were neither vague nor indistinct; on the contrary, Blake insisted that "they are organized and minutely articulated beyond all that the mortal and perishing nature can produce" ("Descriptive Catalogue," p. 795). He was drawing again on his own experience of visions of sculptural exactness and outline. The visions revealed to Blake the vital realities beyond the perishing and illusory shows of nature.

In Blake's theory of the sculptural vision, color was subordinated as a result partly of his early study of casts and engravings of antiques and partly of his sharing Winckelmann's and Reynolds's disparagement of color. Even as the early Neo-Classical critics had permitted imitation in the infancy of art and in the lesser types of work, so Blake considered color the inferior part of painting. An emphasis on color characterized the lower branches of painting, such as genre and portraiture. Both Reynolds and he shared an admiration for the Antique and for Poussin, who was thought to have painted reliefs, and for Raphael and Michelangelo.

On a third point Blake was with his Neo-Classical and Academic predecessors. His opposition to an unselective imitation has been hinted at in his statements about the supremacy of vision or form. For him, as for the portrait-painters and the copiers of natural objects, sight was the most important sense; but Blake directed his eyes inward. One of his most famous critical remarks was a sharp rebuke to Wordsworth: "Natural Objects always did & now do weaken, deaden & obliterate Imagination in Me. Wordsworth must know that what he Writes Valuable is Not to be found in Nature." To clarify his position he referred to Wordsworth's own translation of one of Michelangelo's sonnets with a Platonic theme agreeable to all three poets.

> Heaven-born, the Soul a heaven-ward course must hold;
> Beyond the visible world She soars to seek
> (For what delights the sense is false and weak)
> Ideal Form, the universal mould.
> The wise man, I affirm, can find no rest
> In that which perishes: nor will he lend
> His heart to aught which doth on time depend (pp. 1024–25).

This warning against imitating the transient or mutable, the lower or sensual portions of existence, was to be repeated by almost every English Romantic poet. Frequently the fear of the transitory led them to Grecian sculptors who had represented "spiritual existences" in forms which had survived for centuries.

Exact imitation—the aping of nature in the attempt to deceive the beholder—Blake and Reynolds held to be scarcely more than manual labor, unbecoming in the artist who should work with his mind and "invent." It was no longer permissible, in theory at least, in the enlightened eighteenth century. Blake added the logical capstone to the theory which had been developing for a long time when he proclaimed, "Copiers of Nature are Incorrect, while Copiers of Imagination are Correct." For this position he later gave one of his frequent Scriptural parallels: "Israel deliver'd from Egypt, is Art deliver'd from Nature and Imitation." [16] Egyptian art was barbaric and imitative; imaginative art—whether Hebraic, or Grecian, or entirely Blakeian—intellectual and spiritual.

Declaring war on imitation, Blake exclaimed,

[16] ["Public Address"] and ["Laocoön group"], *Works*, pp. 813, 764. See above, pp. 56 ff.

Shall Painting [and sculpture is included here as in the *Pictura* of the
seventeenth century] be confined to the sordid drudgery of fac-simile representations of merely mortal and perishing substances, and not be as
poetry and music are, elevated into its own proper sphere of invention and
visionary conception? No, it shall not be so! Painting, as well as poetry
and music, exists and exults in immortal thoughts. ("Descriptive Catalogue," p. 794.)

It was no longer the Horatian *Ut pictura poesis* dear to critics before
Lessing, but exactly the opposite—*Ut poesis pictura*. Because poetry,
owing to the nature of its medium, enjoyed a freedom from the representation of matter, Blake believed that it had best preserved the life
of the spirit. Mind alone was the material out of which "romantic"
poets made monuments more lasting than paint or stone.

IMAGINATIVE VISION

By devoting the major portion of his discussions to the cause of
mind and to the necessity for imagination or vision, Blake seemed to
forget the other parts of the Neo-Classical triad of art, namely, dis-
position and elocution, the parts dealing with execution. That those
two elements were less prominent in Romantic criticism, which
concentrated on the invention of the older theory, is not without
an explanation. Because the Academic critics gave ostensibly infallible
recipes and objective measurements for all the sister-arts, the "finding
of the thought"—as Dryden defined invention—now assumed new
importance. Unless one were to be content with the "ivy on the rind
of antiquity," the problem of the artist and poet was to "find" vital,
significant, or interesting ideas.

Yet Blake, the one poet of the Romantic period in England great in
an art other than literature, did not underestimate the importance
of execution. He was too fine an artist not to recognize the necessity
for perfection of technique, even if he did not always achieve it. He
believed that "Mechanical Excellence is the Only Vehicle of Genius"
and that "Execution is the Chariot of Genius." [17] Moreover, he praised
Reynolds whenever the Academician told his students to strive for
exactness of drawing and for definiteness of outline. The sculptor,

[17] "Annotations," p. 981.

with whom Blake had many affinities, illustrated the difficulties facing every artist:

> Silent Milton stood before
> The darken'd Urizen, as the sculptor stands silent before
> His forming image; he walks around it patient labouring.
> (*Milton,* Book I, Part 22, ll. 7–9.)

Again, he was too close to the Academy lectures of Sir Joshua himself and later of his friends, Barry, Fuseli, and Flaxman, not to consider what is called the "practical" side of art. He was constantly experimenting with the materials of his arts. All his life he preached his visions, and near its close he attracted a band of ardent disciples, who called themselves the "Ancients."

Blake insisted as strenuously as Reynolds that to attain to excellence the artist must labor incessantly. "Without Unceasing Practise nothing can be done. Practise is Art. If you leave off you are Lost." [18] Parallel to this excellent advice for labor in the studio was his exhortation to spiritual warfare against the proponents of color and of imitation. Like Milton and Wordsworth, Blake felt that art is the task of dedicated spirits. Like devout ecclesiastics, artists must never "cease from Mental Fight." He exhorted poets, painters, and sculptors to renounce the world:

We are in a World of Generation & death, & this world we must cast off if we would be Painters such as Rafael, Mich. Angelo & the Ancient Sculptors; if we do not cast off this world we shall be only Venetian Painters, who will be cast off & Lost from Art. ("Descriptive Catalogue," pp. 839–40.)

Blake's remarks take on additional significance when one recalls that these were the very artists whom Reynolds had held up to his pupils as the finest exemplars of the grand style. Furthermore, the Torso Belvedere, which Blake conceded to be perhaps "the only original work" remaining of the Greeks, was also regarded by Reynolds as the one ancient statue which all artists must look upon with "a warmth of enthusiasm, as from the highest efforts of poetry." [19]

[18] ["Laocoön group"], p. 766.
[19] See "Descriptive Catalogue," pp. 780–81, and Reynolds, Discourse X.

Both praised that fragment, partly because Michelangelo had termed it his "school." But Reynolds saw in it the perfection of "the science of abstract form": it was a work of mind alone. Blake, on the other hand, saw in the Torso an "original work," since it could not be labeled a portrait or an allegorical figure; the typical trait or characteristic defied discovery! There was some space, however, between the two artists. Reynolds found that Michelangelo, Raphael, and the Grecian sculptors measured up to certain "rules" and that their works belonged to the grand style. Any one of these artists would have been acceptable for the presidency of the Royal Academy. But Blake, praising the same masters, considered them great because they had been artists of the imagination.

It was no longer a question of conceding with Sir William Temple that the Moderns could never equal the Ancients in certain arts, particularly sculpture, even though the English Romantics followed the German critics from Winckelmann to Hegel in considering sculpture the typical classical art. No longer was one to imitate certain Academic writers who either divided the arts into parcels— design to the Ancients and color to the Moderns—or scored works of art by reference to a rigid scale of beauty—"We will give Poussin 18 out of a possible 20 points for Design but only 11 for Expression and 6½ for Colour." [20] From his critical test Blake dropped all the elaborate systems of proportion and ancient canons of the human body, in brief, all those mechanical props for the artist commonly referred to as the "rules."

With imagination the center of artistic as indeed of all perception in Blake's opinion, certain acid tests were to be applied to every work of art: is the poem a product of the spirit? is the statue the bearer of the divine or imaginative vision? If so, ancient or modern, the work of art may be great. When one judged by such a standard, there could be no subserviency to the past, and the quarrel between the

[20] The scale produced by the French critic De Piles was very popular in the eighteenth century among those who needed an "objective" standard for the arts. Similarly Akenside rated the great poets according to such a scale. In 1759, when Blake was only two years old, and a decade before any other great Romantic was born, Sterne had ridiculed the schematic judgments of art; see *Tristram Shandy*, Book I, chap. ix, Book II, chap. iv, and Book III, chap. ii.

Ancients and the Moderns was dissolved as meaningless. Modern and Ancient stood on the same level; each was to be valued according to the degree of his success in presenting visionary conceptions and spiritual existences.

Asserting that the great artists in every age have been alike in possessing imaginative insight, Blake spoke for all "romantic" poets when he declared:

Poetry as it exists now on earth, in the various remains of ancient authors, Music as it exists in old tunes or melodies, Painting and Sculpture as it exists in the remains of Antiquity and in the works of more modern genius, is Inspiration, and cannot be surpassed; it is perfect and eternal. Milton, Shakspeare, Michael Angelo, Rafael, the finest specimens of Ancient Sculpture and Painting and Architecture, Gothic, Grecian, Hindoo and Egyptian, are the extent of the human mind. ("Descriptive Catalogue," p. 798.)

His temple of poetic fame was truly eclectic, and his seizure of imaginative power, wherever found, corresponded to the catholicity of the later Romantic poets in England.

THEORY AND PRACTICE

Blake's theories concerning "historic" art and the "Grecian" workmanship of intellectual inventions organized and embodied in sculptural outlines throw light upon many elements in his work. They help explain the major problem confronting readers of his poetry, namely, the difference between the early lyrics and the prophetic books laden with philosophizing and social meanings. For he carried something like the theory of outline over into the poetry, with disastrous results.

In his *Poetical Sketches* (1769–78, printed in 1783) Blake worked in the forms and used the motifs common to many of the poets of the eighteenth century. As in art, he began in an "academic" spirit; yet several of these poems—"My silks and fine array"; "The wild winds weep"; and the invocation "To the Muses"—show the perfection he could give to old forms. With increasing skill Blake achieved in the *Songs of Innocence* and *Songs of Experience* a lyrical tone distinctly his own; here the simple and concentrated intensity came mainly through the accord of music and clarity of intention or vision. The ideas were simple enough and so clearly outlined, so sculptural according to his theory, that he could give them adequate expression. Thereafter he largely abandoned singing and, with it, the more intelligible style of the lyrics. That first simplicity and clarity reappeared most often in the epigrams and aphorisms, such as the "Auguries of Innocence," where the limited forms forced the philosophy sprawling through the prophetic books to crystallize into an approximation to the earlier brilliance of phrase. As a poet Blake was most felicitous in relatively rigid and traditional patterns, when his energies went into the polishing of statement and the controlling of emotion and rhythm rather than into the discovering of original forms. Yet Blake continued to seek original modes of expression, since he felt that his unique visions required new and original forms for presentation to the world.

A similar development occurred in his art. The period of apprenticeship left its marks on his own efforts in the suggestions of Grecian statues and Gothic effigies, of ancient reliefs and modern works by Michelangelo, Poussin, and Raphael. But even in the use of these motifs his personal idiom became perceptible, and Blake charged the borrowings with so much of himself that one almost forgets their origins. Again the visions needed new and original forms.

Blake's major task became, in short, the attempt to forge a mythological and symbolical system out of the society in which he lived in order to state his judgments on that society. One easily grasps the general plan or scheme, for the outlines are clear: reason or Urizen or materialism or institutional Christianity is the power of evil, while Los or imagination is the true Christlike spirit of good. The two forces clash in an England clouded by "dark Satanic Mills" but ultimately to be "a green and pleasant land." Blake's ideal Albion was not the Athens or Rome of an eighteenth-century gentleman under the spell of Plutarch's republicans, but a new Jerusalem of spiritual liberty where all men would be artists. For him, Christ rather than Apollo or Prometheus was the synonym of the imaginative spirit and the master of all arts. The poems dealing with the revolutions in

America and France were intended as rhapsodic preludes to the establishment of such liberty in England and throughout Europe.

With that "original" invention or design in his own mind, Blake tended to trust his theory that every vision carried its own execution and also to forget that the eyesight of other human beings was less certain, less exact, and less ready for prophecies. Moreover, too many of the huge symbols of his high romance were unprecise; they were less Grecian and less sculptural than he sometimes asserted. The main ideas were obscured by many imperfectly drawn lines, and the total effect was disappointing. He could "invent" a great deal more than he could organize in clear and intelligible forms. The poetry suffered in particular from the assumption that the vision could not exist without its minutely articulated execution. In practice the theory served to justify careless writing, though Blake, like Shelley and Keats, had more trouble with the organization and planning of large units and themes than with the phrasing of individual lines of poetry or the drawing of separate figures or motifs. In the details he often showed a fine draftsmanship, the skill and feeling of a sculptor of reliefs.

The linear medium of engraving best suited the Grecian outline he admired in theory, because the hard and sharp—even though flowing—lines gave determinate bounds to the vision; his grand and daring conceptions needed visual expression. Hence the *Job* illustrations are more satisfying than the epic prophecies *Jerusalem, Milton,* or *The Four Zoas,* since his essentially conceptual imagination was better suited to line and contour than to verse. For a similar reason his illustrations of subjects already complete, such as *Job, Paradise Lost, The Divine Comedy,* Virgil's *Eclogues,* Blair's *Grave,* or Young's *Night Thoughts,* will be preferred to all but his simplest and most effective lyrics and aphorisms. In such illustrations Blake was freed from the necessity of elaborating and defending his original inventions and therefore was able to treat themes already determined for him in a highly personal manner within the given framework. Somewhat the same difference exists between *Prometheus Unbound,* into which Shelley poured his own feelings in treating a story whose outlines were familiar, and *The Daemon of the World* and *The Revolt of Islam* where he was utilizing a system of his own manufacture.

One feels considerable dissatisfaction, then, with Blake's efforts in the longer poems, not only because there was very little song or continuous rhythm in them, but also because he failed to present his visions in carefully organized and delineated shapes. When he left the simplicity to which he was devoted in theory, and which he achieved after the *Songs of Innocence* and *Songs of Experience* only occasionally in lyrics, gemlike aphorisms, and epigrams, he seldom found the relief-like forms suited to his talents outside the subject matter already outlined by other poets and artists.

Blake's reputed "madness" was, then, that he did not write of the tangible objects in nature; that he did not take over the familiar classical system of mythology; that he did not fall in with the elegant trifles and portraits of fashionable art. He turned in particular from the imitation of the classical models he first studied, not, as Damon has suggested, because "the imaginative depicting of great ideas had absolutely vanished," [21] but because the tradition had degenerated into a stereotyped sort of "great ideas" in classical garb. As a "romantic" poet and artist, Blake sought vital or significant or expressive ideas rather than merely "great" ones. Unwilling to use his talents in toying with ideas inherited from the past and compelled by the social and religious spirit, of which there was a forewarning even in early songs, to tackle the problems of his age, Blake thought his task was to mold into form visions instinct with meaning for his own time.

Neo-Classical in preferring fine forms to fine tints, he asserted that no forms were finer than the Grecian. The sculpture of the Greeks was one of the summits of art, not because it had been produced in a free state, though he believed most passionately in Liberty, nor because the Greek sculptors had been universally regarded as the prime masters of the plastic arts, but simply because their works were a great achievement of the human spirit or mind. Mere perfection of form, even that of the ancient statues, was insufficient; hence, the artist-poet insisted that perfectly executed forms must express the

[21] *William Blake; His Philosophy and Symbolism,* p. 137.

spirit working within them. Blake found in the Antique what he saw in all great art: visions expressed in perdurable forms; outlines given to matter by the imagination. "Nature has no Outline, but the Imagination has." In his loyalty to imagination—the vision or insight or intuition of "romantic" aesthetics rather than the intellection or invention or mental architecture of Neo-Classical theory—one finds the source not only of the weakness but also of the strength of his poetry and art.

Blake accepted the Platonic elements of Neo-Classical theory; like Reynolds he was haunted by an inexpressible yet very real Intellectual Beauty, the gleam added to nature, the light that never was on sea or land. The president of the Academy, lecturing on composite beauty, canons of proportion, and lessons derived from the Antique, and "romantic" Blake, convinced that the Greeks had sculptured visions, subscribed to a similar purpose:

The art which we profess has beauty for its object; this it is our business to discover and to express; the beauty of which we are in quest is general and intellectual; it is an idea that subsists only in the mind; the sight never beheld it, nor has the hand expressed it; it is an idea residing in the breast of the artist, which he is always labouring to impart, and which he dies without imparting. (Discourse IX.)

In his art and poetry Blake set out in the Platonic quest for Intellectual Beauty, but he went beyond Reynolds and Plato, adding the wisdom of the Nazarene to that of the ancient world. With him, mind, the core of Neo-Classical theory, became the essence of the supreme artist, the Maker of Eternal Designs. In a Christian spirit he also sought the Divine Vision:

As the breath of the Almighty such are the words of man to man
In the great Wars of Eternity, in fury of Poetic Inspiration,
To build the Universe stupendous, Mental forms Creating.
(*Milton*, Book II, Part 33, ll. 18–20.)

VI. WORDSWORTH AND
COLERIDGE

WORDSWORTH AND SIMPLICITY

WORDSWORTH "hates conchology, and he hates the Venus of Medici"—that was one of the severest charges Hazlitt could make in the notorious account of the Lake Poets in *Lectures on the English Poets*. The brightest star of the Uffizi had never been placed so low (except by "Smelfungus" Smollett), though Aphrodite rising from the sea had traditional associations with conchology. One should notice, however, that on the insistence of Crabb Robinson and others Hazlitt took back the charges about Wordsworth's opinion of the Venus in *The Spirit of the Age,* without admitting that he himself had made them in the first place. The statements, he hoped with uncertain sincerity, were "mere epigrams and *jeux-d'esprit,* as far from truth as they are free from malice." [1] In any case, Wordsworth's reputation as an art-lover was cleared, and he was now entitled to "love" the Venus, if he wished.

Nevertheless Wordsworth had not been especially interested in the arts either in his early days in Cumberland and Westmoreland or in the period of greatest productivity between 1798 and 1807. Even had he possessed *Polymetis* in his boyhood, the plates of Grecian statues would certainly have interested him less than they did Keats and Hunt. Like Byron and Shelley, Landor and Coleridge, they absorbed the classicistic culture of the time in ways that Wordsworth the "northern villager" did not.

On the other hand, Wordsworth approached very closely to the life of "Grecian simplicity" admired from a distance by the connoisseurs and artists of the late eighteenth century who collected and

[1] *Complete Works,* ed. P. P. Howe, V, 163; XI, 93–94.

enjoyed their antiques amid the luxuries of an un-simple London. Away from the city, Wordsworth spent his formative years under the influence of the spirit which he recommended later to all youths:

> A healthy sound simplicity . . .
> A seemly plainness, name it what you will,
> Republican or pious.[2] (*Prelude,* Book III, ll. 399–401.)

Young Wordsworth had been, indeed, almost the incarnation of the antique republican of eighteenth-century taste. The independence and vigorous labor of the free mountain people was

> followed by a train
> Unwooed, unthought-of even—simplicity,
> And beauty, and inevitable grace. (*Prelude,* Book VIII, ll. 108–10.)

In such a life, as among the Greeks and Romans who inspired the ideal, the arts were "unthought of." Wordsworth himself, however, early began to read "venerable books" of ancient history, and when he pictured his early life and the people favored by nature and mountain liberty, the language of the connoisseurs and patriots—the simplicity, the beauty, the inevitable grace of Plutarchian figures and of the Antique—came into his mind.

At Cambridge the

> academic institutes
> And rules . . . held something up to view
> Of a Republic (*Prelude,* Book IX, ll. 224–26),

while in France Wordsworth shared the stirrings of the revolutionary movement, in certain respects another manifestation of the desire for antique simplicity. Robert Jones and William Wordsworth were feted in villages as English "forerunners in a glorious cause" of reviving Liberty on antique patterns.

> My heart
> Responded; "Honour to the patriot's zeal!
> Glory and hope to new-born Liberty!" (*Prelude,* Book VI, ll. 440–42.)

Greece and Rome were much in his mind, for there Liberty had been the presiding genius.

[2] Citations are from *The Prelude,* ed. E. de Selincourt (1926), 1850 text unless otherwise noted.

> 'Tis true, the history of our native land,
> With those of Greece compared and popular Rome,
>
> . . .
>
> Had never much delighted me;

for the English story, Wordsworth felt, lacked the "harmonizing soul" of the "life of manners and familiar incidents" which he found in ancient history and poetry (*Prelude,* Book VIII, ll. 617 ff.). The same ideas were in his mind during his Socratic dialogues with Beaupuy ("Let the name stand near the worthiest of Antiquity") concerning liberty.

> Such conversation, under Attic shades,
> Did Dion hold with Plato. (*Prelude,* Book IX, ll. 408–9.)

But Wordsworth's faith in the French Revolution as the means of reviving the antique *dignitas* and *libertas* ultimately vanished. When his ideal of a "social" or widespread simplicity—similar in conception to that which characterized the nations of idealized, Plutarchian republicans foreseen by many statesmen in the eighteenth century—became impossible of realization, there yet remained a simplicity and dignity and freedom for the individual. That ideal Wordsworth found once more in the humble people of the mountainous regions of his youth, whom he regarded as approximating the early Grecians in many respects, and in a natural piety for himself. Nature restored his faith in himself and in men as he knew them in the north of England.

In this light the poetry of the years before 1805 may be considered the logical result of the eighteenth-century doctrines of simplicity, in forming which the ideas and theories associated with the Antique had had so large a part. *Descriptive Sketches* (1793) was Wordsworth's statement, in the terms of the eighteenth century itself, of this admiration of simplicity. There he employed his limited knowledge of the arts in the manner of Darwin. Using the "pencil" of the connoisseur, he described picturesque scenes, referred to the lyre of Memnon, and rose to the occasion at the Chapel of William Tell.

But, lo! the boatman, overawed, before
The pictured fane of Tell suspends his oar;
Confused the Marthonian tale appears,
While his eyes sparkle in heroic tears.
And who, that walks where men of ancient days
Have wrought with godlike arms the deeds of praise,
Feels not the spirit of the place control,
Or rouse and agitate his labouring soul? (Lines 285-92.)

But the significant expression of simplicity was in *Lyrical Ballads* (1798) and similar poems. It was a result that the connoisseurs could not recognize, because Wordsworth had made moving poetry out of what had been cant and half-believed catch phrases with Academic poets and gentlemen. However, *Lyrical Ballads* was hardly possible without the body of simplicity-lovers; indeed, the eighteenth century had looked ahead to the moment when a great poet should show the antique dignity and simplicity in freedom-loving English "Grecians." The wheel had come full circle: from Milton's praise of the spirit of old Greece one has come to Wordsworth's praise of a "Grecian simplicity" in the men of England. Milton, unconscious father of the cults of simplicity, himself referred but seldom to the fine arts; Wordsworth, his truest heir among the Romantic poets, similarly mentioned art only infrequently in his poetry, at the close of the long tradition.

THE SPIRIT OF GRECIAN RELIGION

In writing of Peter Bell and Goody Blake and Simon Lee, Wordsworth was, however, at some distance from the Antique, much as the Grecian statues had helped create the eighteenth-century taste for simplicity. He might easily have been more popular, had he compared Martha Ray of "The Thorn," for example, to a younger Niobe. But such imagery did not suggest itself; his poems were too "simple" for the world of taste and fashion. Many gentlemen felt that Wordsworth had achieved the "bald" and "sordid" simplicity Pope condemned as dullness. As perhaps the strongest defenders of the refinements of polite society among writers of the Romantic period, Byron and Hazlitt later attacked the "simple" Wordsworth. Coleridge also criticized his friend, though he used carefully reasoned statement rather than Byron's ridicule or Hazlitt's misrepresentation: he seems to have felt that Wordsworth had pushed too far the cause of simplicity in making "low and rustic life" his standard. Other factors besides the criticism of the principles exemplified in *Lyrical Ballads* must be taken into account, but Wordsworth's poetry after the early 1800's was seldom as "simple." In general he either abandoned "incidents and situations from common life" or used them as parts of larger themes. Morality, religion, history, mythology, the story of culture, including the arts—these were the materials for the epic on man and nature and society which Wordsworth set for himself as the crown of his poetic career. He never really betrayed nature, but he extended his interests to include the whole range of experience.

One of the larger themes—in many respects the most important— was the history of society; again he was a child of the eighteenth century. As a "romantic," however, Wordsworth characteristically approached the building of his great cathedral-masterpiece, *The Recluse,* first through a rigid self-appraisal in *The Prelude* ("to record, in verse, the origin and progress of his own powers") and, secondly, through an examination of the place of the religious spirit or belief in a society. Hence in *The Excursion* Greece, with the heroic "spirit of the place" and the "harmonizing soul" of its "life of manners and familiar incidents," became the subject of special study. In order to present his conception of Greece, Wordsworth analyzed the religious spirit of the Greeks, the belief manifested in their mythology and statuary. Thus he became not only "the fountainhead of nineteenth-century poetry on mythological themes"—as Douglas Bush has brilliantly shown [3]—but also the source of considerable poetry about Grecian statuary, especially in its relation to religion. Slight as his own knowledge of specific examples of the Antique seems to have been, he nevertheless turned many poets to the ancient works.

In the account of Grecian mythology in *The Excursion,* one hears the burden of Shaftesbury, Thomson, Akenside, Winckelmann, and others regarding the sculpture of Greece summarized in clear if some-

[3] *Mythology and the Romantic Tradition in English Poetry* (Cambridge, Mass., 1937), pp. 56 ff.

what gaudy verse. The description of the technical process of sculpture is almost too "academic," too Masonian or Darwinian; still, the appreciative tone and the sympathetic picture of the life of the Ancients carry the reader across the flats.

> The lively Grecian, in a land of hills,
> Rivers and fertile plains, and sounding shores,
>
> . . .
>
> Could find commodious place for every God,
>
> . . .
>
> With unrivalled skill,
> As nicest observation furnished hints
> For studious fancy, his quick hand bestowed
> On fluent operations a fixed shape;
> Metal or stone, idolatrously served.
> And yet—triumphant o'er this pompous show
> Of art, this palpable array of sense,
> On every side encountered;
>
> . . .
>
> a SPIRIT hung,
> Beautiful region! o'er thy towns and farms,
> Statues and temples, and memorial tombs.[4]
> (Book IV, ll. 718 ff., 847 ff.)

Everything in Greece showed the working of the one spirit of the time and place; and Wordsworth chose sculpture as its characteristic art. The statues made with "unrivalled skill" had been the works of believing Greeks: the artists were servants of religion, putting belief into the "palpable array" of forms on temples and tombs, which were perceivable by the senses yet expressive of a spiritual life within the "fixed shapes." No wonder Wordsworth sometimes admired Greece for its unity of belief and artistic expression; as he remarked in another case where fancy had worked on reality,

> Hence came a spirit hallowing what I saw
> With decoration and ideal grace;
> A dignity, a smoothness, like the works

[4] See also the sonnet "Tranquillity! the Sovereign Aim Wert Thou" (1833) where the philosophy, tragedy, and sculpture of Greece were said to express the same spirit. See also Coleridge, below, pp. 143 ff.

Of Grecian Art, and purest Poesy.[5]
(*Prelude*, 1805 ed., Book V, ll. 478–81.)

With the same natural piety the sculptor gave shape to "the fair humanities of old religion" and the lonely herdsman summoned forth Apollo, Diana, oreads, nymphs, or Pan himself, "the intelligible forms of ancient poets."

> So might I, standing on this pleasant lea,
> Have glimpses that would make me less forlorn;
> Have sight of Proteus rising from the sea;
> Or hear old Triton blow his wreathed horn.

Yet the belief of the Greeks was pagan and idolatrous; it was an outworn creed. Poets were not to adopt the pagan views, attractive as they were; nor were sculptors to imitate their forms of ideal grace. As Wordsworth said in a sonnet written between 1810 and 1815,

> Brook! whose society the Poet seeks.
>
> . . .
>
> If wish were mine some type of thee to view,
> Thee, and not thee thyself, I would not do
> Like Grecian Artists, give thee human cheeks,
> Channels for tears; no Naiad should'st thou be,—
> Have neither limbs, feet, feathers, joints nor hairs:
> It seems the Eternal Soul is clothed in thee
> With purer robes than those of flesh and blood.[6]

Despite the dubious grammar of the somewhat pedestrian lines, it is clear that the poet was not to give a fixed shape to the brook in the manner of the Greeks, for its soul, he felt, could not be captured in a palpable human form.

[5] De Selincourt (p. 531) believes these lines were probably written in Germany in 1798–99; if so, they may reflect discussions with Coleridge concerning ideas found in some German follower of Winckelmann, possibly Schelling; see also, pp. 321 ff. But he did not read Winckelmann until 1815. If the lines were written later, they may have been colored by Reynolds's *Discourses*, read with interest by Wordsworth in 1804; see letters to Sir George Beaumont, July 20, Aug. 31, and Dec. 25, 1804 (*The Early Letters of William and Dorothy Wordsworth* [1787–1805], ed. E. de Selincourt [1935], pp. 402, 410, 422).

[6] The sonnet may have been intended, in part, as a criticism of Winckelmann's remarks on allegory among the Greek painters; see letter to B. R. Haydon, Jan. 13, 1816 (*The Letters of William and Dorothy Wordsworth* [1806–1820], ed. E. de Selincourt [1937], II, 701–2).

Where the eighteenth-century poets, especially the Academic ones, had admired the physical appearances or external beauties of Grecian forms, Wordsworth admitted their perfection but sought the spirit within. The intimate relationship between the religious beliefs of the Greeks and the forms of their art and poetry was clearly indicated in *The Excursion*. Similarly a "romantic" poet should treat the belief of his own day. In a spirit comparable to that of the Grecian artists and poets (though producing different forms to fit different beliefs), Wordsworth desired to show the harmonizing soul in the manners and familiar incidents of the early nineteenth century: a "pure religion breathing household laws."

FANCY AND GRECIAN ART

The spirit of the religion and morality reflected in the actions of daily life was, for Wordsworth, the most important thing about Greece or any other nation. Few English poets approach him in the ability to apprehend the spiritual temperature of an age—to feel and, what is more, to present·in words the "presence" of a place both in its exterior characteristics and in its inner qualities. Older poets, Wordsworth sometimes felt, had concerned themselves only with imaginary lands and had largely treated what were really "fictions." On the other hand, he was consecrated to reality, to "a simple produce of the common day." His ideal was a presence or motion or spirit instinct with life yet not capable of being defined in a palpable array of sense. That vision was the more awe-inspiring and at the same time the more tantalizing because of its elusiveness:

> Not Chaos, not
> The darkest pit of lowest Erebus,
> Nor aught of blinder vacancy, scooped out
> By help of dreams—can breed such fear and awe
> As fall upon us often when we look
> Into our Minds, into the Mind of Man—
> My haunt, and the main region of my song.
> —Beauty—a living Presence of the earth,
> Surpassing the most fair ideal Forms
> Which craft of delicate Spirits hath composed

> From earth's materials—waits upon my steps;
> Pitches her tents before me as I move,
> An hourly neighbour.[7] (*Recluse,* ll. 788–800.)

The task of revealing the harmonizing soul of his own age—the beauty given to life by the mind of man in communion with the spirit more fair than the forms of Grecian art—was no idle playing with indefinite and loose imaginings. For the skeptical he had only ridicule:

> Call ye these appearances—
>
> . . .
>
> A shadow, a delusion, ye who pore
> On the dead letter, miss the spirit of things;
> Whose truth is not a motion and a shape
> Instinct with vital functions, but a block
> Or waxen image which yourselves have made,
> And ye adore! (*Prelude,* Book VIII, ll. 293, 296–301.)

His partly pietistic and puritanical horror of images made him fear any "fixed shape" for the "realities" of the spirit, which were to be apprehended by the mind, not by the senses.

Not long after Wordsworth had announced that the beauty waiting upon his steps surpassed the ideal forms of the skillful Grecian artists, he began to show more interest than ever before in those very forms of earlier art and literature. The works of the mind of man in ancient life as well as in contemporary events rivaled the presences of the earth. The regions of fancy—explored in classical literature and history with intense delight by the boy Wordsworth, who had been instinctively responsive to "primitive paganism" [8]—were in part drawing him from an avowed intention of laying bare the beauty—the spirit or harmonizing soul or unifying imaginative principle—operating within the forms of his own day. Partly as a relief from the very great strain of that ambitious attempt, Wordsworth turned to the classical world, and references to ancient fables, heroes, mythology,

---

[7] The description of the "ideal Forms" made out of "earth's materials" suggests Akenside; see above, p. 83.

[8] See the Foreword to the "Ode to Lycoris" (1817), *The Prelude* (De Selincourt), p. 506, and Bush, *Mythology and the Romantic Tradition,* pp. 57, 62.

art, history, and literature became more frequent after 1805-6. *The Excursion* is the symbol of the change, with its mixture of passages written under the influence of the earlier devotion to common life and "the living Spirit of this earth" and passages reflecting the attractiveness of ancient, especially Grecian, mythology and art. Antique fables were no longer merely "fictions" but were sympathetically described as the expression of the "real" sentiments of another age: in the account of Greece, Wordsworth saw how human beings had made beauty from their beliefs. As the epic cathedral of contemporary life, which was to have been his lifework, seemed less likely to be completed, the poet withdrew somewhat reluctantly into fancy's maze. *The Excursion* corresponded to the retreat from the position of extreme simplicity in the *Lyrical Ballads,* a position partly abandoned almost as soon as it had been announced.

The writing of *The Excursion* (from 1795 to 1814 but mostly between 1808 and 1811) coincided with considerable reading in the classics and concern for the fine arts, especially painting, with the guidance of Sir George Beaumont. "Dion" and "Laodamia," written in the year *The Excursion* was published, 1814, also resulted from reading in ancient works. Moreover, the passage on the Grecian artists in *The Excursion* is reflected in "Laodamia" when Protesilaus describes the "happier beauty" of the Elysian fields:

> [He] spake of heroic arts in graver mood
> Revived, with finer harmony pursued.

Not an active participant in the controversy over the Elgin Marbles, Wordsworth in 1815 nevertheless was on the edge of the discussion. From Rydal Mount he wrote to Benjamin R. Haydon, the leading proponent of the sculptures, a letter which indicates his acquaintance with the works (December 21, 1815). "I am not surprised that Canova expressed himself so highly pleased with the Elgin Marbles. A man must be senseless as a clod, or perverse as a fiend, not to be enraptured with them." Then he inquired whether Haydon had read Winckelmann on the Antique; for he had himself just read a copy of the Glasgow (1766) translation of *Reflections concerning the Imitation of the Grecian Artists in Painting and Sculpture, in a Series of*

Letters which he had discovered on a bookstall at Penrith. He was unable to understand how Winckelmann's "high reputation among the most judicious of the German criticks" could have been founded upon such a "superficial" work.[9]

In the "Thanksgiving Ode" of 1816 ("When the soft hand of sleep had closed the latch") Wordsworth fused his classical, aesthetic, and patriotic interests when thoughts of Grecian art came surging into his mind as appropriate antique models for English memorials to the victory of Liberty over the tyranny of Napoleon.

> Victorious England! bid the silent Art
> Reflect, in glowing hues that shall not fade,
> Those high achievements; even as she arrayed
> With second life the deed of Marathon
>   Upon Athenians walls;
> So may she labour for thy civic halls:
>   And be the guardian spaces
>   Of consecrated places,
> As nobly graced by Sculpture's patient toil;
> And let imperishable Columns rise
> Fixed in the depths of this courageous soil;
> Expressive signals of a glorious strife,
> And competent to shed a spark divine
> Into the torpid breast of daily life (ll. 94–107).[10]

Wordsworth's inspiration was literary, with Plutarch and Pausanias supplying the "deed of Marathon" and the general impression of statues, temples, and columns. There was only the faintest suggestion

[9] Wordsworth probably heard of Winckelmann during his visit to Germany, but he seems not to have read any of his works before the time of the letter; see above, p. 126n. The discussion of the ideas of the German critic apparently ended with the query.

[10] The "deed of Marathon" was the mural painting of the Battle of Marathon, formerly attributed to Panainos. Wordsworth had already mentioned it in *Descriptive Sketches*, see above, p. 123, while "The Painted Tower of Tell" (1820) drew an effusion with similar reference to the "fine skill as did the meed bestow on Marathonian valour." (See also "Composed at Cora Linn" [1814] for references to Grecian heroism.) Wordsworth was familiar with the accounts of the work in Pliny and Pausanias, the chief sources of information about the painting; he may have read also Hayley's lines in *An Essay on Painting*, Book I, ll. 190–97 (*Poems and Plays* [1788 ed.], I, 11). See Mary H. Swindler, *Ancient Painting* (New Haven, 1929), pp. 209 ff. For Landor's use of the "deed of Marathon," see below, p. 248.

of his memories of the Elgin Marbles. As almost always, Wordsworth was primarily concerned with the theory of art, with works of sculpture which should be "expressive signals" or symbols of a heroic spirit, such as the simplicity of the ancient Greeks. Again their art was the servant of religion and morality. Even as the arts as well as nature had influenced the daily lives and morality of Greece, so now they were to show similar powers in England.

Wordsworth mentioned no specific ancient sculpture in the "Thanksgiving Ode," and in general the Antique seems to have interested him more on the printed page than in the gallery and more in theory than in actual representational examples. He left no record of antiques seen in his visits to the "spectacles" of London in 1791 but only "those carved maniacs" of Bedlam "perpetually recumbent" and heroes in the parks (*Prelude,* Book VII, ll. 132 ff.). The Harmodius-Aristogiton reference (*Prelude,* Book X, ll. 198–99), along with his translation of an Athenian song in their honor, may imply a glimpse of the statues, but Wordsworth was probably thinking of classical historians rather than art. In writing of Coleridge's sojourn in Sicily and Malta (*Prelude,* Book XI, ll. 461 ff.), Wordsworth was happy that his friend would be "a glad votary"—

> Not in vain
> Those temples, where they in their ruins yet
> Survive for inspiration, shall attract
> Thy solitary steps:—

though he preferred to read the ancient poets at home in Freedom's "only sanctuary." Poetry was definitely the mistress of the arts for Wordsworth.

In Paris in 1820 he showed less interest in statues and pictures at the Louvre than in the wonders of Le Jardin des Plantes. During the remainder of that tour on the Continent, architecture aroused his interest to some extent, though the Antique drew his attention less than it did that of any other Romantic poet. Yet in "Stanzas Composed in the Simplon Pass" he longed with a truly Renaissance spirit

> To range through the Temples of PAESTUM, to muse
> In POMPEII preserved by her burial in earth.

He returned, however, to England without having seen the paintings and statuary.

> The beauty of Florence, the grandeur of Rome,
> Could I leave them unseen, and not yield to regret?

In 1825 the Pillar of Trajan called forth some noteworthy lines on Roman sculpture in the exercise Wordsworth wrote, perhaps to show his son John at Oxford how he might win the Newdigate Prize, since the award for the following year was given to a poem on that subject. As a statement of his own response to that famous work "The Pillar of Trajan" is excellent: he was led to "study Trajan as by Pliny seen," and he wrote of a grandeur that cannot be put in "outward symbol." A very uneven poem, "The Pillar of Trajan" has lines of prosaic description, such as

> Historic figures round the shaft embost
> Ascend, with lineaments in air not lost . . .

Yet the images of "Group winding after group with dream-like ease" and the "spiral grace" of the woodbine on a lofty elm tree hardly redeem the account of the imagined action on the pillar in the poorer sort of Byronic style in *Childe Harold*. Still, with his characteristic skill in rounding off a subject, Wordsworth balanced some of the weaker couplets with an effective conclusion:

> Still are we present with the imperial Chief,
> Nor cease to gaze upon the bold Relief
> Till Rome, to silent marble unconfined,
> Becomes with all her years a vision of the Mind (ll. 70–73).[11]

In 1837 Wordsworth visited Florence and Rome,

> With those rich stores of Nature's imagery,
> And divine Art

he had long wished to see, only to fall asleep before Raphael's painting of John the Baptist—"sitting," he confessed, "with my back towards the Venus de Medici"! [12] "Daddy" Wordsworth took a very

[11] For Wordsworth's indebtedness to Forsyth's *Remarks on Antiquities,* see *Poetical Works,* ed. William Knight (1896), VII, 138 ff.
[12] See *Memorials of a Tour in Italy* (1842), Sections XXVI, ll. 3–4, and XX, Foreword.

sensible view of his affront to the goddess—especially unpardonable in a poet. He was "not ashamed" to admit that he had been exhausted from strenuous sight-seeing. More revealing, perhaps, is the fact that the Baptist, not the Venus, got his poem.

"The Egyptian Maid" (1830) deserves brief mention as a poem "suggested by the beautiful work of ancient art, once included among the Townley Marbles, and now in the British Museum." But the work of art was merely the starting place for the poet; fancy rather than aesthetic feeling attracted Wordsworth to this romance of the water lily. With his poetic spirit thus at work, one is scarcely surprised to find in one of his last poems, "Love Lies Bleeding" (1845), an image drawn from no less an antique statue than the Dying Gladiator. In describing the drooping but not prostrate flower, Wordsworth adopted again the "academic" manner of *Descriptive Sketches:*

> Even thus stoops
> (Sentient by Grecian sculpture's marvellous power)
> Thus leans, with hanging brow and body bent
> Earthward in uncomplaining languishment
> The dying Gladiator. (ll. 5-9).

Though Wordsworth's poetic style had reverted to its earliest form, the controlling spirit of his work was still "romantic." Only three years before "Love Lies Bleeding" he had strongly defended nature against art and artifice, "imported with other impertinences from the Germans," and in "A Poet!—He Hath Put His Heart to School" had advanced the "romantic" conception of poetry as a living organism:

> the grandeur of the Forest-tree
> Comes not by casting in a formal mould,
> But from its *own* divine vitality.

That was close to the core of Wordsworth's "romantic" position; and in so far as he wrote of Grecian sculpture, he found it valuable, not for the "formal moulds" and "fixed shapes"—made, he admitted, with greatest art and unrivaled skill—but for the divine vitality of the poetic principle. In Grecian art as in lofty poetry, of whatever age, a "harmonizing soul" or organic simplicity revealed itself. Under the influence of such Wordsworthian and "romantic" aesthetics, many an English poet sought to penetrate through the forms of the Antique to the inner or essential spirit.

COLERIDGE AS CONNOISSEUR

Young and optimistic, Samuel Taylor Coleridge in *Religious Musings* (1794–96) pictured Imagination leading mankind from pastoral simplicity to a sense of property, in whose train followed not only the vices (Luxury, War, Superstition) but also the virtues (Love, Science, Freedom) with

> all the inventive arts that nursed the soul
> To forms of beauty (ll. 208–9).

Like Akenside, one of his favorite poets at the time, the young writer saw all the "inventions" of mind—reason and philosophy, poetry and the fine arts—directing the progress of man. Almost too familiar to readers of the verse of the eighteenth century are the allegorical machinery and the overwrought theorizing on the intellectual and moral history of humanity.

Coleridge likewise had the taste for the picturesque which was expected in every poet. Though usually applied to landscapes, this sensitivity also turned to works of art. The earliest mention of a specific antique statue—and it is the only one in his poetry apparently—appeared in Coleridge's contribution to the first edition (1796) of Southey's once-famous epic *Joan of Arc*. There Coleridge described a personified Ambition in the manner of his eighteenth-century masters:

> A dazzling form, broad-bosomed, bold of eye,
> And wild her hair, save where with laurels bound.
> Not more majestic stood the healing God,
> When from his bow the arrow sped that slew
> Huge Python (ll. 433–37).[13]

In a footnote he identified the figure as the Apollo Belvedere.

[13] Coleridge thought enough of these heroics to incorporate them into a didactic poem, "The Progress of Liberty; or, the Visions of the Maid of Orleans," which was neither published nor even finished though the fragment appeared as "The Destiny of Nations" in the volume *Sibylline Leaves*, 1817. The original title, "The Progress of Liberty," indicates the tradition to which the lines belonged.

While traveling in Germany three years later, Coleridge constantly viewed the scenery with the appreciative eye of a connoisseur. Once, indeed, he surpassed his contemporaries by discovering a "sculptural" scene to add to the picturesque. Of some peasant women sowing fir-seed he reported in a letter to Thomas Poole (May 19, 1799), "Never did I behold aught so impressively picturesque, or rather *statue-esque*, as these Groups of women in all their various attitudes—The thick mist, thro' which their figures came to my eye, gave such a soft *Un-reality* to them!" Here the word "statue-esque" is especially interesting since this was its first use by an English man of letters.

Coleridge the connoisseur next appeared in 1804 in London where he visited galleries and studied painting in anticipation of his secretary-ship in Malta. In order to obtain information about Sicily he called on no less a man of taste than Richard Payne Knight, who showed him Hackart's views of Sicily and a large collection of ancient bronzes. The figure of a Venus—"as from the bath, on one leg, putting on her sandal on the upraised leg"—"absolutely enamoured" Coleridge.[14] "I have seldom in my life," he reported to Sir George Beaumont, who had given him the introduction to Knight, "experienced such a burst of pleasurable sense of *beauty*. . . . I am not afraid of the charge of using violent language when I say you will be enchanted."

On the way to Malta, Coleridge thought Gibraltar could furnish a number of Hogarthian "character-paintings," but his growing interest in the arts had to wait until he halted in Italy on his return from the secretaryship. Now conscious of the power of art, the student of all knowledge began in earnest to learn the alphabet of the fine arts amid classical scenes. "By my regular attention to the best of the good things in Rome, and association almost wholly with the artists of acknowledged highest reputation, I acquired," he wrote Daniel Stuart of the *Morning Post*, "more insight into the Fine Arts

[14] *Memorials of Coleorton; Being Letters from Coleridge, Wordsworth and His Sister, Southey, and Sir Walter Scott to Sir George and Lady Beaumont of Coleorton, Leicestershire, 1803 to 1804*, ed. William Knight (Edinburgh, 1887), I, 55–57. The figure admired by Coleridge is officially listed by Henry B. Walters in the *Catalogue of the Bronzes, Greek, Roman, and Etruscan, in the Department of Greek and Roman Antiquities, British Museum* (1899) as an Aphrodite Fastening Her Sandal, of the Roman period, No. 1083, p. 193. See also *Unpublished Letters*, I, 317, for Coleridge's interest in art in 1804.

in three months than I could have done in England in twenty years." [15]

Moreover, as in Germany, Coleridge associated nature with art, so that in one of the few notes remaining from his short stay one finds him describing the setting of Naples in terms borrowed from the antiquities.

Naples, view of Vesuvius, the Hail-Mist—Torre de Greco—bright amid darkness—the mountains above it flashing here and there from their snows; but Vesuvius, it had not thinned as I have seen at Keswick, but the air so consolidated with the massy cloud curtain, that it appeared like a mountain in basso relievo, in an interminable wall of some pantheon.

Very much in the fashion of James Thomson, Shelley, and Byron, then, Coleridge looked upon the Italian scene with "a poet's eye," gathering the beautiful images of classical magnificence as well as of nature, which he later called up often in conversation with Gillman.[16]

A pilgrim of culture, Coleridge apparently filled a journal with comments on landscape and the antiquities, expecting to publish them. Fate intervened, however, and the projected "Notes on Art and Travel" disappeared during the return from Italy, after Coleridge received warning that Napoleon had issued orders for his arrest. Whether the "Notes" were with the books not returned by the sea captain or were with those lost in customs, or whether Captain Derkheim of the Yankee brig *Gosport* compelled the author to throw overboard his literary labors in order to lighten the load when the ship was chased by the French, Coleridge neglected to inform his friends.

A few records of the Italian visit of Coleridge survive, however, and, though scanty, indicate both the nature of his thoughts about art and also what may well have been the burden of the lost observations on art, artists, and Mediterranean scenery. The American painter

---

[15] See *Letters from the Lake Poets to Daniel Stuart* (1899), pp. 38, 40–41, and 60.
[16] See James Gillman, *The Life of Samuel Taylor Coleridge* (1838), I, 179, 181n. With Joseph Cottle, however, Coleridge seems not to have talked about Rome or the antiquities; see *Early Recollections, Chiefly Relating to the Late Samuel Taylor Coleridge, during his Long Residence in Bristol* (1837), II, 82–83n.

Washington Allston reported that poet and student of art explored with gusto what Coleridge termed the "silent" city. The young painter added,

But I never could think of it as such while with him; for meet him when or where I would, the fountain of his mind was never dry; but like the far-reaching aqueducts, that once supplied the mistress of the world, its living streams seemed especially to flow for every classic ruin over which we wandered.[17]

To the eager American, Coleridge was no less than a Plato discoursing of beauty in a new Academe.

On one ramble through the city, or perhaps in the famous Caffè Greco, the rendezvous of foreign artists and travelers, Coleridge tried to convince Allston that he should study Gothic art rather than the Grecian models which were then the staples in the education of an artist. "Grecian architecture," he urged, "is a thing, but the Gothic is an idea. . . . I can make a Grecian temple of two bats and a cocked hat." [18] Coleridge's remark was significant, not because a fifth-rate painter chose to disregard the advice and continued to paint in the grand style of the Academicians, but because Allston was one of the first recipients of what was to be a favorite Coleridgean antithesis between Gothic—that is, Christian or "romantic"—and Grecian— that is, pagan or "classical"—art. Occurring repeatedly in the lectures on the drama and the fine arts, this opposition became one of the principal bases upon which Coleridge formed his aesthetics. Years later Wordsworth wrote that Coleridge and Sir George Beaumont had taken "great delight in referring to Mr. Allston's observations upon art and the works of the great masters they had seen together in Rome, and the admiration was no doubt mutual from the commencement of their acquaintance." [19] Echoes of Coleridge are audible, if faint, in Allston's posthumous *Lectures on Art.*

[17] See Allston's *Lectures on Art and Poems,* ed. R. H. Dana (New York, 1850), p. v.

[18] See Jared B. Flagg, *The Life and Letters of Washington Allston* (New York, 1892), p. 65. Flagg added in language reminiscent of eighteenth-century men of taste like Walpole, "It were unjust to suppose that Coleridge was insensible to Grecian beauty; Plato and Socrates could charm his intellect, but Christ and the Church captivated his heart and soul."

[19] See letter to R. H. Dana, Sr., Oct., 1843, *ibid.,* p. 369.

In an account tallying with the advice to the American painter, Coleridge himself described, in a letter to Samuel Rogers (March 28, 1804), certain of his ideas about art while in Italy. He was most awed neither by the classicistic works of the famous Canova, with whom he was acquainted, nor by the false modesty of the Venus de Medici—to generations of connoisseurs and Academic critics the beau ideal of feminine grace—but by the sublimity of the works of Michelangelo, especially the Moses. Unlike many gentlemen of the eighteenth century who had scorned religion as "superstition," Coleridge proudly asserted his Christian spirit. Indeed, the Triumph of Death frescoes in the Campo Santo at Pisa and the Moses were "deeply interesting" to him precisely because they *were* Christian:

the one as the first and stately upgrowth of painting out of the very heart of Christendom, underived from the ancients, and having a life of its own in the spirit of that revolution of which Christianity was effect, means, and symbol; the other the same phenomenon in statuary, but unfollowed and unique (for there is no analogy to it in the unhappy attempt at picture petrifactions by Bernini, in whom a great genius was bewildered and lost by excess of fancy over imagination, the aggregative over the unifying faculty).

Sir Joshua Reynolds had condemned Bernini and exalted Michelangelo for the same reasons, but he had turned back finally to the classical rather than the Christian world. To Coleridge the "romantic," however, Michelangelo was more interesting than the Antique, since the Florentine stated the truths of Christianity with the imaginative simplicity which in the late eighteenth century many men of taste had begun to demand in art, ancient and otherwise. Coleridge was applying to modern sculpture a distinction which, foreshadowed in his important letter to William Sotheby (September 10, 1802), was to be the core of his psychology of art, namely, the distinction between fancy and the imagination proper: Bernini was a sculptor of fancy; Michelangelo, a truly imaginative artist.

Through the mental processes indicated in these observations, Coleridge in time arrived at one of the pivotal positions in his "romantic" logic, namely, that as a Modern he must prefer an art expressing the sentiments of Christianity. Yet like many other Romantic poets he was not unaffected by classical art, and traces of his connoisseurship reappeared throughout his works. A man of great learning, he mentioned classical art in table talk and letters as well as in essays on aesthetic subjects. His association with the Wedgwoods presumably gave him some acquaintance with the antiquities; and in the first of the *Essays on the Fine Arts* he generously applauded "the transfusion of the fairest forms of Greece and Rome into the articles of hourly domestic use by Mr. Wedgwood." [20] In the same essay Coleridge listed the Venus de Medici and the Apollo Belvedere among "the noblest productions of human genius" along with the Pantheon and the works of Michelangelo, Milton, Shakespeare, Raphael, and Homer. Had he included Phidias and the statue known as the Torso Belvedere, "the school of Michelangelo," he would have agreed completely with Walpole, perhaps the greatest of the English connoisseurs, and with Reynolds, first president of the Royal Academy, as well as with "Gothic" Blake! All four ordinarily meant the Hellenistic and Greco-Roman statues when they referred to the Antique, whether or not they mentioned Phidias.

Coleridge was, at times at least, even something of a collector of virtu, though in a very minor way, of course, when compared with Samuel Rogers, who was one of his friends. In 1819 he displayed considerable interest in his collection of casts from ancient cameos and intaglios, writing in a letter (October 28), perhaps to Mrs. Aders, that "every little gem is associated with my recollections, or more or less recalls the images and persons seen and met during my own stay in the Mediterranean and Italy." Under less kindly stars Coleridge might easily have become a connoisseur like Richard Payne Knight or a poet on the order of Darwin, Rogers, or Hayley!

SCULPTURE IN THE COLERIDGEAN AESTHETICS

The abbreviated version of the antithesis between Grecian or classical and Gothic or modern art which Coleridge announced to Allston

[20] See "On the Principles of Genial Criticism concerning the Fine Arts, More Especially Those of Statuary and Painting, Deduced from the Laws and Impulses Which Guide the True Artist in the Production of His Works," *Biographia Literaria*, ed. J. Shawcross (1907), II, 220.

in Rome was, in the final analysis, a new manifestation—rather, a continuation—of the Ancients-Moderns controversy which has plagued Europeans since the Renaissance at least. Encouraged by the universal interest in theories of milieu, especially the notion that a unique national or racial spirit shows itself in the works of every nation, people, and epoch of culture, late in the eighteenth century the Romantic critics in Germany popularized the theory that ancient art was to be compared to sculpture while modern art was to be associated with painting. The scarcity of ancient paintings aided the cause of these theorists, and, fortunately for them, archaeologist and historian had not unearthed the information that has since upset their neat schemes.

Coleridge, therefore, was sharing contemporary thought—in particular A. W. Schlegel's lectures on the drama—when he accepted this facile summary of two eras of human culture and employed it in several lectures and essays. In his philosophizing about art both in Germany and in Italy he had been groping toward the "romantic" antithesis between the ancient and the modern spirits; but he first clearly advanced the analogy of literature to the fine arts in a lecture in 1811, in which he contrasted the small number of figures in the abstract and sculptural dramas of the Greeks with the crowded, pictorial "canvases" of modern dramatists.[21] Two years later he contributed the word "statuesque" (which he had been using since 1799) to the terminology of English criticism, when he contrasted Shakespeare with the Ancients, asserting that the productions of the Greek stage "were, therefore (if the expression may be allowed), *statuesque*. The moderns we may designate as *picturesque*." The unfamiliar word translated the *plastisch* of the German critics, and the whole statement was borrowed, in this case from Schlegel.[22]

In the eighteenth century the eagerness to study Grecian models

[21] See *Coleridge's Shakespearean Criticism*, ed. Thomas M. Raysor (Cambridge, Mass., 1930), II, 159, 262. Of course the antithesis was a conclusion easily drawn from the absorption of Winckelmann and Lessing in the sculpture of the Ancients.

[22] For the history of the word "statuesque," see my article, "Critical Terms from the Art of Sculpture," *Notes & Queries*, April 3, 1937, pp. 239–40. See also *Coleridge's Shakespearean Criticism*, II, 262, and the sources referred to there. The Schlegel statement is (*Werke*, ed. Bocking, V, 10): "der Geist der gesammten antiken Kunst und Poesie ist plastisch, so wie der modernen pittoresk."

had led not only to the Academic copying of antiques but also to the praise of the peoples and societies possessing the "simple" morality which had produced the unsurpassed art and civilization of the ancient world. Nature and the Greeks were potent watchwords in the latter years of the Enlightenment: poet and patriot, artist and man of taste admired Grecian simplicity. But soon writers and critics recognized that the forms of the Ancients, however perfect, were unsuitable vehicles for what the Moderns desired to express. Without rejecting or condemning completely the old forms, many English Romantic poets sought not only to charge classical forms and themes with new meaning but also to draw from them whatever suited their purposes. The primary concern of "romantic" writers became, there-fore, not the "progress" of the arts but the content or expressiveness of a work of art. In Coleridge, more strikingly than in any other English writer of the early nineteenth century except Wordsworth, may be seen the "romantic" tendency to emphasize the content or expressiveness of art. Throughout his life he unswervingly preached that the artist should seek to reveal the spirit within objects—a spirit which the artificer might discover in his intuitive participation in the phenomena of human and physical nature.

Interested in expression beyond all else, as a Platonist Coleridge included all creative activity under Poesy, agreeing with Diotima in the *Symposium* (502) that "all creation or passage of non-being into being is poetry or making, and the processes of all art are crea-tive; and the masters of arts are all poets or makers." [23] As a "ro-mantic" aesthetician he went on to specify that Poesy mediated be-tween man and nature; for the imaginative principle was the unifying faculty revealing the oneness in the multiplicity of experience. The poet had, therefore, two goals: to discover the spirit working within objects in nature, that is, "to make nature thought"; and to force the thought, derived either from penetrating the phenomena of nature or from intellection having no reference to external objects, into forms which should then be perceptible to other men, in other words,

[23] See also Coleridge's *Treatise on Method*, ed. Alice D. Snyder (1934), pp. 35–36 and notes.

"to make thought nature." By following these principles the poet, having worked the "sensible impressions" which he received from nature into "a bright, and clear, and living Idea," earned the title of "maker" or "creator" of individual forms in which truth is clothed. His ideas existed with the validity of objects in nature: the products of his creative activity had assumed shape; nonbeing had passed into being.[24]

To illustrate his very "romantic" theories Coleridge turned, very much in the manner of Blake and Shelley, to the Antique. Presumably the choice was partly a sign of his own familiarity with the ancient masterpieces and partly a realization that the Grecian statues were the works of art best known to his readers. In any case the Apollo Belvedere and the Venus de Medici served as admirable precedents for his statements. The ancient sculptors had followed the Coleridgean formula: they had made "nature" into "thought," and they had turned ideas into a second "nature."

Even as the ancient Apollo and Venus were the exemplars of the ideal in art, so sculpture itself—and Coleridge had in mind the Antique—became for him the best illustration of his theories of expression. "Light, manhood, simplicity, wholeness . . . the *entelechy* of Phidian Genius"—these were the very qualities to be achieved by the unifying imagination of "romantic" aesthetics. From Schlegel came the final statement of Coleridge's principle:

The ideal of earnest poetry consists in the union and harmonious melting down, the fusion of the sensual into the spiritual, of the man as an animal into man as a power of reason and self-government, which we have represented to us most clearly in the plastic art, or statuary, where the perfection of form is an outward symbol of inward perfection and the most elevated ideas, where the body is wholly penetrated by the soul, and spiritualized even to a state of glory.[25]

For such a "romantic" theorist as Coleridge, the perfect illustration of the art-process, the essential spirit or organic form showing itself

---

[24] *Ibid.*, pp. 62–63. See also *Biographia Literaria* (Shawcross), II, 258 ff., 317, and *Coleridge's Miscellaneous Criticism*, ed. Thomas M. Raysor (1936), pp. 204 ff.

[25] See, respectively, letter to J. H. Green (January 16, 1819) and "Lecture on the Greek Drama," *Coleridge's Shakespearean Criticism* (Raysor), I, 170–71.

in the art-form—*forma formans per formam formatam translucens*
—was Greek sculpture.

The language of Coleridge's discussions of the imagination, as
indeed of all his theorizing in the field of aesthetics, indicates that
he was never far from theology. Always concerned with the question
of organic form, that is, the spirit underlying and giving significance
to the external form in art, he turned easily and early to study the
connection between the fine arts and religion. To what extent, he
constantly asked, had the religious beliefs of the Greeks aided in
effecting their masterpieces? Of the various interpretations of the
Antique in the light of the institutions, morality, and climate of the
Greek state, which Shaftesbury, Montesquieu, Winckelmann, and
others had propagated, the relation of the religion of the Greeks to
their art most interested Coleridge. Even the vaunted freedom of the
ancient state meant little to him; after his youthful flirtations with
the Revolutionary Muse he grew conservative. In dealing with the
religion of the Greeks, moreover, he thought only of the spiritual
bases of the old cults and mysteries, not of rites and ceremonials. In
the eighteenth century, however, critics and gentlemen had been interested in the school of anatomy and the athletics encouraged by the
festival games and rites. But Coleridge regarded the religious exercises
of the ancient Greeks as neither picturesque nor diverting. He sought,
rather, to lay bare the spiritual impulse of which the rites and games
had been the manifestation.

As early as the famous lines which he introduced into *The Piccolomini* (1799–1800), a free translation of Schiller's drama of the
same name, Coleridge sketched what developed into his characteristic
interpretation of Greek mythology and religion:

> The intelligible forms of ancient poets,
> The fair humanities of old religion,
> The Power, the Beauty, and the Majesty,
> That had their haunts in dale, or piny mountain,
> Or forest by slow stream, or pebbly spring,

Or chasms and wat'ry depths; all these have vanished.
They live no longer in the faith of reason (II, iv, 123–29)! [26]

In these splendid lines written out of his special interest in mythology, he was thinking of the way in which the poets and sculptors had given concrete form to the beliefs of the Greeks. Strongly suggestive of sculpture, the phrases, the "fair humanities" of old religion and the "intelligible forms" of ancient poets, indicate that he regarded the ancient artists as instruments of the religious spirit of the Greeks.

In the essays of *The Friend* (1809–10 and 1818) and in the *Treatise On Method* (1818) Coleridge elaborated the relationships of religion and sculpture, even attributing the whole intellectual development of mankind to inspirations coming from the Divine Spirit. The "progress" of the arts in Greece, where they had flowered as nowhere else, was owing to the tutelage of religion.

The mysteries and the mythical Hymns and Paeans shaped themselves gradually into epic Poetry and History on the one hand, and into the ethical Tragedy and Philosophy on the other. Under their protection, and that of a youthful liberty secretly controlled by a species of internal Theocracy, the Sciences and the sterner kinds of the Fine Arts; viz. Architecture and Statuary, grew up together: followed, indeed, by Painting, but a statuesque and austerely idealized painting, which did not degenerate into mere copies of the sense, till the process, for which Greece existed, had been completed.[27]

The arts endured, moreover, according to Coleridge, until Greece no longer believed in its gods. The bonds of religion became weaker, and, as sophistry and cosmopolitanism spread in the state, the Greeks lost the greatness which characterized them in the Periclean age. The arts were no longer imaginative but imitative: Hellenistic works of art became mere copies of the sense.

This outline of Greek culture was, in brief, Coleridge's equivalent for the eighteenth-century explanations of the Greek decline through

[26] See also Bush, *Mythology and the Romantic Tradition in English Poetry,* pp. 54–55, and Wordsworth, above, pp. 124 ff.

[27] *The Friend,* Essay IX (1818), III, 232–33. The ideas had been developing in the earlier *Friend.* See also *Treatise,* pp. 48–49, for more details about sculpture, especially the improvement by the Greeks upon "the lifeless Statuary of the Egyptians." Throughout these passages Coleridge is eighteenth century in tone.

luxury and the loss of freedom. He warned his countrymen against a similar course of events in England, urging them to preserve "old England, the spiritual, Platonic old England" which he feared was being transformed into a new, "commercial Great Britain." [28]

Coleridge's speculations on the spiritual bases of art culminated in the plan for an "essay on the Connection of Statuary and Sculpture with Religion," which was to have been written in 1825. Addressing his friend John Flaxman as the "first" of "all modern sculptors," he announced the project in a letter, dated January 24, 1825, asking both for permission to visit the sculptor's studio and for information in regard to the antiquities in London. What the nature of the treatise was to have been is clearly seen from the prospectus sent to Flaxman.

The origin of statuary as a fine art, that is, as a form or species of Poesy (which I distinguish from poetry as a genus from one of its species). This origination or new birth is beyond controversy, the result of the Grecian mind. I then proceed to the re-action of sculpture after its escape from the caves and temples of Egyptian and Indo-European hieroglyphical idolatry into Greece on the religious conceptions and imaginations of men and in what way it joined with philosophy and the mysteries in preparing the Graeco-Roman world for Christianity, and that great article of the *Divine* HUMANITY and its meditative offices. Lastly, on the true essence of the ideal, and its intimate connection with the symbolic.

Some of this material went into the essay *On the Prometheus of Aeschylus,* also written in 1825, and Coleridge probably planned to use Flaxman's lectures on sculpture at the Royal Academy (delivered between 1810 and 1826) for information about the art.

The most significant aspect, finally, of the theorizing in *The Piccolomini, The Friend,* and the letter to Flaxman was the fact that Coleridge indicated the direction which the interest in Greek sculpture was to take among the late Romantics and the poets of the later nineteenth century. Though these poets continued to employ the cant phrases and ideas handed down by the earlier critics, and though they related in some form or other the "progress" or history of the

[28] *Anima Poetae,* ed. E. H. Coleridge (1895), p. 128. See also *The Friend,* No. 24 (1810), pp. 389 ff.; and the 1818 ed., II, 180–81; III, 116–17, 130–31.

arts, their best poetry on the sculpture of the Greeks expressed their personal and sensitive response. Theory became subordinated to interpretation, and statues were not objects to be described in terms of technique and rules but rather symbols of the spiritual powers wielded by the artist.

Coleridge, like Wordsworth, went even further and showed that the religious beliefs of the sculptors had been important, and he sought to reveal how the Divine Spirit had moved the artists. Largely because of the efforts of Coleridge and Wordsworth, many English poets tried to discover how religion had helped to create the masterpieces of Greek sculpture—the finest art according to the majority of the critics of the nineteenth century. By such an analysis they hoped to learn to work in a similar spirit so that they might mold the life of their own times into forms worthy to be classed with those of the Ancients.

In devoting his energies to analyzing the beliefs of the Ancients in the attempt to discover the psychology of their religion (his own term would be their "mental initiative"), Coleridge was prophetic of the interests of the poets and critics of the nineteenth century. Writing, too, at the height of the various cults of the classical—the movements led by the Dilettanti, Flaxman and the Wedgwoods, James Barry and the painters of history, Canova, Thorwaldsen, and others—he raised one of the loudest protests against the undervaluation of the modern or Christian spirit. Interested not only in the painters, sculptors, and writers of his acquaintance but also in seeing great works of art produced in his day, he warned artists away from the Antique. Though he was addressing the modern sculptors in particular, the following remarks summarized very well his complex and carefully reasoned attitude toward classical art.

Imitation of the antique may be too exclusive, and may produce an injurious effect on modern sculpture;—1st, generally, because such an imitation cannot fail to have a tendency to keep the attention fixed on the externals rather than on the thought within;—2ndly, because, accordingly, it leads the artist to rest satisfied with that which is always imperfect, namely, bodily form, and circumscribe his views of mental expression to the ideas of power and grandeur only;—3rdly, because it induces an effort to combine together two incongruous things, that is to say, modern feelings in antique forms;—4thly, because it speaks in a language, as it were, learned and dead, the tones of which, being unfamiliar, leave the common spectator cold and unimpressed;—and lastly, because it necessarily causes a neglect of thoughts, emotions and images of profounder interest and more exalted dignity, as motherly, sisterly, and brotherly love, piety, devotion, the divine become human,—the Virgin, the Apostle, the Christ.[29]

Altogether Coleridge's advice to sculptors constituted a splendid statement of the case of "romantic" critics, not against the classical masterpieces, but against the "academic" tendency to worship ancient forms and to neglect sentiments and emotions arising from the Christian spirit. The feelings and circumstances of the nineteenth century demanded something other than an easy acceptance of classical externals—the learned language which the weight of tradition tended to impose on educated gentlemen. "Romantic" writers saw their task, then, as the more difficult one of endowing with form the spirit operative in the world in which they lived. They were to accomplish their aim neither by foisting mere abstractions on the world nor by utilizing Grecian outlines, ready-made according to "academic" principles; instead, they were to "write from a principle within," said Coleridge: they were to reveal the significance of the phenomena of their own world.[30] Coleridge's position became widely prevalent later in the nineteenth century, even among poets and artists who ransacked the storehouse of antiquity for themes and images.

With all his warnings against the dangers of overzealous admiration of antiquity, and despite his recognition that the classical writers and artists were silent about many matters of great significance in

[29] "On Poesy or Art," *Biographia Literaria* (Shawcross), II, 260–61. For the indebtedness to Schelling, see *Notes and Lectures upon Shakespeare and Some of the Old Poets and Dramatists,* ed. Sara Coleridge (1849); Shawcross, II, 317 ff.; and *Coleridge's Miscellaneous Criticism* (Raysor), pp. 204 ff. Schelling's remark (quoted by Shawcross from *Werke* [1860 ed.], II, 295)—"They [the works of antiquity] leave you colder than the works of nature, if you have not the spiritual insight to penetrate the husk and to feel the power that is operative in them"—very nearly summarizes the feeling of most English Romantic poets toward the sculpture of Greece.

[30] *Coleridge's Shakespearean Criticism* (Raysor), II, 261: "One character attaches to all true poets: they write from a principle within." Of his contemporaries, Coleridge regarded only two as successful "poets" according to this remark: Wordsworth had written from within, while Allston, friend of his days in Rome, was doing the same in painting. See Flagg, *The Life and Letters of Washington Allston,* pp. 114–15.

his own age, Coleridge admitted the greatness of the Greeks. "Plain sense, measure, clearness, dignity, grace over all—these made the genius of Greece." [31] Yet no "romantic" writer expected those qualities to return in Grecian forms. He found them, rather, in poets like Wordsworth, who discovered a simplicity, dignity, and grace in modern life comparable to that of the Greeks. Coleridge left no doubt that the "romantic" writers felt that they were not and never could be Greeks.

[31] *Anima Poetae*, p. 150.

VII. BYRON

BYRON AND ART

ACCORDING to his early biographer John Galt, Byron "affected" to possess "no feeling for art." [1] "Affected" was precisely the word, for on many occasions the poetic lord revealed an unmistakable sensitivity to works of art. The descriptions of Athens, Rome, and Florence in *Childe Harold* and the account of the Coliseum in *Manfred* were consciously written as set pieces—patches as purple as Byron could make them; they are some of the best as well as most familiar sections of his more florid verse. Gothic art, particularly architecture, also interested the part of Byron which delighted in Newstead Abbey and in the gloomy effects achieved by Mrs. Radcliffe and other romancers. Nevertheless, he was primarily classical in taste.

Byron repeatedly protested ignorance of the fine arts, from the announcement in 1810, "I am not a collector or admirer of collections," to his remark to Trelawny at Ithaca in 1823, "I detest antiquarian twaddle." [2] Yet he added notes to *Childe Harold* referring to various popular travel books and authorities on antiquities, and he took great pride in the *Historical Illustrations of the Fourth Canto of Childe Harold* written by his friend John Cam Hobhouse in 1818. Compared either to Hobhouse or to Rogers, he was indeed, as he said, "a poor virtuoso." [3] Byron belonged to the tribe of connoisseurs, however, in his references to the fine arts and, more conspicuously, in his devotion to the beau ideal and in his habit of seeing resemblances between actual persons and works of art. An early example of his

[1] *The Life of Lord Byron* (1830), p. 109.
[2] *Works of Lord Byron; Poetry*, ed. E. H. Coleridge (1898–1901), II, 170–72, and E. J. Trelawny, *Recollections of the Last Days of Shelley and Byron* (1858), p. 204.
[3] Letter to Thomas Moore, Nov. 7, 1818 (*Works; Letters and Journals*, ed. R. E. Prothero [1898–1901], III, 387).

connoisseurship occurs in the letter concerning the Greeks met in his travels: "I like the Greeks, who are plausible rascals . . . some are brave, and all are beautiful, very much resembling the busts of Alcibiades." [4] Clearly Lord Byron protested too much his ignorance of the arts.

To anyone familiar with the contradictions between the poses and the practices of Byron, his assertions of ignorance of the arts suggest, then, that the poet probably prided himself on his acquaintance with and his feeling for the arts. Perhaps the first critic to notice the discrepancy between Byron's statements and his poetry was Professor John Wilson ("Christopher North"), who remarked in reviewing Canto IV of *Childe Harold* on its appearance,

Byron has gazed upon these masterpieces of art with a more susceptible, and, in spite of his disavowal, with a more learned eye, than can be traced in the effusions of any poet who had previously expressed, in any formal manner, his admiration of their beauty.[5]

Few critics today would follow Wilson in considering Byron more akin to the genius of ancient Greece than Keats or Shelley; yet his suggestion that the art of sculpture had influenced Byron's solitary and heroic figures is an interesting comment, even though Milton and his so-called "Grecian" or sculptural creations, which had been so much praised during the eighteenth century, probably exerted as much influence as any ancient works.

More of a connoisseur than he was willing to admit, Byron was, of course, no very serious student of the arts. Like practically all poets, he was primarily concerned with the general effect of works of art —that is, the imaginative or emotional or associational qualities he could utilize in poetic description and imagery. Certainly the effervescent Byron, the passionate participant in the Oriental narratives and the adventures of Don Juan, was not likely to admire statues and paintings in preference to flesh-and-blood Leilas, Zuleikas, and Haidées. On the other hand, largely through his vociferant defense of

---

[4] Letter to Henry Drury, May 3, 1810 (*Letters*, I, 266). As a connoisseur and collector he wrote later, "I have brought home some marbles for Hobhouse;—for myself, four ancient Athenian skulls, dug out of sarcophagi . . ." (Letter to Drury, July 17, 1811 [*Letters*, I, 318]).

[5] *Edinburgh Review*, XXX (June, 1818), 103.

the "classical" tradition, Byron was more in sympathy with the
various ideas associated with sculpture by earlier critics and poets
than were other writers of the Romantic period, with the exception
of Shelley or such a lesser figure as Rogers. Both in the number of
descriptions of works of art and in the frequency with which he
employed and made reference to the large body of political, moral,
and aesthetic ideas, which gentlemen of varying degrees of classical
culture and taste had linked with Greek sculpture for more than a
century, Byron easily surpassed the other important Romantics, his
friend Shelley alone excepted. The several comments on sculpture
in his letters and criticism as well as in his poetry sincerely expressed
significant aspects of his personality; what is more, they were perfectly
consistent with his attitude toward other arts and with his conception
of the nature of the artistic and poetic processes. In short, sculpture
was the favorite art of Byron as it was of Shelley, and each of them
was moved deeply, at times at least, by such statues as the Venus de
Medici and the Apollo Belvedere.

BYRON AND THE ELGIN MARBLES

Byron first showed his preference for the familiar Greco-Roman
antiques when he attacked Lord Elgin for bringing the Parthenon
sculptures to England. Though he had traveled in Greece and had
responded enthusiastically to classical remains, including what was
left of the Parthenon, he still considered the Academic favorites superior to the Elgin Marbles; for the world of fashion to which Byron
belonged tended to cling to the Apollo and the Venus. Among connoisseurs and the educated public in general, there was then, as often
in the history of movements in art, what may be termed a "lag" in
taste and knowledge of art, so that Byron, like many gentlemen and
ladies, preferred the well-known antiques even after the Elgin Marbles
had found a resting place in the British Museum. Consequently Byron
furnishes a more accurate indication of Regency taste than other
poets, since he crystallized the opinions of his contemporaries concerning the arts of the Greeks as the better poets did not. That most
of his criticism of the Elgin Marbles had little or nothing to do with
the artistic merits of the masterpieces does not alter the fact that his

disapproval of the sculpture brought to England by Lord Elgin was thoroughly in accord with the views about the arts, especially sculpture, which he expressed at other times.

In 1809 in *English Bards and Scotch Reviewers* Byron began his condemnation of the Elgin Marbles with all the arrogant effrontery he could muster.

> Let ABERDEEN and ELGIN still pursue
> The shade of fame through regions of Virtù;
> Waste useless thousands on their Phidian freaks,
> Misshapen monuments and maimed antiques;
> And make their grand saloons a general mart
> For all the mutilated blocks of art (ll. 1027–32).[6]

Byron's scorn of the "freaks" from the Parthenon rose to an even higher pitch in his note: "Lord Elgin would fain persuade us that all the figures, with and without noses, in his stoneshop, are the works of Phidias! 'Credat Judaeus!'" The remark seems somewhat more reasonable when one remembers that the question of whether or not the sculptures were genuinely Phidian was one of the principal subjects of discussion in the controversy over the actions of Lord Elgin, and also that Byron's position was that of many critics and connoisseurs.

At approximately the same time Byron was also composing the stanzas scourging Elgin which appeared in Canto II of *Childe Harold* in 1812. Without touching on the art of the sculptures from Greece, the young poet even more strenuously beat the "Pictish peer." Picturesquely perched on the "massy stone, the marble column's yet unshaken base," of the Temple of Jupiter Olympius, Childe Harold hurled five stanzas (x–xv) at the despoiler of the Parthenon:

> Blush, Caledonia! such thy son could be!
>
> . . .
>
> But most the modern Pict's ignoble boast,
> To rive what Goth, the Turk, and Time hath spared:
> Cold as the crags upon his native coast,
> His mind as barren and his heart as hard,

[6] George Hamilton Gordon, Earl of Aberdeen, who had traveled in Greece in 1801–3, founded the Athenian Society in 1803. See Richard Payne Knight's *Specimens of Antient Sculpture* (1809).

> Is he whose head conceived, whose hand prepared,
> Aught to displace Athenae's poor remains.[7]

Then he slid into an elegiac vein, and, somewhat as Milton questioned why the nymphs had failed to save Lycidas, Byron called on the guardians who should have protected the Parthenon from Elgin.

> Where was thine Ægis, Pallas! . . .
>> Where Peleus' son? . . .
>> What! could not Pluto spare the Chief once more,
>> To scare a second robber from his prey?
>> Idly he wander'd on the Stygian shore,
> Nor now preserved the walls he loved to shield before.

Still in the spirit of "Lycidas" Byron wrote a quiet lament followed by a curse like that by St. Peter.

> Cold is the heart, fair Greece! that looks on Thee,
>> Nor feels as Lovers o'er the dust they loved;
>> Dull is the eye that will not weep to see
>> Thy walls defaced, thy mouldering shrines removed
>> By British hands, which it had best behoved
>> To guard those relics ne'er to be restored,
>> Curst be the hour when from their isle they roved,
>> And once again thy hapless bosom gored,
> And snatched thy shrinking Gods to Northern climes abhorred!

The *Childe Harold* stanzas with their mixture of the satirical and the elegiac opened a vein which Byron continued to exploit in *The Curse of Minerva,* the broadside fired at Elgin in 1811 and circulated privately soon afterward, but withheld from print until 1828 though pirated editions appeared in England, America, and France.[8]

At least two contemporary poets wrote similar denunciations of Elgin, but Byron's inspiration came from better sources. In the celebrated attack of Cicero on Verres for his spoliation of Sicily—an incident to which Byron referred in his own notes to *Childe Harold,* Canto II—he had a precedent in a favorite classical author.

[7] See also the Latin lines condemning the infamous Scot, *Works,* ed. E. H. Coleridge, I, 462.

[8] The poem as printed later included the first fifty-four lines of Canto III of *The Corsair* (1814), one of Byron's best descriptions of the scenery of Greece. Thomas Moore (*The Works of Lord Byron,* II, 145) suggests that either Lord Elgin himself or "some of his connections" persuaded Byron to withhold the poem.

In Pope's *Dunciad* and *The Rape of the Lock* he might also have found many hints for the tone of his work and for certain elements in its execution.

Writing *The Curse of Minerva* near the site of Elgin's depredation, Byron lashed out at the barbarian, expressing the indignation and regret which even admirers of the nobleman's acts must have sometimes felt in witnessing how casually one supposedly civilized nation can appropriate the treasures of a helpless people. Suddenly the giant form of Minerva stood before him—

> Not such as erst, by her divine command,
> Her form appeared from Phidias' plastic hand:
> Gone were the terrors of her awful brow,
> Her idle Ægis bore no Gorgon now (ll. 77–80).

Minerva came to curse not merely the Scottish Elgin and his accomplices in the rape of Athens but even the English admirers of the sculpture, especially Benjamin West, president of the Royal Academy yet supporter of the Marbles against the attacks led by Payne Knight (whom Byron favored). Turning the ideas of Knight, the most influential connoisseur of the time, into brilliant poetry, Byron reached the climax of the work in the actual curse, in lines brightened by the spirit of Pope.

> "First on the head of him who did this deed
> My curse shall light,—on him and all his seed:
> Without one spark of intellectual fire,
> Be all the sons as senseless as the sire:
>
> . . .
>
> Meantime, the flattering, feeble dotard, West,
> Europe's worst dauber, and poor Britain's best,
> With palsied hand shall turn each model o'er,
> And own himself an infant of fourscore.
> Be all the Bruisers culled from all St. Giles',
> That Art and Nature may compare their styles;
> While brawny brutes in stupid wonder stare,
> And marvel at his Lordship's 'stone shop' there" (ll. 163–66, 175–82).[9]

---

[9] Byron's own notes to these lines read: "Mr. West, on seeing the 'Elgin Collection' . . . declared himself 'a mere tyro' in art" and "poor Crib was sadly puzzled when the marbles were first exhibited at Elgin House: he asked if it was not 'a stone

Though Byron said little about the actual sculptures, his estimate of their artistic merit was none the less clear. He felt, first of all, that the grand figures from the Parthenon were not—and he was quite correct—the graceful forms that he was accustomed to seeing in the familiar Greco-Roman works; they were, for him, huge and brawny "bruisers" suited for a prize fight instead of a gentleman's gallery or a lady's boudoir. The Theseus might pass as a wrestler, but he could never serve as the model of Childe Harold, Don Juan, or Mazeppa. The Byronic hero was to be molded after the elegant classicistic figures of Regency fashion. One wonders whether Byron had ever actually looked at the works he so roundly condemned, but his description of the Parthenon figures as "bruisers" is understandable in the light of his devotion to "academic" art.

The poet disliked the Theseus, the Three Fates, and the Ilissus, moreover, because he thought they were too close to nature: in such works art had not improved upon nature, and the statues did not fit the canons of the Neo-Classical Ideal Beauty. They were not the composite beauties praised by the Academic theorists. In stressing the "naturalness" of the Elgin Marbles, Byron was superficially in accord with admirers of the sculptures like Haydon, Hazlitt, and Keats; for they also maintained that the figures were close to nature. In the interpretation of that "naturalness," however, they were at opposite poles: Haydon and his friends admired that approximation to living forms, while Byron condemned the statues because they were not, he felt, of a beauty higher than that of nature.

Byron's position was, in fact, that of the most intransigent "academic" critics, and in 1811 he apparently had the weight of their opinion behind him, though West had bowed to the Elgin Marbles. The attacks on the merit as well as the authenticity of the Parthenon sculptures did not collapse, as a matter of fact, until 1816 when the Italian sculptor Canova—whom Byron effusively praised many times

---

shop?'—He was right; it *is* a shop." For West's statements, see William R. Hamilton, *Memorandum on the Subject of the Earl of Elgin's Pursuits in Greece* (2d ed., 1815), pp. 42 ff., and Appendix A with West's letters (1809, 1811) to Elgin. The brawny brutes staring in stupid wonder included Tom Crib, the famous prize fighter, an old friend of Byron, who said he liked "energy—even animal energy–of all kinds."

and whose word dominated European taste in the fine arts at the time—expressed the opinion that the statues were genuine.[10] Even then for many Englishmen the purchase of the Marbles merely meant that the sculptures were accepted as "Phidian," not that they were superior to the Apollo and the Venus. Writing *The Curse of Minerva* before the statues had been pronounced genuine or been approved by Canova, Byron advanced the argument that the imperfect condition of the sculptures proved that they were poor works of art compared to the familiar Greco-Roman works. He preferred the smooth perfection and the elegant grace of the Apollo and the Venus, and the Elgin Marbles could not make him change his mind.

What most concerned him was not the aesthetic value of the sculptures but the way in which they had come to England. The stealing from a prostrate people was shocking enough, but a greater crime was that the thief had been a Scotchman. Yet even a matter of such seriousness could not hold Byron's attention for long in *The Curse of Minerva*, so that at the height of the execration of Elgin he slipped into some excellent lines poking fun at the combination of sensuality and prudery which passed for morality among his countrymen. In Lord Elgin's "stone shop" he sketched the amusing scene of amorous English maidens eyeing with ill-disguised delight the statues modeled from finer physiques than those of the Regency dandies who strolled in St. James' Park.

> "Round the thronged gate shall sauntering coxcombs creep
>   To lounge and lucubrate, to prate and peep;
>   While many a languid maid, with longing sigh,
>   On giant statues casts the curious eye;
>   The room with transient glance appears to skim,
>   Yet marks the mighty back and length of limb;
>   Mourns o'er the difference of *now* and *then;*
>   Exclaims, 'These Greeks indeed were proper men!'
>   Draws slight comparisons of *these* with *those,*

[10] The effect of Canova's praise upon the struggle between the defenders and the opponents of the Elgin Marbles is told most interestingly by Haydon in his *Autobiography and Memoirs*, ed. Tom Taylor ([new edition with notes and introduction by Aldous Huxley, 1926], chaps. xv–xvi, pp. 209–40). See also John T. Smith, *Nollekens and His Times* (1828) and A. H. Smith, "Lord Elgin and His Collection," *Journal of Hellenic Studies*, XXXVI (1916), 163 ff.

And envies Laïs all her Attic beaux.
When shall a modern maid have swains like these?
Alas! Sir Harry is no Hercules!" (Lines 183–94.)

Altogether *The Curse of Minerva* was the longest and the best
poem in a satirical vein which had yet been inspired by English interest in Greek sculpture. Pope and other poets of the eighteenth
century had ridiculed the foibles and affectations of connoisseurs;
but Byron easily outdid them in the vigorous couplets of *The Curse*.
The poem, moreover, was noteworthy in Byron's career, since he was
for the first time successful in what were to be his characteristic moods
in satire—the invective hurled upon Elgin and the ridicule of the
scene in the "stone shop." A great admirer of Greece, he protested
against the bringing to England of what is one of the finest monuments to the genius of the ancient Greeks. A censor wielding a double-
edged pen, he concluded that only occasionally was there a man of
sense like himself who would speak out against the infamy of the
monstrous Scot.

> "And last of all, amidst the gaping crew,
> Some calm spectator, as he takes his view,
> In silent indignation mixed with grief,
> Admires the plunder, but abhors the thief.
> Oh, loathed in life, nor pardoned in the dust,
> May Hate pursue his sacrilegious lust!" (Lines 195–200.)

Though the phrase "admires the plunder" suggests that Byron
wanted to qualify the judgments on the artistic merits of the sculpture
given earlier in the poem, he gave no specific praise to the Elgin
Marbles elsewhere in his work, despite several favorable mentions
of the Parthenon and of Phidias.[11] For the parting thrust Minerva
screamed at Lord Elgin,

[11] But in the *Letter on the Rev. W. L. Bowles's Strictures on the Life and Writings
of Pope* he wrote, "I opposed, and will ever oppose, the robbery of ruins from
Athens, to instruct the English in sculpture . . . but why did I do so? The *ruins*
are as poetical in Piccadilly as they were in the Parthenon; but the Parthenon and its
rock are less so without them. Such is the Poetry of art." Then he carefully enumerated
the Apollo, the Laocoön, the Venus de Medici, the Hercules, the Dying Gladiator, the
Moses of Michelangelo, and "all the higher works of Canova," works of sculpture
"as *poetical* as Mont Blanc or Mount Aetna, perhaps still more so, as they are direct
manifestations of mind, and *presuppose* poetry in their very conception," adding

"So let him stand, through ages yet unborn,
Fixed statue on the pedestal of Scorn" (ll. 207–8).

BYRON'S DESCRIPTIONS OF STATUES

Foremost among the statues possessing the beauty Byron failed
to find in the Elgin Marbles were the trio of Academic favorites, the
Venus de Medici, the Apollo Belvedere, and the Laocoön, with the
celebrated enchantress of the Uffizi appropriately first in the favor
of the gallant poet. Only slightly less interesting to him were the
Niobe, the Hercules Farnese, and the Dying Gladiator. Other works
of Roman as well as Greek art came in for miscellaneous praise, so
that an analysis of the body of remarks, both in verse and in prose,
gives one a good insight into Byron's theories of sculpture.

The principal description of the Venus occurred in the well-known
passage on the galleries of Florence and Rome in Canto IV of *Childe
Harold* (1818). In Italy during the two years previous as a pilgrim
more passionate than learned, Byron boasted at first that he had no
interest in Florence; nevertheless he had to admit that no gentleman
on the Grand Tour could fail to see the Venus. Once he stood before
the statue itself, though, every doubt vanished; in the fashion of
Gibbon he learned at the feet of the Venus what beauty in art really
was! He returned from the gallery "drunk with beauty," realizing
that what he had contemptuously dismissed as the "cant" of the
criticism of art actually had some justification.[12] Indeed, he was soon
repeating the ideas and stock phrases of the connoisseurs so frequently that Hazlitt belabored him for using the stale language of
the Academies.

In *Childe Harold,* therefore, the Venus drew great praise from a
poet who, almost in spite of himself, had discovered that sculpture
could arouse his enthusiasm. Inspired in part, perhaps, by Thomson's

---

rather casually in parentheses "those of ancient Greece, still extant in that country,
or transported to England." See *Letters,* V, 547–48.

[12] See letters to Moore, April 11, 1817, and to John Murray, April 26, 1817
(*Letters,* IV, 104 ff., 113). The phrase "drunk with beauty" appeared later in the
stanzas on the Venus in *Childe Harold,* for Byron frequently incorporated phrases and
ideas from his letters and journals into his verse.

lines on the Venus de Medici in *The Seasons,* Byron endowed the figure with an energy and vitality lacking in the eighteenth-century accounts of her beauty; he far exceeded Thomson in using what Hobhouse termed "the sexual imagination of the descriptive poet." [13] In a manner suggesting Shelley's passionate accounts of ancient statues, he presented the admired lady as a lover of the "romantic" school:

> the Goddess loves in stone, and fills
> The air around with Beauty—we inhale
> The ambrosial aspect, which, beheld, instils
> Part of its immortality—the veil
> Of heaven is half undrawn—within the pale
> We stand, and in that form and face behold
> What mind can make, when Nature's self would fail;
> And to the fond Idolaters of old
> Envy the innate flash which such a Soul could mould:
>
> We gaze and turn away, and know not where,
> Dazzled and drunk with Beauty, till the heart
> Reels with its fulness; there—for ever there—
> Chained to the chariot of triumphal Art,
> We stand as captives, and would not depart.
> Away!—there need no words, nor terms precise,
> The paltry jargon of the marble mart,
> Where Pedantry gulls Folly—we have eyes:
> Blood—pulse—and breast, confirm the Dardan Shepherd's prize.
>
> Appear'dst thou not to Paris in this guise?
>
> . . .
>
> Glowing, and circumfused in speechless love—
> Their full divinity inadequate
> Their feeling to express, or to improve—
> The Gods become as mortals—and man's fate
> Has moments like their brightest; but the weight
> Of earth recoils upon us;—let it go!
> We can recall such visions, and create,
> From what has been, or might be, things which grow
> Into thy statue's form, and look like gods below.

[13] "Historical Notes to Canto the Fourth," p. 14, "The Venus of Medicis," *Works,* II, 489–90. Hobhouse's remarks indicate that no one could look at the statue without thinking of and, perhaps, reciting Thomson's lines.

> I leave to learnèd fingers and wise hands,
>> The Artist and his Ape, to teach and tell
>> How well his Connoisseurship understands
>> The graceful bend, and the voluptuous swell:
>> Let them describe the undescribable:
>> I would not their vile breath should crisp the stream
>> Wherein that Image shall for ever dwell—
>> The unruffled mirror of the loveliest dream
> That ever left the sky on the deep soul to beam.
>
> (Canto IV, stanzas xlix–liii.)

While his approach to the statue of Venus was primarily that of a "romantic" poet, Byron was no less an "academic" critic in these stanzas; for he joined the favorite ideas of the connoisseurs to the impressionistic rhapsody of the kind one finds also in the writings of Hazlitt, Hunt, and Shelley. Though he was concerned with the general effect and the poetical associations of the Venus, he put a considerable amount of theory into verse. Moreover, after having specifically condemned the artists and their apes, the critics, who used the "precise terms" and "words" of criticism, Byron approved the learned notes of his friend Hobhouse, who referred in a long note on the Venus stanzas to no less an authority than Winckelmann. The remarks on sculpture in the *Letter to John Murray, Esq., on the Rev. W. L. Bowles's Strictures on the Life and Writings of Pope,* published three years later, suggest likewise that Byron probably had had more detailed knowledge of "the paltry jargon of the marble mart" when he wrote Canto IV than he wanted to admit in his role of a sensitive soul responding to the magical allurements of the goddess of love.

The theories which Byron was unwilling to leave to pedants and connoisseurs were, withal, the common and the central ideas in Academic writings on art. Above all else he felt that the Venus had a beauty beyond that in nature; the Venus in *Childe Harold* was the "higher" or "composite" beauty admired by every classicistic artist and critic.[14] Corollary to such theories was the Academic view of sculpture as the expression of an abstract or typical quality or char-

---

[14] In the *Letter on Bowles's Strictures on Pope* (*Letters,* V, 549) Byron wrote: "Of sculpture in general, it may be observed, that it is more poetical than nature

acteristic of a person or thing. That a similar view was in Byron's mind when he worshiped the Venus as the personification of feminine beauty is made evident by his repetition of the same notion in *Don Juan* where the lovely Haidée called to mind the marble embodiment of grace. In the face of the Grecian maiden

> The ruling passion, such as marble shows
> When exquisitely chiselled, still lay there,
> But fixed as marble's unchanged aspect throws
> O'er the fair Venus, but for ever fair.
> (Canto IV, stanza lxi, ll. 1–4.)

In these lines, as in his other mentions of the Venus, the language was very close to that of such masters of connoisseurship as Joseph Spence.

Almost as "academic" as the account of a Venus beyond the powers of nature was Byron's thinking of the statue as a living figure. Poets had often talked of "breathing stones," but he elaborated the phrase "the Goddess loves in stone" at such length that the trite expression was lost in his "romantic" enthusiasm. The chief proof of the surpassing beauty of the Venus was its emotional effect on the beholder, and Byron was moved to sympathize with the passion she expressed and to revel in her feelings. In his intoxication with the beauty of Love herself given a body in sculptured flesh, he insisted that he needed no study by art-historian or critic; merely to gaze and adore was enough, as the lava kisses from her lips were "Showered on his eyelids, brow, and mouth, as from an urn!"

Childe Harold thought, moreover, that the creation of the statue of the Venus had resulted from an artistic process that was similar to religious revelation. The work of sculpture was in fact a vision: in an ecstatic moment of insight or intuition the superhuman quality of the Venus had been revealed to a human being who, fortunately for mankind, had possessed the power to enshrine that glorious vision in a stone body which might last for ages. Flashes of intuition such as the sculptor had known, or such as those which poets like Byron

itself, inasmuch as it represents and bodies forth that ideal beauty and sublimity which is never found to be in actual Nature."

felt in the presence of the surpassing loveliness of the Venus, made up the noblest portions of the experience of human beings.

Interesting as the sentiments of Childe Harold themselves were, they have the additional significance of showing how easily Byron, in writing of Grecian sculpture, mingled the language of the Academies with the new and "romantic" theories of the imagination of Shelley and Wordsworth. With no feeling of strain he wrote of the Ideal Beauty of Neo-Classical and Academic tradition in one line, and in the next advanced an idea or theory stemming from Romantic aesthetics. To Wordsworth's lines on mythology in *The Excursion* (Book IV, ll. 717–887)—a passage to which nearly every Romantic poet was in some way indebted—Byron may have owed the conception of the "fond idolaters of old" embodying their beliefs in statues like the Venus. The tone of the description of the artist's recollection of his mighty visions probably owed something to *Tintern Abbey* and other statements of Wordsworth's theory of the creative process.

Yet the language in which Byron praised the power of the mind in portraying things beyond the reach of nature makes it apparent that the spirit of Shelley rather than Wordsworth hovered over Byron's description of the Venus. Such impassioned sentiments as the feeling of human insufficiency in the presence of great beauty or the "recoil" after moments of revelation were derived from Shelley's Platonism. The idea of the plastic stress working in the object of his contemplation was also Shelleyan; for Byron was paraphrasing his friend's idea that gazing upon a beautiful form, such as that of the Venus, tends to give the sensitive beholder a portion of its beauty. Shelley likewise conveyed to Byron something of his own preference for the art of sculpture because of its directness or immediacy of appeal. Henry Joy, who visited Byron in Italy in 1817, wrote,

He contended that Sculpture, as an art, was vastly superior to Painting;— a preference which is strikingly illustrated by the fact that, in the fourth Canto of *Childe Harold* [written at this time], he gives the most elaborate and splendid account of several statues, and none of any pictures; although Italy is, emphatically, the land of painting, and her best statues are derived from Greece.[15]

[15] Quoted by Moore in *Works*, IV, 57–58. See also below, pp. 171 ff., 184–85.

Byron's contention was the same as Shelley's, and he was following his friend's statements about the art of sculpture. His emphasis, both in the account of the Venus and in a majority of his other descriptions of statues, upon the "energy" and "life" of the sculptured figures corresponded, moreover, to the emotional vitality Shelley felt in the statuary discussed in his *Notes on Sculptures in Rome and Florence*.

The Apollo Belvedere was another favorite, although it was hardly in the class of the Venus de Medici, since Byron, unlike Shelley, always waxed most eloquent over female figures. The formal description of the famous statue came in *Childe Harold*:

> the Lord of the unerring bow,
> The God of Life, and Poesy, and Light—
> The Sun in human limbs arrayed, and brow
> All radiant from his triumph in the fight;
> The shaft hath just been shot—the arrow bright
> With an Immortal's vengeance—in his eye
> And nostril beautiful Disdain, and Might
> And Majesty, flash their full lightnings by,
> Developing in that one glance the Deity.
>
> But in his delicate form—a dream of Love,
> Shaped by some solitary Nymph, whose breast
> Longed for a deathless lover from above,
> And maddened in that vision—are exprest
> All that ideal Beauty ever blessed
> The mind with in its most unearthly mood,
> When each Conception was a heavenly Guest—
> A ray of Immortality—and stood,
> Starlike, around, until they gathered to a God!
>
> And if it be Prometheus stole from Heaven
> The fire which we endure—it was repaid
> By him to whom the energy was given
> Which this poetic marble hath arrayed
> With an eternal Glory—which, if made
> By human hands, is not of human thought—
> And Time himself hath hallowed it, nor laid
> One ringlet in the dust—nor hath it caught
> A tinge of years, but breathes the flame with which 'twas wrought.
>
> (Canto IV, stanzas clxi–clxiii.)

This account is perhaps the best summary in verse of the Academic interpretations of the Apollo; it might have been written by Winckelmann. Characteristically Byronic in tone, however, was the explanation of the origin of Apollo's "delicate form": the nymph who, maddened by her dream of love, conceived the beau ideal of manly beauty that later became the god himself! The work of the sculptor repaid the debt mankind owed to heaven; the artist gave the Apollo Belvedere back to heaven as payment for Prometheus's theft of fire. So enduring, felt Byron, was this masterpiece produced by a human artist's mental "energy."

Byron also reverenced the Apollo as the statue of

> the poets' God
> In all his marble-chiselled beauty.
> (*Marino Faliero*, II, i, 388–89.)

In *The Deformed Transformed* he gave the figure even greater praise: the noblest shape one could imagine was that of Apollo,

> The Poet's God, clothed in such limbs as are
> Themselves a poetry (I, i, 368–69).

In the spirit of Hunt and Shelley he expressed further admiration by describing the ancient heroes who appeared in Faustian visions in exactly the same language he had used to picture the Apollo Belvedere. Demetrius Poliorcetes, who interested Byron because he had in 307 B.C. liberated Greece from the tyranny of Ptolemy and Cassander, wore an especially Apollonian appearance:

> Blooming and bright, with golden hair and stature,
> If not more high than mortal, yet immortal
> In all that nameless bearing of his limbs,
> Which he wears as the Sun his rays—a something
> Which shines from him, and yet is but the flashing
> Emanation of a thing more glorious still.
> (*The Deformed Transformed*, ll. 247–52.)

To describe the shade of Mark Antony in the same work, Byron again employed a combination of a reference to sculpture and an identification of himself with the ancient hero. The figure of him who "lost the ancient world for love" came into the poet's mind in the guise of the Hercules Farnese.

> What's here? whose broad brow and whose curly beard
> And manly aspect look like Hercules,
> Save that his jocund eye hath more of Bacchus
> Than the sad purger of the infernal world,
> Leaning dejected on his club of conquest,
> As if he knew the worthlessness of those
> For whom he had fought.
>
> (*The Deformed Transformed*, ll. 231–37.)

Dejected, jaded, and aware that the game had not been worth the struggle, a Byronic Hercules-Antony arose. Both in the Apollonian Demetrius and in the Herculean Antony, Byron expressed elements of his personality, giving an individual interpretation to the ancient heroes and statues.

The Laocoön, of course, received the praise expected from one of so many "academic" sympathies as Byron; nevertheless, Childe Harold gave a rather undistinguished report of the statue:

> go see
> Laocoön's torture dignifying pain—
> A Father's love and Mortal's agony
> With an Immortal's patience blending:—Vain
> The struggle—vain, against the coiling strain
> And gripe, and deepening of the dragon's grasp,
> The Old Man's clench; the long envenomed chain
> Rivets the living links,—the enormous Asp
> Enforces pang on pang, and stifles gasp on gasp.
>
> (Canto IV, stanza clx.)

For a brief relation of the famous incident before Troy as represented in the statue, the lines have more rhetorical weight than they can carry. Byron managed the reference to the Laocoön better in *Don Juan* (Canto IV, stanza lxi, ll. 4–8), presenting the statue as "eternal" in energy: the vitality caught by the sculptor and rendered in stone would endure forever.

Of practically the same nature and merit as the two mentions of the Laocoön were the two passages dealing with the statue known as the Dying Gladiator. In *Don Juan* (Canto IV, stanza lxi, ll. 4–8) the marble fighter displayed an "air" which was eternal in its energy, while in *Childe Harold* (Canto IV, stanza cxl, ll. 2–9) he received the more rhetorical but less interesting description. The writing was vigorous, but in picturing the "life" of the Gladiator, Byron's pen flowed more easily than usual. Because of this facility the passage appeared until recently in schoolboy declamations.

The Niobe drew from Byron an expression of sympathy similar to that he felt for the Dying Gladiator. Even though he gave no full account of her tragedy, the figures of Niobe and her children came to his mind on several occasions. In *The Age of Bronze* (l. 643) the Mother Church was a Niobe, weeping "o'er her offspring—Tithes," and in *Childe Harold* Rome was

> The Niobe of nations! there she stands,
> Childless and crownless, in her voiceless woe.
> (Canto IV, stanza lxxix, ll. 1–2.)

More significant, however, was the description of Zuleika in *The Bride of Abydos* where the statue served to localize the poet's conception of the beautiful Oriental maiden.

> Zuleika, mute and motionless,
> Stood like that Statue of Distress,
> When, her last hope for ever gone,
> The Mother hardened into stone;
> All in the maid that eye could see
> Was but a younger Niobé. (Canto II, stanza xxii.)

Here Byron made poetical use of an image from sculpture with a felicity more characteristic of Keats and Shelley.

The serious descriptions of statues, however, were not the only good ones in the poetry of Byron; for sooner or later he made fun of every object or ideal which he ever regarded with gravity. His "farcical" treatments of Grecian statuary and the ideas of the connoisseurs were not so numerous as the "heroical" ones; yet they were of a high order of poetic merit. From his streak of facetiousness, we have seen, sprang the account of the "stone shop" of Lord Elgin in *The Curse of Minerva,* his first contribution to the tradition of satirizing English interest in antiques. The most effective lines in the comic vein dealing with ancient sculpture were the familiar ones in *Don Juan* (Canto II, stanza cxciv, ll. 5–8) describing the dalliance of the hero and the maiden Haidée:

> She sits upon his knee, and drinks his sighs,
>   He hers, until they end in broken gasps;
> And thus they form a group that's quite antique,
> Half naked, loving, natural, and Greek.

The inspiration for the amusing lines came apparently from certain groups in the Uffizi, since Byron reported that there he had seen what he chose to call "one or two not very decent groupes in marble." In the poetry very likely he had in mind a Cupid and Psyche, imaginatively giving life and naturalness to the figures and posing them to suit the picture he desired.[16] Almost as fine was the account of the amorous Dudù in Canto VI, when Don Juan was hiding in a harem:

> A kind of sleepy Venus seemed Dudù,
>   Yet very fit to "murder sleep" in those
> Who gazed upon her cheek's transcendent hue,
>   Her Attic forehead, and her Phidian nose: (Stanza xlii, ll. 1–4.)
>
>   . . .
>
> She looked (this simile's quite new) just cut
>   From marble, like Pygmalion's statue waking,
> The mortal and the marble still at strife,
> And timidly expanding into Life. (Stanza xliii, ll. 5–8.)

The transition from the "heroical" to the "farcical" was an easy one for Byron.

BEAUTY REAL AND IDEAL

Both in his "heroical" and "farcical" descriptions of Grecian sculpture and in his theorizing about that art, Byron's personal sympathies

[16] See Letter to John Murray, April 26, 1817 (*Letters*, IV, 113). If the lines were suggested in the way proposed here, the group Byron had in mind was probably the Cupid and Psyche shown in Plate XLIII, *Reale galleria di Firenze, serie IV, statue, bassi relievi, busti e bronzi* (Firenze, 1817–24), I [Plates], 134. The winged figures are standing, locked in a Byronic embrace.

and experiences stood out conspicuously; for his statement that painting interested him only if "it reminds me of something I have seen,
or think possible to see"[17] was applicable to every subject he touched.
One result of the tendency thus to relate everything to his own experience was his practice of thinking of actual women in terms of the
statues he admired. With the Venus de Medici as the canon of a
sublimity and ideality by which to judge his feminine friends, apparently he observed how closely these women approached the human form divine displayed by the Greco-Roman antiques! He began
the search early, too, for Margaret Parker, who inspired him in 1800
to write his first verses, was unforgettable with "her dark eyes—her
long eye-lashes—her completely Greek cast of face and figure!" [18]
Mary Anne Chaworth, the first really to command the attentions
of the young lord when he was fifteen, was no less than "the *beau
idéal* of all that my youthful fancy could paint of the beautiful." [19]
The daughter of the widow of the late British consul at Athens, the
maid of Athens, was "a pale and pensive-looking girl, with regular
Grecian features." [20] Lady Charlemont, whom he compared to Helen
of Troy when he first met her, possessed "all that sculpture could
require for its ideal"; she was surpassed only by the Venus itself.[21]
In Rome in 1817 he wrote, "The Apollo Belvedere is the image of
Lady Adelaide Forbes—I think I never saw such a likeness." [22] That
was a compliment no one would covet today, but the Lady Adelaide
was doubtless pleased.

[17] Letter to Murray, April 14, 1817 (*Letters*, IV, 107). This comment comes from
his remarks on painting as "the most artificial and unnatural" of the arts; yet two
weeks later he was succumbing to the "cant" of criticism reflected in *Childe Harold*.
In the *Letter on Bowles's Strictures on Pope* he defended the "artificial" in the arts,
writing of the bust of Antinous: "The poetry of this bust is in no respect derived
from *nature*, nor from any association of moral exaltedness; for what is there in
common with moral nature, and the male minion of Adrian? The very execution is
not natural, but *super*-natural, or rather *super-artificial*, for *nature* has never done so
much" (*Letters*, V, 557).

[18] *Works*, I, 5n.

[19] See Thomas Medwin, *Journal of the Conversations of Lord Byron* (1824), p. 35.

[20] See Galt, *The Life of Lord Byron*, p. 119.

[21] *Letter on Bowles's Strictures on Pope* (*Letters*, V, 549).

[22] Letter to Moore, May 12, 1817 (*Letters*, IV, 22). See also *Don Juan*, Canto II,
stanza cxix, ll. 2–8 (*Works*, VI, 116).

Miss Milbanke, who became the Lady Byron satirized as Donna Inez in *Don Juan,* called forth no sculptural descriptions from the connoisseur of feminine beauty, though the Contessa Guiccioli, one of the comforts of his Italian years, was close to the beau ideal. "Her figure is, perhaps, too much *embonpoint* for her height, but her bust is perfect; her features want little of possessing a Grecian regularity of outline." The Contessa attracted him in some degree, at least, through her Grecian or ideal or statuesque quality in much the same way that Emilia Viviani interested Shelley. Similarly related to his admiration of the feminine type of beauty suggesting sculpture was the conversation with Medwin where the poet discussed the relative beauty of English and Italian women.[23] Thirty out of every hundred English women, he generously allowed, were handsome; in Italy, however, only one of a hundred was handsome, but that one Italian lady was incomparably superior to the thirty English ladies. The Italian paragon was "one who, like the Florence Venus, has no rival, and can have none in the North."

The sensibility evident in Byron's statements concerning the beauty of his female acquaintances created the women of his poetry: "My writings, indeed, tend to exalt the sex; and my imagination has always delighted in giving them a *beau idéal* likeness, but I only drew them as a painter or statuary would do,—as they should be." [24] Therefore, he gave Zuleika and Haidée a loveliness like that of the Academic favorites, a beauty beyond the reach of nature. Under the shaping influence of the goddess of love, Byron gave form in *Childe Harold* to the creatures seen by his imagination in a way suggesting the ancient sculptors:

> Of its own beauty is the mind diseased,
> And fevers into false creation:—where,
> Where are the forms the sculptor's soul hath seized?
> In him alone. Can Nature show so fair?
> (Canto IV, stanza cxxii, ll. 1–4.)

[23] Medwin, *Journal of the Conversations of Lord Byron,* pp. 10 and 15.
[24] *Ibid.,* p. 44. "It is the great scope of the Sculptor to heighten nature into heroic beauty; *i.e.,* in plain English, to surpass his model" (*Letters,* V, 550).

In the theater, too, Byron applied the same sort of criticism. For him as for other Romantic critics, Mrs. Siddons was the beau ideal of actresses, and J. P. Kemble was a statuesque actor reminding him of a Plutarchian hero treading the boards in Grecian dignity.[25] On his last journey to Greece Byron probably expected to find a few Apollo-like Greeks out of the pages of Plutarch throwing off the yoke of the tyrannous Turks.

In all his talk about the beau ideal Byron was fumbling toward some sort of Platonic scale of beauty, such as Shelley might have talked about. The shifting of his focus from the real to the ideal and vice versa was an ambiguity characteristic of Byron, even though one thinks of him as usually having stopped with earthly and tangible beauty. Admiration of flesh-and-blood human beings led finally, however, in *Don Juan* to the beauty beyond nature:

> as in the niche
> A lovely statue we almost adore,
> This sort of adoration of the real
> Is but a heightening of the *beau ideal*.
> (Canto II, stanza ccxi, ll. 5–8.)

At other times Byron's fervent adoration of the real led him to exclaim that no artist, no painter or sculptor, could ever equal nature —a position he could maintain in the facetious or satirical works. Hence it was that Haidée in *Don Juan* was

> one
> Fit for the model of a statuary
>   (A race of mere impostors, when all's done—
> I've seen much finer women, ripe and real,
> Than all the nonsense of their stone ideal).
> (Canto II, stanza cxviii, ll. 4–8.)

Though sometimes taken as Byron's final word on art, the lines clearly express the sentiments of the moment; for the poet had written some of the best "nonsense of their stone ideal." Thus, even in *Beppo*

---

[25] See Preface to *Marino Faliero;* note 1 (*Works,* IV, 338–39); Medwin, *Journal of the Conversations of Lord Byron,* pp. 91 ff.; and Clement T. Goode, *Byron as Critic* (Weimar, 1923), pp. 257–58. Kean displayed the realism of nature in contrast to the

when he was working in the "farcical" vein and attacking Ideal Beauty—"that fine name"—Byron turned naturally to a work of art (the so-called Family of Giorgione in the Manfrini Palace) to describe his conception of the "real" beauty of a woman, "*such* a woman! Love in life!*" To such Browningesque praise he added his own version of the theory of Platonic reminiscence, marveling at the "love in full life and length" in almost the same terms with which he described the women in whom he had seen reflections of the beau ideal (stanzas xii-xiv).

However much he protested, then, works of art—Greco-Roman statues, Italian paintings, the works of Canova—came into his mind as he sought for the ideal loveliness. Real women interested him, apparently, to the extent that they made him think of the supernal beauty he hoped to find in beautiful forms on earth. The Venus de Medici remained the standard by which to judge womankind in life and in art!

Even as Byron fluctuated between the "heroical" or idealistic accounts of the Venus and the Apollo in *Childe Harold* and the "farcical" or satirical passages about statues in *The Curse of Minerva* and *Don Juan,* so he was equally at home in alternating between the beau ideal and the "real." Joining the loosely Platonic ideas derived from Neo-Classical theories of art and from the "romantic" theorizings of Shelley, Wordsworth, and Coleridge to the strong emphasis on nature and simplicity and reality, likewise found both in the "academic" and in the "romantic" positions, Byron was bound to attract nearly every reader. No wonder then that Thomas Moore could write,

That Lord Byron, though despising the imposture and jargon with which the worship of the Arts is, like other worships, clogged and mystified, felt deeply, more especially in sculpture, whatever imaged forth true grace and energy, appears from passages of his poetry, which are *in every body's memory,* and not a line of which but thrills alive with a sense of grandeur

---

"classical" art and perfection of Kemble, though Byron developed the contrast at less length than Hazlitt or Hunt and, of course, in a vein more favorable to the "classical" spirit.

and beauty such as it never entered into the capacity of a mere connoisseur even to conceive.[26]

Few connoisseurs have, indeed, attempted to express either their sensibility or their learning in verse, so that Byron, who had in him elements of the antiquarian, the scholar, and the connoisseur along with his spontaneous, nature-loving, and satanic qualities, could take over many of their ideas and theories and disseminate them in his poetical, amateur, and popular appreciation of the sculpture of ancient Greece.

Sensitive to influences and responsive to prevailing tastes, Byron in his poetry exhibits an exceptionally clear illustration of the way in which a large body of critical ideas finds its way into literature. As a frequent and loud defender of the liberty of the Greeks he condemned the "freaks" stolen by Lord Elgin and extolled the Greco-Roman statues admired by the world of fashion. As a sensitive visitor to the galleries in Florence and Rome he felt the attractiveness of several statues, describing them in a very personal combination of the theories of "academic" connoisseurs and "romantic" thinkers like Shelley. In the passages on the Greco-Roman antiques Byron's position as the most vocal continuator of the Academic tradition among the poets of the early nineteenth century is more clearly seen than anywhere else. No other English poet of the time so vigorously supported the opinions of the Academic critics, to which he gave almost as brilliant a statement as Keats gave to the ideas of Haydon and Hazlitt concerning the Elgin Marbles.

At the same time that he was "academic," Byron was also very much a "romantic"; and since some of his statements of the theories of the Academies appeared in the language of "romantic" poets, this ambivalence was one of his most striking traits. Mainly under the influence of Shelley, Byron summed up his most "romantic" ideas in *The Prophecy of Dante* (1819). There (Canto IV, ll. 10 ff.) he

---

[26] *Works*, IV, 210–11. Italics added. Moore talked of Byron's expressing "heretically his opinions" concerning painting and sculpture in his letters, but the "heresy" is difficult to discover. One wonders, too, what constitutes the "due appreciation of these arts" which Byron lacked.

said that poetry was not a definite technique or work but a spirit or feeling,

> Many are Poets but without the name;
>   For what is Poesy but to create
>   From over-feeling Good or Ill.

Byron went on to parallel Shelley's *Defence of Poetry* in such lines as:

>   all they
>   Whose Intellect is an o'ermastering Power
> Which still recoils from its encumbering clay
>   Or lightens it to spirit, whatsoe'er
>   The form which their creations may essay,
> Are bards.

In recoiling from the clay that encumbers and in lightening it to spirit, the poet of Byron's statement was a thoroughgoing Platonist of the "romantic" school. The change of nonbeing into being, the endowing of matter with form or spirit is Poesy. The process is the same for all arts, moreover, and sculpture has a prominent place here as in Shelley's theorizings:

>   the kindled Marble's bust may wear
>   More Poesy upon its speaking brow
>   Than aught less than the Homeric page may bear;
> One noble stroke with a whole life may glow,
>   Or deify the canvass till it shine
>   With beauty so surpassing all below,
> That they who kneel to Idols so divine
>   Break no commandment, for high Heaven is there
>   Transfused, transfigurated: and the line
> Of Poesy, which peoples but the air
>   With Thought and Beings of our thought reflected,
>   Can do no more.[27]

Then Byron put into the mouth of Dante—whom Shelley had hailed as "the morning star of the Renaissance"—a lament over the world's treatment of its Genius, followed by a prophecy of the beginning of the world's great age anew—

[27] See also Byron's "The Dream," ll. 19–22 (*Works*, IV, 33–34) and Shelley, below, pp. 183 ff.

Within the ages which before me pass
    Art shall resume and equal even the sway
    Which with Apelles and old Phidias
She held in Hellas's unforgotten day.
    Ye shall be taught by Ruin to revive
    The Grecian forms at least from their decay.

In admiring the Grecian forms recovered in the Renaissance, Byron took front rank among the Romantics who felt a kinship with artists and poets in every period of enlightenment. From an appreciation of the achievements of the Greeks in literature and the arts these writers were to advance to an emulation of the Grecian state and way of life. Both the Grecian hatred of tyranny and the devotion to liberty were to be admired and, what is more, to be revived in a world Byron felt was in great need of regeneration.

Sovereigns shall pause amidst their sport of war,
    Weaned for an hour from blood, to turn and gaze
    On canvass or on stone; and they who mar
All beauty upon earth, compelled to praise,
    Shall feel the power of that which they destroy.

VIII. SHELLEY

GREECE: "THE CRYSTALLINE SEA OF THOUGHT"

WHETHER angel or demon, Percy Bysshe Shelley beat his luminous wings in no void. On the contrary, he concerned himself so passionately with the problems of his own time that only a few of his lyrics can be read without a fairly extensive examination of his intellectual milieu. Nowhere, perhaps, is an understanding of his theories concerning history, morality, aesthetics, philosophy, and government more necessary than in a study of his interest in the fine arts and, more particularly in this book, in his responses to Greek sculpture. Even though other poets may rival him both in the number and in the quality of the poems and lines directly inspired by Greek statues and vases, Shelley gave a more comprehensive treatment of the various strands in the tradition of interest in ancient art than any other important poet of the Romantic period. In his verse many historical, moral, and aesthetic "ideas" associated with the sculpture of Greece glow with a life which they had possessed only occasionally before.

Shelley believed, first of all, that the moral temper or condition of a nation will always be seen in its arts and in its social organization and political institutions—in what the poet called its "forms." Accordingly, the worth or value of a state may be judged by the mental "forms" which it creates or sustains: "A summary idea may be formed of the worth of any political and religious system, by observing the comparative degree of happiness and of intellect produced under its influence." [1] In the works and institutions of every age there is reflected likewise a time-spirit, which artists as well as political and

---

[1] "Essay on the Literature, the Arts, and the Manners of the Athenians," *Shelley's Literary and Philosophical Criticism*, ed. J. Shawcross (1909), p. 35.

moral leaders cannot but express. "Poets, not otherwise than philosophers, painters, sculptors, musicians, are, in one sense, the creators, and in another, the creations, of their age."

The Golden Age of fifth-century Greece seemed to Shelley to be the period with the noblest "forms" and the highest time-spirit. In that favorable atmosphere the human mind and the human form reached their greatest height. Following Platonic philosophers like Shaftesbury and Winckelmann and historians like Montesquieu in stressing the influence of physical nature and climate upon the public morality and spirit, Shelley saw in Periclean Greece the twofold perfection of the arts and the social scheme:

Homer and the cyclic poets were followed at a certain interval by the dramatic and lyrical Poets of Athens, who flourished contemporaneously with all that is most perfect in the kindred expressions of the poetical faculty; architecture, painting, music, the dance, sculpture, philosophy, and we may add, the forms of civil life. . . . Never at any other period has so much energy, beauty, and virtue, been developed; never was blind strength and stubborn form so disciplined and rendered subject to the will of man, or that will less repugnant to the dictates of the beautiful and the true, as during the century which preceded the death of Socrates. Of no other epoch in the history of our species have we records and fragments stamped so visibly with the image of the divinity in man.

The godlike qualities in human shapes, the ideal of the possible perfection of humankind, Shelley found in the "forms" of Greece (its "action" as well as the "language" of its arts), that is, in the deeds of heroes, in philosophy, and in poetry and the ancient sculptures, "faultless productions, whose very fragments are the despair of modern art." [2]

A love of thought expressing itself in beautiful "forms" constituted, according to Shelley, the Greek time-spirit. Thus, his conception of the Greek ideal of the beautiful was a truth which reveals the harmonious working of the order of the universe. Every revelation of the divine order is poetry; for the poetical power expresses itself in the "forms" of society as well as in those of art—"language, colour,

---

[2] *A Defence of Poetry* (Shawcross, p. 132), and Preface to *Hellas*, in *The Complete Poetical Works of Percy Bysshe Shelley*, ed. Thomas Hutchinson (1927), p. 442.

form, and religious and civil habits of action, are all the instruments and material of poetry." [3] In Greece a "mental beauty" spread its sunlike influence through the clear atmosphere so that "every human being then caught a splendour not his own" from his surroundings.[4] Then indeed every artist (or poet) easily participated in the divine or intellectual beauty—the Eternal, the Infinite, the One. Since they revealed the indestructible order of the world, artists must have been more than mere musicians, dancers, architects, statuaries, painters, or writers. In Shelley's Greece they were more nearly the cornerstone of society, "the institutors of laws, and the founders of civil society." Men of thought had been most highly honored in Greece, and philosophers had actually been rulers there. "The study of modern history is the study of kings, financiers, statesmen, and priests. The history of ancient Greece is the study of legislators, philosophers, and poets; it is the history of men, compared with the history of titles." [5]

Greece represented, then, in the feelings of Shelley, the prime illustration of the reign of thought or light, the rule of the spirit of Apollo, god of reason, music, and poetry. It was ever the

> antique region, on which fell
> The dews of thought in the world's golden dawn
> Earliest and most benign, and from it sprung
> Temples and cities and immortal forms
> And harmonies of wisdom and of song,
> And thoughts, and deeds worthy of thought so fair.
> (Prologue to *Hellas*, ll. 32–37.)

The enduring glory of Greece was its supremacy in the creation of mental "forms":

[3] *A Defence of Poetry* (Shawcross, pp. 124–25).

[4] See letter to Thomas Love Peacock, Jan. 24, 1819 (*Complete Works*, ed. Ingpen and Peck [1929], *Letters*, X, 22–23), where Shelley commented on some paintings at Herculaneum and suggested that even inferior artists could draw power from the atmosphere. The idea may be applied as well to Shelley's idealized conceptions of Greece and Greek artists.

[5] "Essays on the Literature . . . of the Athenians" (Shawcross, pp. 36–37). See also Preface to *Prometheus Unbound* (*Poetical Works*, ed. Hutchinson, p. 203), Preface to *The Revolt of Islam* (*Works*, pp. 35–36), and a passage in the spirit of Winckelmann in the letter cited in note 4.

Greece and her foundations are
Built below the tide of war,
Based on the crystalline sea
Of thought and its eternity. (*Hellas,* ll. 696–99.)

"THE GENUINE ELEMENTS
OF HUMAN SOCIETY"

The contrast between the Greece of Apollonian thought and the England of the early nineteenth century shocked Shelley. What place was there in his native land for the poet or artist? he asked in a spirit felt by nearly all his contemporaries. Yet poetry itself offered almost too feeble an instrument with which to set forth the ideal social scheme, and in a letter to Peacock (January 24, 1819) he wrote, "I consider poetry very subordinate to moral and political science, and if I were well, certainly I should aspire to the latter; for I can conceive a great work, embodying the discoveries of all ages, and harmonizing the outstanding creeds by which mankind have been ruled." Shelley also hoped, according to the Preface to *Prometheus Unbound,* sometime to "produce a systematical history of what appear to me to be the genuine elements of human society." In his fondness for reviewing civilization, "that cyclic poem written by Time upon the memories of men," Shelley resembled many poets of the eighteenth century, especially Schiller. Pageants of history had been common in verse and prose for nearly two hundred years.

Shelley's "systematical history" was never written; his dream remained incomplete, as had the similar ones of Pope, Gray, and Collins. Nevertheless, many of the elements which doubtless would have gone into the projected history appear in his poetry repeatedly. In *Laon and Cythna; or, The Revolt of Islam* (1817), the "Ode to Liberty" (1820), and *Hellas* (1821) in particular, one perceives the outlines of an account of civilization comparable to the "progress" of the arts and of Liberty related by Thomson and other poets. Shelley's poetry represents the finest use which had yet been made of the considerable body of "ideas" concerning culture which had attracted so many English poets.

Briefly, Shelley's "progress" runs as follows. Before the coming of
Liberty the civilizer, man was "savage, cunning, blind, and rude."
While he was covered with the dark pall of Tyranny, the arts re-
mained undiscovered.

> On the unapprehensive wild
>   The vine, the corn, the olive mild,
> Grew savage yet, to human use unreconciled;
>   And, like unfolded flowers beneath the sea,
>   Like the man's thought dark in the infant's brain,
>   Like aught that is which wraps what is to be,
>   Art's deathless dreams lay veiled by many a vein
> Of Parian stone; and, yet a speechless child,
>   Verse murmured, and Philosophy did strain
>   Her lidless eyes for thee [Liberty].
>   ("Ode to Liberty," ll. 51–60.)

Then Athens arose, more lovely and divine than the shimmering
dream-city Shelley adorned with his characteristic imagery of clouds
and winds:

>   Athens, diviner yet,
>   Gleamed with its crest of columns, on the will
> Of man, as on a mount of diamond, set;
>   For thou [Liberty] wert, and thine all-creative skill
> Peopled with forms that mock the eternal dead
>   In marble immortality, that hill
>   Which was thine earliest throne and latest oracle.
>   ("Ode to Liberty," ll. 69–75.)

Poetry, sculpture, and philosophy—here especially the Greeks had
given form to thought. The images of "deathless dreams," or statues
within the marble hills awaiting the sculptors, and the "forms" of
"marble immortality" on the Acropolis reflect Shelley's customary
stress on sculpture in passages of this kind.

Liberty endured in Greece until despotism, luxury, and sophistry
destroyed the poetical faculty, and the decline manifested itself in the
"forms" of art as well as of society. Shelley linked Hellenistic or
Alexandrian art to the "lettered tyrants" of Sicily and Egypt.[6] Earlier

---

[6] *A Defence of Poetry* (Shawcross, p. 138). See also the Preface to *The Revolt of
Islam* and Coleridge's remarks of a similar nature in *The Friend* (above, p. 144).

poets had similarly interpreted the course of events, asserting that Liberty and the arts always depart together.

Rome, suckled on Liberty, passed through stages similar to those in Greece, though it never became an empire of thought, and it added but little to the arts. Luxury and tyranny brought about the ruin of Rome. Again Shelley pointed out the parallel between the public morality and the spirit of poetry and the arts.

The monstrous figures called Arabesques, however in some of them is to be found a mixture of a truer and a simpler taste, which are found in the ruined palaces of the Roman Emperors, bear, nevertheless, the same relation to the brutal profligacy and killing luxury which required them, as the majestic figures of Castor and Pollux, and the simple beauty of the frieze of the Parthenon, bear to the more beautiful and simple manners of the Greeks of that period.[7]

In Shelley's account Rome occupied a position like that it had held in the "progress-pieces" of eighteenth-century verse: Rome had been no creator but merely the transmitter of works derived from Greece.

After Rome came the "blight" of Christianity, which served as Shelley's equivalent for the "Gothick sleep," the ages of barbarism and superstition which many Augustan and Academic poets had anathematized. This was the tune which Shelley first began to play in *Queen Mab* (1812):

> Where Athens, Rome, and Sparta stood,
> There is a moral desert now. (Sec. II, ll. 162–63.)

In republican Italy the arts finally came to life again, awakened by Dante, the morning star of the Revival of Learning and the Arts.

> Art, which cannot die,
> With divine wand traced on our earthly home
> Fit imagery to pave heaven's everlasting dome.
> ("Ode to Liberty," ll. 133–35.)

The nineteenth century was to see "the world's great age begin anew." In prophetic vision Shelley, like Blake, saw all the nations throwing off the yoke of kings and the chains of tyranny. The Greek

---

[7] This was Shelley's note on Plato, *Republic*, III, 401, where artists are forbidden "to employ their skill upon forms of an immoral, unchastened, monstrous, or illiberal type." See *Complete Works, Prose*, VII, 261–62.

struggle for independence heralded mighty events elsewhere. There was to be political and social revolution, but Shelley made it clear that the really important changes would spring from the poetical faculty expressing itself in thought, both in the arts and in society. Man was in the service of Apollo, god of light and poetry,

> bearer of the quiver,
> Whose sun-like shafts pierce tempest-wingèd Error.

Almost against the day when his hopes should be fulfilled, Shelley listed the greatest figures in the advance of civilization, the finest servants of Apollo, the human beings who have contributed "the genuine elements" of society.

It exceeds all imagination to conceive what would have been the moral condition of the world if neither Dante, Petrarch, Boccaccio, Chaucer, Shakespeare, Calderon, Lord Bacon, nor Milton, had ever existed; if Raphael and Michael Angelo had never been born; if the Hebrew poetry had never been translated; if a revival of the study of Greek literature had never taken place; if no monuments of ancient sculpture had been handed down to us; and if the poetry of the religion of the ancient world had been extinguished together with its belief.[8]

The paramount idea in Shelley's conception of "the genuine elements of human society" was, then, his belief that error will vanish from the individual and then from the social body when light is revealed. That hope was likewise one of the cardinal assumptions of a large number of English poets in the early nineteenth century; for it was the appropriate culmination of the countless poetic and philosophical discussions of civilization during the Renaissance, and most intensely in the "Age of Reason" or Enlightenment. Thought—in the fine arts, in poetry, in philosophy, in society—Shelley believed was not only its own excuse for being, but it was also an Apollonian force making for goodness.

> Let there be light! said Liberty,
> And like sunrise from the sea,
> Athens arose! (*Hellas,* ll. 682–84.)

[8] *A Defence of Poetry* (Shawcross, p. 151). See above, pp. 115, 145, for similar statements by Blake and Coleridge.

Once Shelley even gave divine sanction to the cause of Liberty. In *Hellas* he represented the Saviour as beseeching His Father—in the name of Plato and Greece—to end the slavery of the Hellenic people.

> by Plato's sacred light,
> Of which my spirit was a burning morrow—
> By Greece and all she cannot cease to be,
> Her quenchless words, sparks of immortal truth,
> Stars of all night—her harmonies and forms,
> Echoes and shadows of what Love adores
> In thee, I do compel thee, send forth Fate.
>
> (Prologue, ll. 94–100.)

Throughout his "progress" of the arts and Liberty Shelley omitted, one notices, almost all the details concerning the techniques of the several arts and neglected their histories and their "rules." He used, to be sure, an occasional "breathing marble" and a "stone warmed to life." His view of sculpture implied, as we shall see, something very close to technique. In general, however, the critical cant of Academic poetry had been sloughed off, since the poetical faculty or principle interested him more than the story of the technical advance of sculpture. Shelley's treatment of history was likewise more "poetic" (or "philosophical" or "aesthetic") than that of such a forerunner as Thomson. Desirous of praising the light and spirit of ancient statuary, Shelley reflected his imaginative and emotional responses to works of art in odes and lyrical dramas; whereas the eighteenth-century poet, though possessing a truly poetic feeling for sculpture, nevertheless wrote in *Liberty* what remained for the most part a treatise on the ancient arts.

Shelley's procedure takes on added significance in the light of the fact that the Romantic poets had a larger body of information on which to draw. Winckelmann's ideas and knowledge were now commonplaces among English connoisseurs, travelers, scholars, and critics of art. His aesthetic opinions pervaded the writings of such authors as Wieland, Madame de Staël, Barthélemy, and A. W. Schlegel, with whose works Shelley was acquainted. From Italy the poet himself sent long letters concerning the antiquities, and he jotted down in his journals a series of observations on the sculptures at Florence and Rome. He read with somewhat connoisseur-like eyes popular books of travel like Eustace's *Classical Tour through Italy* (1813), Forsyth's *Remarks on Antiquities, Arts, and Letters, during an Excursion in Italy in the Years 1802 and 1803* (1813), and the *Historical Illustrations of the Fourth Canto of Childe Harold* published by Hobhouse in 1818.

On the other hand, Shelley never considered himself either scholar or historian, archaeologist or antitiquarian. Instead, in the roles of poet and philosopher, he wished to express his own feelings and reflections rather than to give information. Though memories of Madame de Staël's *Corinne,* love story and guidebook rolled into one mediocre novel, came into his mind when he wrote of antiquities in Italy, and though echoes of his reading appeared in his poetry, he left the "science" of sculpture to others, in much the same fashion as did Byron in *Childe Harold* (Canto IV, stanza liii). "Romantic" poets felt almost an obligation to describe their feelings in the presence of ancient masterpieces, to treat philosophically the more general "ideas" associated with the Antique, and, wherever possible, to capture the feeling of sculpture through figurative and imaginative means. Only the lesser poets continued to versify information about statuary without giving evidence that they had in some fashion personally "experienced" works of art.

THE SHELLEYAN VIEW OF SCULPTURE: THE PLASTIC SPIRIT

The philosophy behind all Shelley's discussions of the artistic power or faculty was ultimately Platonic; for that faculty, as he conceived it, was essentially love or a begetting in the spirit. A poet attempts to identify himself with an admired object, and his poetry expresses that sympathy. Moreover, since everyone is influenced by the forms he beholds—being lowered or raised, as the case may be, to the stature of the form contemplated—he should surround himself with harmonious and beautiful forms. From the noble forms everywhere about them, the Greeks had created the preëminent beauty of their civilization.

Throughout most of his life Shelley was imitating the Greeks, he felt, by seeking beauty

> in the words
> Of antique verse and high romance,—in form,
> Sound, colour (*Epipsychidion,* ll. 209-11)—

that is, in poetry and in sculpture, music, and painting. The art of "form" was sculpture, and in Shelley's works the word "form" often stood for "statue" or "statuary." The "immortal forms" of Greece in *Hellas* and elsewhere were really the "immortal statues" of the ancient sculptors. "Forms" and "statues" were interchangeable words in the prose. At times Shelley had sculptures about him to inspire his writing. In the house at Great Marlow where *The Revolt of Islam* was written Shelley had two life-size statues. Leigh Hunt reported, "He used to sit in a study adorned with casts, as large as life, of the Vatican Apollo and the celestial Venus." [9] Among the pleasures of residing in Venice, the Julian of "Julian and Maddalo," who was Shelley himself, numbered works of poetry, painting, and sculpture. Of his room he says:

> books are there,
> Pictures, and casts from all those statues fair
> Which were twin-born with poetry (ll. 554-56).

The forms of Grecian sculpture were more than pleasant objects to behold. They influenced the lives of those who beheld them, for the forms of art and morality interacted upon each other. Shelley agreed with Lessing—

Be it fable or history that Love made the first essay in the plastic arts, it is certain that it never wearied of guiding the hands of the masters of old. . . . As beautiful men produced beautiful statues, so the latter reacted upon the former and the state became indebted to beautiful statues for beautiful men.

Such a sentiment lay behind the lines of *Prometheus Unbound,*

---

[9] *Autobiography,* II, 34. See also Edward Dowden, *The Life of Shelley* (1886), II, 111, "the youthful Apollo and Venus, in casts of ample size, made the room, as it were, a temple of beauty and radiant force." The Venus may have been the celebrated Medici figure, though the word "celestial" might suggest another statue. Ilse O'Sullivan-Köhling (*Shelley und die bildende Kunst* [Bad Sulzungen, 1927], pp. 32-33) indicated the Capitoline Venus.

And mothers, gazing, drank [from marble forms or statues
          made divine] the love men see
Reflected in their race, behold, and perish (II, iv, 83–84).[10]

Shelley's account of the great Florentine artists in *Marenghi* could
be applied to all artists.

The light-invested Herald Poesy,
Was drawn from the dim world by thee [Florence].

And thou in painting didst transcribe all taught
    By loftiest meditations; marble knew
The sculptor's fearless soul—and as he wrought,
    The grace of his own power and freedom grew (ll. 33–38).

The plastic spirit worked upon the artist as well as upon his material,
and the creative process had an effect upon the artist. The best account, perhaps, of the Shelleyan view of the influence of the plastic
spirit of sculpture is Mrs. Shelley's description of the origin and
composition of *Prometheus Unbound,* part of which may be quoted
here.

The charm of the Roman climate helped to clothe his thoughts in greater
beauty than they had ever worn before. And as he wandered among the
ruins made one with nature in their decay, or gazed on the Praxitelean
shapes that throng the Vatican, the Capitol, and the palaces of Rome, his
soul imbibed forms of loveliness which became a portion of itself.[11]

For a sensitive beholder like Shelley, the aesthetic quality of sculptural forms was inseparably linked with a morality of Platonic coloring.

The arts were, moreover, intercessors between man and nature,
even as in the theory of Coleridge art was "the mediatress between,
and reconciler of, nature and man." To Prometheus, Shelley gave the
statement of his similar theory in regard to the sister-arts of painting,
sculpture, and poetry:

[10] See *Laokoon* (*Selected Prose Works of Lessing,* translated by E. C. Beasley and
Helen Zimmern, ed. Edward Bell, 1890), pp. 11–14. Swinburne explained the
passage from *Prometheus Unbound* thus: "Women with child gazing on statues (say
on the Venus of Melos) bring forth children like them–children whose features
reflect the passion of the gaze and perfection of the sculptured beauty" (*Poems of
Shelley,* ed. Locock, 1911, I, 614).

[11] See *Works,* p. 270.

The wandering voices and the shadows these
Of all that man becomes, the mediators
Of that best worship love, by him and us
Given and returned; swift shapes and sounds, which grow
More fair and soft as man grows wise and kind,
And veil by veil, evil and error fall (III, iii, 57–62).[12]

In sculpture, Shelley wrote, the poetical faculty or power speaks through form. Sculpture is the expression of thought, with the lofty conceptions of a mind revealed in marble corresponding to the language of poetry or the color of painting. In *The Daemon of the World* the equation of sculpture and poetry lay behind the lines describing a "divinest form"

> Whose outline is as fair as marble clothed
> In light of some sublimest mind (ll. 16–17).[13]

The rarest sculptures seen in a vision by Marianne (Mrs. Hunt) attested the skill of the Shelleyan sculptor:

> And as she looked, still lovelier grew
>   Those marble forms;—the sculptor sure
> Was a strong spirit, and the hue
>   Of his own mind did there endure
> After the touch, whose power had braided
> Such grace, was in some sad change faded.
>   ("Marianne's Dream," stanza xx.)

The thought expressed by sculptors in enduring forms or statues drew the poet's attention, especially in Italy, as he brooded among his loved ruins:

> Around me gleamed many a bright sepulchre
> Of whose pure beauty, Time, as if his pleasure
> Were to spare Death, had never made erasure;
>   But every lineament was clear
>   As in the sculptor's thought.
>   ("Ode to Naples," stanza i, ll. 12–16.)

[12] See also above, pp. 140–41.

[13] In the earlier version in *Queen Mab*, Sec. I, ll. 16–17 (*Works*, p. 755), the lines were less exact; they were "academic," and they lacked the Shelleyan phrase "clothed in light." Almost any eighteenth-century poet might have written
>   "That lovely outline, which is fair
>   As breathing marble."

Shelley's theories of the nature of sculpture appeared even more explicitly in *The Revolt of Islam*. The temple to which floated Laon and the Woman—the latter vaguely statuesque and of "marmoreal bosom"—was a stupendous pile. Unlike Pope, Shelley declined to visualize the grandiose edifice; indeed, no artist could body forth its appearance,

> nor in painting's light, or mightier verse,
> Or sculpture's marble language, can invest
> That shape to mortal sense. (Canto I, stanza l, ll. 5–7.)

Nevertheless, "that vast Fane's aerial heap" had sculptured ornamentation; statues or friezes on the

> roof of moonstone carved, did keep
> A glimmering o'er the forms on every side,
> Sculptures like life and thought; immoveable, deep-eyed.
> (Canto I, stanza li, ll. 7–9.)

Later Laon, wandering with the orphan Cythna, found many a "monument Vital with mind" (Canto II, stanza xxvi, ll. 5–6).

Shelley's finest poetic statement of his conception of the place of thought in sculpture—as in all the arts and in poetry—was in *Prometheus Unbound,* where he made surprisingly lyrical verse out of ideas difficult to present in poetry. Apparently the intensity with which he felt his theory of art gathered even aesthetic theorizing into the sweep of his rhapsodic, if somewhat rhetorical, lines. The Earth proclaimed that the man of harmonious soul—when love rules the helm of his will, "a tempest-wingèd ship"; or when the "divine intelligence . . . visible only to the mind" is really "the pilot of the soul"—possesses mighty powers.

> All things confess his strength. Through the cold mass
> Of marble and of colour his dreams pass;
> Bright threads whence mothers weave the robes their children wear;
> Language is a perpetual Orphic song,
> Which rules with Daedal harmony a throng
> Of thoughts and forms, which else senseless and shapeless were.
> (IV, 412–17.)

Sculpture is, then, the embodiment of the dreams of the artist, the giving of form to thought. Product of visionary insight and of labor in giving form or shape perceptible to the senses, sculpture expressed the indestructible order of the universe, the abstract, intellectual beauty. That was the burden of the chorus of Promethean spirits who created the arts:

> We come from the mind
> Of human kind,
>
> . . .
>
> From the temples high
> Of Man's ear and eye,
> Roofed over Sculpture and Poesy;
> From the murmurings
> Of the unsealed springs
> Where Science bedews her Daedal wings.[14]
> (*Prometheus Unbound*, IV, 93–94, 111–15.)

Thought—as it reveals itself in the fine arts, in poetry, in science or philosophy—was Shelley's lamp of freedom and the concrete expression of the spirit of beauty and goodness.

> 'Our toil from thought all glorious forms shall cull,
> To make this Earth, our home, more beautiful,
> And Science, and her sister Poesy,
> Shall clothe in light the fields and cities of the free!' [15]

Moreover, after poetry and philosophy, the art of sculpture seems most to have interested Shelley, like many English poets since the seventeenth century. His preference for sculpture rather than painting was partly owing to his notion, which Medwin reports, that no special training or previous study is necessary for its appreciation. The effects of sculpture are immediate, direct, and unified in contrast to those of painting. Of sculpture, Medwin concluded, "the Roman peasant is perhaps as good a judge as the best academician or anatomist." [16] As the art of form, sculpture presents works to be apprehended by the senses. Though the poet's *Notes on Sculptures*

[14] See also Coleridge's remark, "To make nature thought, and thought nature,— this is the mystery of genius in the Fine Arts" (above, p. 141).

[15] *The Revolt of Islam*, Canto V, ll. 2253–56, after stanza li (*Works*, p. 91). See also *The Masque of Anarchy*, ll. 254–57 (p. 339).

[16] *Memoir of Shelley* (1833), p. 54. See also letter to Leigh Hunt, Sept. 3, 1819 (*Letters*, X, 76), and Melvin T. Solve, *Shelley; His Theory of Poetry* (Chicago, 1927), p. 196.

in Rome and Florence show both some use of "the faculty of comparison" and some "previous study," in general they reflect an immediate and sensuous response. Certainly Medwin had in mind Shelley's own opinion of the way to look at sculpture when he announced that the *Notes* were "far surpassing in eloquence anything Winckelman [*sic*] has left on this subject." Their eloquence was apparently more spontaneous:

. . . these notes were written in pencil, and thrown off in the gallery, in a burst of enthusiasm, proving that thoughts struck out in the fire of the moment, have a more inherent force of truth—give birth to a natural eloquence that defies all that study and after meditation can produce.[17]

Yet Shelley was probably attracted to sculpture quite as much by the Shaftesbury and Winckelmann interpretation of the Antique in the light of the Grecian way of life—the ancient statues as the expression of the spiritual and mental "forms" of Greek society. The Grecian statues as manifestations of the Grecian poetical faculty interested him very much as they did Wordsworth in *The Excursion,* though Shelley's concern was with their artistic power for its own sake rather than for its relation to mythology and religion. "Statuary was his passion," said Medwin, and *"there* he was at home." In a more extended account Medwin showed Shelley's emphasis on the relationship between art and morality and society in Greece, which was of a sort he hoped might be revived in the nineteenth century.

He contended, "that the slaughter-house and dissecting-room were not the sources whence the Greeks drew their perfection." It was to be attributed to the daily exhibition of the human form in all its symmetry in their gymnasia. Their sculptors were not mere mechanicians: they were citizens and soldiers animated with the love of their country. We must rival them in their virtue before we can come up to them in their compositions.[18]

[17] *Memoir of Shelley,* p. 56, and Medwin, *Life of Shelley,* ed. H. B. Forman (1913), pp. 222–23. Medwin considered the descriptions of antique statues in Schiller's *Brief eines Residentes Danes,* "pale and lifeless" compared to Shelley's.

[18] *Memoir,* pp. 55–56. In the *Life* (Forman), pp. 197 and 216, "inspiration" takes the place of "perfection," while the other sentence refers to "the daily exhibitions of the human form in all its ease and symmetry in their gymnasia." "Virtue" also becomes "virtues." Such statements make it clear that "his guide and master in the study of ancient art was Winckelmann" (Dowden, *The Life of Shelley,* II, 248), whose ideas he seems to have found in books like *Corinne.*

The "immortal forms" of Grecian sculpture were almost as splendid reminders of the glory of Grecian virtue or morality or thought as its "harmonies of wisdom and of song."

The wrecks and fragments of those subtle and profound minds, like the ruins of a fine statue, obscurely suggest to us the grandeur and perfection of the whole. . . . Their sculptures are such as we, in our presumption, assume to be the models of ideal truth and beauty, and to which no artist of modern times can produce forms in any degree comparable.[19]

On the basis of such statements, one is tempted to class Shelley as the most enthusiastic admirer of the Grecian statues among the English Romantic poets.

Since Greek sculpture was the high expression of the minds, not of artisans or mechanicians but of poets or philosophers, it was also the manifestation in marble forms of the Ideal or Intellectual Beauty. For Shelley sculpture, like all workings of the poetical faculty, had to capture a portion of the eternal loveliness or, in more Platonic language, had to reflect the Idea of beauty. Prometheus again became Shelley's mouthpiece in describing the creative process in the arts:

> lovely apparitions, dim at first,
> Then radiant, as the mind, arising bright
> From the embrace of beauty, whence the forms
> Of which these are the phantoms, casts on them
> The gathered rays which are reality,
> Shall visit us, the progeny immortal
> Of Painting, Sculpture, and rapt Poesy,
> And arts, tho' unimagined, yet to be (III, iii, 49–56).

In putting into verse this account of the artistic process Shelley made almost a "rule" out of his Neo-Platonic theories, even as Plato himself gave rationalistic scales of beauty and descriptions of the plastic powers. Most noteworthy, however, is the fact that the poet thought less of an architectural design or archetypal idea-in-the-mind, such as one meets in Neo-Classical and Academic theory of art and criticism, than of an intuitive and direct penetration into the realm of abstract beauty to be followed by an active, personal, and perhaps

[19] "Essay on the Literature . . . of the Athenians" (Shawcross, pp. 32–33).

even sensory participation in the One. Following this Plotinean "communion in Ideal-Form," the poet returned to clothe his thought with
some measure of the Ideal Beauty he had beheld.[20] Since that thought
—a portion of the eternal Beauty—almost worked itself into a lovely
shape according to the processes of organisms in nature, the artist
might be said to have produced

> Forms more real than living man,
> Nurslings of immortality! (I, 748–49.)

In a letter to Maria Gisborne (October 13 or 14, 1819) written during
the period when he was finishing *Prometheus Unbound,* Shelley
stated explicitly that he had studied the arts of painting and sculpture
as guides in the formulation of a theory of art.

The gallery [at Florence] I have [a] design of studying piecemeal; one
of my chief [objects] in Italy being the observing in statuary and painting
the degree in which, and the rules according to which, that ideal beauty,
of which we have so intense yet so obscure an apprehension, is realised in
external forms.

The poetical faculty acted as a plastic spirit molding into form the
"idea" or thought gained by the artist in the moments when he penetrated the regions beyond reality. Like many German and English
Romantic poets, Shelley used sculpture to illustrate the process of art:

This instinct and intuition of the poetical faculty is still more observable in
the plastic and pictorial arts; a great statue or picture grows under the
power of the artist as a child in the mother's womb; and the very mind
which directs the hands in formation, is incapable of accounting to itself
for the origin, the gradations, or the media of the process.[21]

Unfortunately, the poet was unable to reveal more concerning the
nature of the formative or plastic power belonging to the artist. Apparently he agreed with Blake that idea or thought or spiritual vision
includes its own execution, that is, includes an element which compels
the vision to put on communicable shape. In any case, the plastic
spirit is a sort of internal necessity forcing ideas to achieve form, with

[20] See *The Ethical Treatises of Plotinus,* translated by Kenneth MacKenna (1917),
I, 80 ff.
[21] *A Defence of Poetry* (Shawcross, p. 154).

the artist serving as the means of clothing the conceptions with the forms they wear. Ultimately the object thus created by the plastic spirit exists by itself and has a life of its own.

Shelley versified this process in the terms of sculpture in *The Witch of Atlas* where the lovely lady-witch "within a cavern, by a secret fountain" created a perfect hermaphroditic being of an ideal sexless beauty. With his mind on the sculptures he had seen in Florence and Rome, Shelley described the activity of creation thus:

> Then by strange art she kneaded fire and snow
> Together, tempering the repugnant mass
> With liquid love—all things together grow
> Through which the harmony of love can pass;
> And a fair Shape out of her hands did flow—
> A living Image, which did far surpass
> In beauty that bright shape of vital stone
> Which drew the heart out of Pygmalion.
>
> A sexless thing it was, and in its growth
> It seemed to have developed no defect
> Of either sex, yet all the grace of both,—
> In gentleness and strength its limbs were decked;
> The bosom swelled lightly with its full youth,
> The countenance was such as might select
> Some artist that his skill should never die,
> Imaging forth such perfect purity (Stanzas xxv–xxxvi).[22]

Inexplicably yet with admirable skill, it seems, the artist or poet images forth ideal, intellectual forms beyond nature. Of Raphael's Saint Cecilia, Shelley wrote to Peacock (November 9, 1818),

It is of the inspired and ideal kind, and seems to have been conceived and executed in a similar state of feeling to that which produced among the ancients those perfect specimens of poetry and sculpture which are the

[22] See also *The Revolt of Islam,* Canto X, stanza xxiii, l. 9, for an oblique reference to the Pygmalion story—"Like forms which sculptors carve, then love to agony"— and the *Notes on Sculptures,* especially Notes XIV, "An Athlete," XXIX, "Bacchus and Ampelus," XXXVII, "Ganymede," and XLVIII, "The Figure of a Youth Said to Be Apollo" (*Prose,* VI, 315 ff.). For a full survey of the mythological material in *The Witch of Atlas,* see Douglas Bush, *Mythology and the Romantic Tradition in English Poetry,* pp. 138 ff. The present discussion complements Mr. Bush by suggesting that "the creative imagination of the poet" is the same as "the spirit of love and beauty in nature and the mind of man."

baffling models of succeeding generations. There is a unity and perfection in it of an incommunicable kind.

The Grecian sculptures were models, neither for rules and canons of beauty nor for proportions of anatomy, but for illustration of the poetical expression of spirit and mind, light and thought, the unity and perfection of the One.

To mankind Prometheus gave the arts and the ability to measure all things in thought. In sculpture Shelley saw the advance mentioned also by Jonson and Dryden, by Reynolds and Blake.

> human hands first mimicked and then mocked,
> With moulded limbs more lovely than its own,
> The human form, till marble grew divine (II, iv, 80–82).[23]

Man has thus at his command an instrument capable of achieving divine forms by improving upon nature. That was the core of Shelley's view of the nature and theory of sculpture, and it was all he needed to know of the art in his role of poet.

SHELLEYAN "SCULPTURES"

Of Shelley's pleasure in ruins, architecture, and statuary in Italy, Mrs. Shelley remarked, "There are many passages in the *Prometheus* which show the intense delight he received from such studies, and give back the impression with a beauty of poetical description peculiarly his own." [24] In other poems as well, of course, Shelley gave evidence of his strongly personal response to sculptural figures, mostly Grecian, which he often endowed with the emotional vitality and the Ideal Beauty admired by many Romantic poets. The comments in his *Notes on Sculptures in Rome and Florence* (written, perhaps, in the spring of 1819 at Rome and at Florence in the autumn) aid the reader in discovering the peculiarly Shelleyan elements in his poetic use of the antiques in imagery and his imaginative re-creations of sculpture.

Among the Grecian sculptors Shelley's favorite was Praxiteles.

---

[23] See also above, pp. 49, 56–57, 91, 110–11, and Solve, *Shelley; His Theory of Poetry*, p. 115.

[24] Note on *Prometheus Unbound* (*Works*, p. 270).

Mrs. Shelley noted that "Praxitelean shapes" attracted him most; and even when the poet beheld statues by some other ancient artist, he seems to have been interested in their "Praxitelean" qualities. Various comments in the *Notes on Sculptures* leave no doubt that the tenderness or softness, the sensitive delicacy, and the flowing grace associated with the works of the Greek artist were the qualities he most admired in sculpture. Shelley's characteristic fondness for images of swiftness, airiness, and flight—the sensations of winds and tempests and, in direct contrast, of cloudlike repose and floating dreams—manifested itself in his feeling for sculpture.

In *Prometheus Unbound* a temple "beyond the peak of Bacchic Nysa" was imagined as

> populous with most living imagery,
> Praxitelean shapes, whose marble smiles
> Fill the hushed air with everlasting love (III, iii, 164–66).

In the prose fragment "The Coliseum," modeled to some extent on Madame de Staël's *Corinne,* Shelley introduced his characters silently contemplating the scene from a fallen column,

the eyes of the girl were fixed upon her father's lips, and his countenance, sublime and sweet, but motionless as some Praxitelean image of the greatest of poets, filled the silent air with smiles, not reflected from external forms.[25]

In a similar key was Shelley's note on a Ganymede of "surpassing beauty":

These hands and fingers are so delicate and light that it seems as if the spirit of pleasure, of light, life and beauty that lives in them half lifted them, and deprived them of the natural weight of mortal flesh. The roundness and fulness of the flowing perfection of his form is strange and rare. The attitude and form of the legs and the relation borne to each other by his light and delicate feet is peculiarly beautiful.[26]

---

[25] Medwin (*Life* [Forman], pp. 215–16) wrote that Shelley "has left us a picture of the Coliseum, which, though in prose, surpasses all metrical poetry; and here it was that he laid the scene of a tale that promised to rival *Corinne*." He regarded the tale as "the Torso of some exquisite statue" and read it many times on the very spot described by his friend.

[26] *Prose,* VI, 324. The Ganymede is probably a Roman copy from the Praxiteles Sauroktonos; see Ilse O'Sullivan-Köhling, *Shelley und die bildende Kunst,* p. 190.

Only once in the poetry did Shelley mention Phidias or his works. In *Prometheus Unbound* there was a second temple where the Spirit of the Hour was to rest

> gazed upon by Phidian forms
> Of thee, and Asia, and the Earth, and me.
> (III, iv, 112–13.)

Phidian suggested greater size and grander shape than Praxitelean.[27] Shelley beheld the sculptures from the Parthenon, praising them on at least one occasion. His enthusiasm, however, like Byron's, was excited by the "old antique," of which he had casts at Great Marlow and which he beheld in the Italian galleries and elsewhere. No important Romantic poets were more attached to the Greco-Roman statues which had pleased connoisseurs for centuries.

Since Shelley seldom mentioned (outside the *Notes on Sculptures* and the letters on antiquities penned in Italy) specific antique statues, the works singled out for praise or utilized imaginatively in his poetry represented particularly strong and often very individual feelings on his part. The following examples illustrate the peculiarly Shelleyan response to Grecian statues. The mysterious stranger in "The Coliseum" was of a strikingly sculptural beauty of the kind which the poet liked to associate with himself.

His form, which, though emaciated, displayed the elementary outlines of exquisite grace, was enveloped in an ancient chlamys, which half concealed his face; his snow-white feet were fitted with ivory sandals, delicately sculptured in the likeness of two female figures, whose wings met upon the heel, and whose eager and half-divided lips seemed quivering to meet. It was a face, once seen, never to be forgotten. The mouth and the moulding of the chin resembled the eager and impassioned tenderness of

---

The *Notes,* as Dowden has said (II, 283–84), were "the criticisms of a poet, who endeavours to penetrate to the centre of emotional life in each marble form, to catch the spirit which flows through the limbs and animates the countenance." See above, p. 183, and Byron, p. 160.

[27] See also letter to Peacock, March 23, 1819 (*Letters,* X, 43). Shelley was at the British Museum in 1815 with Mary and Hogg to see the statuary (though not the Elgin Marbles). Three years later Mary at least visited the Museum to look at the Elgin Marbles and, on another day, saw "the casts from Phidias"; see Mrs. Julian Marshall, *The Life and Letters of Mary Wollstonecraft Shelley* (1889), I, 113, 209; and Dowden, *The Life of Shelley,* II, 183.

the statues of Antinous; but instead of the effeminate sullenness of the eye, and the narrow smoothness of the forehead, shone an expression of profound and piercing thought; the brow was clear and open, and his eyes deep, like two wells of crystalline water which reflect the all-beholding heavens. Over all was spread a timid expression of womanish tenderness and hesitation, which contrasted, yet intermingled strangely, with the abstracted and fearless character that predominated in his form and gestures.[28]

A statue of a hermaphrodite, presumably the figure at Florence though definite testimony is lacking, fascinated the English poet and teased him out of thought. In the *Epipsychidion* fragments one finds these lines:

> And others swear that you're a Hermaphrodite;
> Like that sweet marble monster of both sexes,
> Which looks so sweet and gentle that it vexes
> The very soul that the soul is gone
> Which lifted from her limbs the veil of stone (ll. 57–61).

Apparently Shelley felt that the statue had possessed a soul which had torn away the veil of stone and become pure spirit or Ideal Beauty.[29] The fanciful conception of ancient poets, philosophers, and artists of an ideal being of mixed or bisexual nature was certain to attract Shelley more than any other Romantic poet.

In his enthusiasm for statues of Apollo, Shelley was with earlier poets and his contemporaries; for the Apollo Belvedere had long rivaled the Venus de Medici in the affections of poets and gentlemen of classical taste. The Belvedere statue contributed to Shelley's conception of the god of all light in nature and in art, partly from Byron's account in *Childe Harold,*

> the Lord of the unerring bow
> The God of life, and poesy, and light—

[28] *Prose,* VI, 299–300. Shelley probably had in mind the famous Antinous of the Belvedere, but see also Ilse O'Sullivan-Köhling, *Shelley und die bildende Kunst,* pp. 164–65. Note XXIII, "Mercury," should also be read for a similar idealization of Shelley.

[29] With this description compare the hermaphrodite in *The Witch of Atlas* (above, p. 192), and Note LI, "Olinthus," "another of those sweet and gentle figures of adolescent youth in which the Greeks delighted." See also Edward Carpenter and George Barnefield, *The Psychology of the Poet Shelley* (New York, 1925), pp. 88 ff.

The Sun in human limbs array'd, and brow
All radiant from his triumph in the fight;
The shaft hath just been shot—

and partly from his visits to the gallery. Almost inevitably, therefore, memories of the Apollo came into his mind in connection with the Byron of *Adonais,* as William Michael Rossetti pointed out. Byron dispersed the critics of Keats, "the herded wolves,"

When, like Apollo, from his golden bow
The Pythian of the age one arrow sped
And smiled! (Stanza xxviii, ll. 6–8.)

The "smile" of contempt came directly from the description of the Apollo of the Vatican by Winckelmann, Byron, and others. Though Shelley wrote no note upon the Apollo Belvedere, he regarded it as the union of "the sublimity of lofty and impetuous passion" and "the grandeur of enthusiastic imagination"—qualities he sometimes associated with himself.[30]

Grecian statues were likewise the inspiration of Shelley's portrait of himself in *Adonais* as a Dionysus,

A pardlike Spirit beautiful and swift—
A Love in desolation masked—

. . .

His head was bound with pansies overblown,
And faded violets, white, and pied, and blue;
And a light spear topped with a cypress cone,
Round whose rude shaft dark ivy-tresses grew
Yet dripping with the forest's noonday dew,
Vibrated, as the ever-beating heart
Shook the weak hand that grasped it (Stanzas xxxii–xxxiii).

[30] See above, pp. 163–64, and *Adonais,* ed. W. M. Rossetti (1890, 1924 ed.), pp. 129–30. Four of the *Notes on Sculptures* (XXVI, XXVII, XXXI, XLVIII) were on statues of Apollo. The second expressed "the intense energy and god-like anima- tion" admired in these statues by Shelley, while the former, a copy of the Praxiteles Sauroktonos, had been restored with the right arm lifted, "as if in triumph, at the success of the arrow." Shelley referred to Apollonius Rhodius's (*Argonautica,* II, 705 ff.) Apollo "when the dazzling radiance of his beautiful limbs suddenly shone over the dark Euxine," *Prose,* VI, 318 ff. See also letter to Peacock, March 23, 1819 (*Letters,* X, 37), and O'Sullivan-Köhling, *Shelley und die bildende Kunst,* pp. 177– 78, 182–83, 194–95.

That idealized Shelley was dramatically presented in the spirit of the figures of Bacchus seen in Italy and described in lyrical prose in the *Notes on Sculptures*. The ivy coronal of Bacchus has been supplanted by the Shelleyan flowers, pansies and faded violets, while a cypress cone takes the place of a pine cone on the thyrsus in a funereal touch typical of the poet. Still, Shelley saw himself as a Bacchus-statue or figure on a vase possessing "immortal beauty." The accounts of Bacchus were among the finest "Notes" both as impressionistic and emotional descriptions and as imaginative self-portrayals.

A bronze cast of the Borghese Vase contributed the following details to the Shelleyan figure of Bacchus: "Bacchus with a countenance of calm and majestic beauty surrounded by the tumultuous figures whom the whirlwinds of his Deity are tossing into all attitudes, like the sun in the midst of his planets; power calm amid confusion." The Bacchus and Ampelus at Florence gave the poet other elements with which to fill in the conception of Bacchus outlined earlier.

[Bacchus and Ampelus] are walking as it were with a sauntering and idle pace, and talking to each other as they walk, and this is expressed in the motions of their delicate and flowing forms . . . [Bacchus] is crowned with vine leaves laden with their crude fruit, and the crisp leaves fall as with the inertness of a lithe and faded leaf over his rich and over-hanging hair, which gracefully divided on his forehead falls in delicate wreaths upon his neck and breast. . . . The countenance of Bacchus is sublimely sweet and lovely . . . It has a divine and supernatural beauty, as one who walks through the world untouched by its corruptions, its corrupting cares; it looks like one who unconsciously yet with delight confers pleasure and peace. . . . Like some fine strain of harmony which flows round the soul and enfolds it, and leaves it in the soft astonishment of a satisfaction, like the pleasure of love with one whom we most love, which having taken away desire, leaves pleasure, sweet pleasure.[31]

Shelley's identification of himself with Bacchus gains in interest, if, as Medwin suggested, the poet was thinking of his boyhood strolls

[31] Notes III and XXIX (*Prose*, VI, 311, 319-20). For the general conception, see also Note XXIII, "Mercury." The parallel between the Shelley in *Adonais* and a Bacchus-statue was originally suggested by Professor Charles G. Osgood. In Naples, Shelley had seen another Bacchus "more sublime than any living being" (Letter to Peacock, Dec. [22], 1818 [*Letters*, X, 19]). The note on a statue of Minerva (XXXIV) includes a description of maenads that may profitably be compared with passages in *Adonais* and the "Ode to the West Wind."

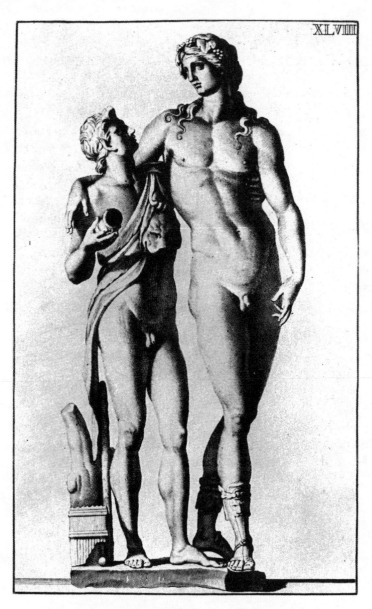

BACCHUS AND AMPELUS

with Medwin when he described the Bacchus and Ampelus group, "a younger and an elder boy at school walking in some remote grassy spot of their play-ground with that tender friendship towards each other which has so much of love." [32] One notices, too, that Shelley condemned a Bacchus by Michelangelo because the statue was unlike his conception of the Greek ideal of beauty in sculpture and because the Italian artist was far from the Shelleyan conception of Bacchus. He granted the boldness and energy of the work but added, "It wants as a work of art unity and simplicity; as a representation of the Greek Deity of Bacchus it wants every thing." [33]

Shelley, like many English Romantic poets, enjoyed adorning edifices, especially temples, with sculptures, even though he described them in less detail than Keats and Landor. In *Prometheus Unbound* a temple, reminiscent of the Pantheon, showed reliefs, where

> The likeness of those winged steeds will mock
> The flight from which they find repose (III, iv, 120–21).

In "Marianne's Dream" (54 ff.) the towers, columns, and domes were "all bright with workmanship" of dream sculptures. The temple in *The Revolt of Islam* (Canto I, stanzas lii–lvii) was amply decorated with ten thousand columns, paintings on jasper walls, and sculptures. The Imperial House in the same work also had sculptured walls. Laon and Cythna passed

> thro' portals sculptured deep
> With imagery beautiful as dream. (Canto V, stanza xxvi, ll. 2–3.)

The Altar of the Federation was a marble pyramid, wearing "the light of genius":

> its stair
> With female quires was thronged: the loveliest
> Among the free, grouped with its sculptures rare.
> (Canto V, stanza xliii, ll. 1–3.)

On the platform three rather Blakeian statues of Giant, Woman, and "Image" crushing Faith kept marble watch around the shrine

[32] Note XXIX (*Prose*, VI, 319) and Medwin, *Life* (Forman), p. 23.
[33] *Prose*, VI, 329. See also O'Sullivan-Köhling, *Shelley und die bildende Kunst*, pp. 197–98, and Felix Rabbe, *Shelley; the Man and the Poet* (1888), II, 137–38.

(Canto V, stanzas xlix–l). Shelley displayed a similar delight in halls "pavilioned round with Parian stone" in *Rosalind and Helen* (l. 1113).

The peculiarly Shelleyan character of these figures was that they were all dreamlike and of a visionary quality. In *The Revolt of Islam* Shelley typified the figures he had in mind with bodies

> shrouded in their long and golden hair,
> As if not dead, but slumbering quietly
> Like forms which sculptors carve, then love to agony.
> (Canto X, stanza xxiii, ll. 7–9.)

Perhaps the best of his original imaginative sculptures in this vein was the procession—as on a bas-relief—which occurred in the scene of the triumph of the powers of oppression in the same poem, a scene suggesting a drawing by Blake.

> And, one by one, that night, young maidens came,
> Beauteous and calm, like shapes of living stone
> Clothed in the light of dreams, and by the flame
> Which shrank as overgorged, they laid them down,
> And sung a low sweet song, of which alone
> One word was heard, and that was Liberty;
> And that some kist their marble feet, with moan
> Like love, and died; and then that they did die
> With happy smiles, which sunk in white tranquillity.
> (Canto X, stanza xlviii.)

Another of his most statuesque figures was the Witch of Atlas, who

> saw the constellations reel and dance
> Like fire-flies—and withal did ever keep
> The tenour of her contemplations calm,
> With open eyes, closed feet, and folded palm. (Stanza xxviii, ll. 5–8.)

But Shelley's most subtle criticism of sculpture came, not from such embodiments of dreams and thought, but from his stress on the living or passionate quality of the antiques seen in Italy. For the emotional vitality he found in the figures led him beyond most of his contemporaries to write of statues "in the round." That is, the poet discovered that certain statues at least were more than linear reliefs to be read like words and were to be seen from successive points of view as one walked around the figures. The size of the Niobe, as of any other work of art, "rather adds to its beauty," he felt, "because it allows the spectator the choice of a greater number of points of view, in which to catch a greater number of the infinite modes of expression of which any form approaching ideal beauty is necessarily composed." [34]

Shelley, like other poets, also used sculpture and "marble" in a more general fashion in order to suggest at different times coldness, permanency or obduracy, and radiance, and to summon visions of classical lands. He was seldom more happy than among ruins, like those surrounding the figures in "The Coliseum." " 'Around us lie enormous columns, shattered and shapeless—and fragments of capitals and cornice, fretted with delicate sculptures.' "

Sculpture also interested Shelley as an important agent in the "progress" of man. To him, its masterpieces, expressing as they did the power of the poetical faculty, marked the general advance of mind. Like almost all poets, however, he considered poetry superior to sculpture and painting—not because poetry, being unconfined, like sculpture, to the showing of one moment or attitude or pose, can show progression and action and life, but because its material is entirely mental and spiritual.

Still, of all the arts sculpture was most like poetry in permanence. The ruins of Rome and Greece and the East attracted Shelley, not so much as symbols of physical power or signs of the grandeur of ancient empires, but as "monuments vital with mind" and testimony to the conquest of matter by the mind of man. Through thought in word and in stone man triumphs over time, and the poet or artist may be calm amid decay. Stone is more enduring than sound and more lasting than color; but thought outlasts marble and brass. Shelley's estimate of the relative endurance of the materials of the

[34] *Prose,* VI, 330 ff. Harry Buxton Forman, in his separate edition of the *Notes on Sculptures* ([1879], p. 42), pointed out the similarity between the close of *The Cenci* and a portion of the note on the Niobe. Presumably the note was written after the drama, and Shelley described the statue with memories of his own lines in *The Cenci.*

several arts may be found in a letter to Peacock (November 9, 1818)
concerning the fading of some pictures at Bologna.

These are symptoms of the mortality of man, and perhaps, few of his
works are more evanescent than paintings. Sculpture retains its freshness
for twenty centuries—the Apollo and the Venus are as they were. But
books are perhaps the only productions of man coeval with the human
race. . . . The material part, indeed, of their works must perish, but they
survive in the mind of man, and the remembrances connected with them
are transmitted from generation to generation.

Thus Laon in *The Revolt of Islam* could speak of ideals "sculptured
in human hope" outlasting brass. The thought expressed in all the
arts survives longer than the material element, and the work of the
poets is most widely spread and most easily renewed.

Even as Shelley saw himself in *Adonais* as a spirit of "love in desolation masked," so in the ruins instinct with thought and grandeur
he communed with the harmony of the universe. That, for him, was
the attraction of ruins:

> His wandering step,
> Obedient to high thoughts, has visited
> The awful ruins of the days of old:
>
> . . .
>
> Among the ruined temples there,
> Stupendous columns, and wild images
> Of more than man, where marble daemons watch
> The Zodiac's brazen mystery, and dead men
> Hang their mute thoughts on the mute walls around,
> He lingered, poring on memorials
> Of the world's youth. (*Alastor,* ll. 106–8, 116–21.)

Prometheus Unbound was partly written among the ruins of Rome,
and their influence is felt in many passages.

There was, moreover, a vaguely religious element in Shelley's
"experience" of ruins: "It is because we enter into the meditations, designs and destinies of something beyond ourselves, that the contemplation of the ruins of human power excites an elevating sense of awful-
ness and beauty." [35] That Longinus-like feeling for the sublime, that

[35] "The Coliseum," *Prose,* VI, 304. For the general spirit, see also Madame de
Staël's *Corinne.*

joy in nature and in art, was for Shelley always love. Thus he identified himself with the artists or makers or poets defined for Socrates by Diotima in the *Symposium*—with all "those great minds," ancient sculptors and modern poets, who have forged links in the great chain of poetry which "strips the veil of familiarity from the world, and lays bare the naked and sleeping beauty, which is the spirit of its forms."

IX. KEATS

KEATS, THE ''GREEK''

SHELLEY is reputed to have said that John Keats was a "Greek," though he was the son of a livery-stable keeper.[1] And, indeed, with very little training in the classical languages he surpassed most of his contemporaries in writing on mythological themes and classical antiquities. Byron recognized the fact, writing in *Don Juan* (Canto XI, stanza lx) that

> [Keats] without Greek
> Contrived to talk about the Gods of late
> Much as they might have been supposed to speak.

Landor termed him "the most Grecian of all." Moreover, he found a classical (and Shakespearean) felicity of expression in Keats's poetry; he belonged with the Greek authors: "A few hours in the Poecile with the Tragedians would have made him all he wanted —majestically sedate." [2]

Yet the "Greekness" of Keats has always led to difference of opinion. With Wordsworth's description of the "Hymn to Pan" in *Endymion* as "a very pretty piece of Paganism"—despite the tone of disapproval, an admission that Keats had achieved a definitely Grecian or pagan quality—one balances Lockhart and Wilson's attack on the poet as no Grecian but "a young Cockney rhymester, dreaming a fantastic dream at the full of the moon," and their statement that *Endymion* "has just as much to do with Greece as with 'old Tartary the fierce.'" [3] In answer to the *Quarterly* critics John Hamilton Reyn-

---

[1] Richard Henry Horne, *A New Spirit of the Age* (1844), II, 8.

[2] Quoted by Horne, I, 75.

[3] See the discussions of the reviews of *Endymion*, as in Amy Lowell, *John Keats* (Boston and New York, 1925), I, 346 ff. For the Wordsworthian and "romantic" character of the "Hymn to Pan," see Douglas Bush, *Mythology and the Romantic Tradition in English Poetry*, pp. 101–2, and H. W. Garrod, *Keats* (1926), p. 81. Still, in referring to Wordsworth's influence on the "Hymn," one must not neglect

olds argued that "the genius of Keats is peculiarly classical," an opinion shared by other friends of the poet such as Richard Woodhouse.[4]

Taking his cue from the Romantic poets and critics, Horne continued the lyrical praise of "the pure Greek wine of Keats" among the early Victorians: "Keats . . . saw divine visions, and the pure Greek ideal, because he had the essence in his soul." [5] Lord Houghton felt that the poet had possessed a "natural consanguinity . . . of intellect" with the Greeks.[6] Later in the century Matthew Arnold found the "little town" stanza of the "Ode on a Grecian Urn" bright yet clear, objective, sculptural—"as Greek as a thing from Homer or Theocritus." Basing the Greek element in Keats on similar qualities, Palgrave remarked that the poet had displayed simplicity, "the gift of absolutely direct and, as it were, spontaneous expression of the thought, whether of description or of emotion, before the poet." Keats had been "a true son of Hellas," furthermore, in that he had thought of beauty as "the first word and the last of Art." Yet that worship of beauty, Palgrave added, was Renaissance rather than Hellenic in spirit.[7]

In his well-known edition of the poems of Keats (1905), Ernest de Selincourt, like Horne, described Keats as innately Greek. The poet had delighted in such Hellenic traits as "the expression of truth in forms essentially beautiful, the spontaneous unquestioning delight in the life of nature and its incarnation in forms human but of more than human loveliness"—sympathies which proved "his essential kinship with the thought of Greece." In brief, Keats "has resumed, un-

---

to notice the attraction that "Grecian paganism" had for him. Wordsworth seems to have meant that he regarded Keats as having stressed outward forms and appearances without getting at the inner spirit of Grecian belief; see above, pp. 124 ff.

[4] See Claude L. Finney, *The Evolution of Keats's Poetry* (Cambridge, Mass., 1936), I, 335.

[5] *A New Spirit of the Age,* I, 315; and II, 9.

[6] *The Life and Letters of John Keats* (1848), "Everyman's Library," p. 13. See also pp. 16–17, 22–23. In Keats "was realised the medieval legend of the Venusworshipper, without its melancholy moral."

[7] Arnold, *On the Study of Celtic Literature and On Translating Homer* (1867), p. 165; Palgrave, *The Poetical Works of John Keats,* "Golden Treasury" series (1919 ed.), pp. 267 ff.

consciously, something of the naïveté of the ancient world." Yet, on the heels of such statements, de Selincourt wrote that since Keats was no scholar he "could know nothing . . . of the literature in which the Greek spirit found true expression"; hence, it was "through his kinship with the Elizabethans that he became the poet of ancient Greece." [8] Though neglecting the remarks about the innate Hellenic spirit of Keats, Paul Elmer More approved the judgment of de Selincourt but proceeded to find a "more essential relationship" between Keats and the Elizabethans in "that faculty of vision in his mind which, like theirs, beheld the marriage of the ideas of beauty and death." [9] Amy Lowell developed the suggestions of these two critics into sweeping assertions of an exactly contradictory nature: "Keats never had the slightest knowledge or comprehension of the true Greek spirit," and "Keats is so seldom in the least Greek." [10]

Though many have refused the name of "Greek" to Keats, and though the majority of critics prefer to regard him as a sort of Elizabethan-Grecian, the popularity of the poet, particularly among poets and critics, in the twentieth century has sprung in large measure, I believe, from the feeling that Keats is the most "classical" and presumably the most "Greek" of the English Romantic poets.

Now when Keats is regarded as the most "Greek" of the Romantic poets (some critics extend the remark to include all English poets), the judgment may mean any of a number of things. First of all is the fashion, set by the poet's own friends, of describing him as Greek in appearance. According to Benjamin Bailey, "the form of his head was like that of a fine Greek statue:—and he realized to my mind the youthful Apollo, more than any head of a living man whom I have known." George Felton wrote similarly, "A painter or sculptor might have taken him for a study after the Greek masters." [11] But since various poets of the nineteenth century were likened to antique

---

[8] Pages xliii–lxvi.

[9] *Shelburne Essays*, Series 4 (New York and London, 1906), p. 102.

[10] *John Keats*, I, 346, 483. Miss Lowell (II, 248) corrected Arnold by pointing out that "'this little town' stanza is not so much Greek as Japanese. The Greek presentation is simple, single, clear, but it is not quite this simplicity or clarity."

[11] See Sidney Colvin, *John Keats* (1917), pp. 25, 143, or Finney, *The Evolution of Keats's Poetry*, I, 11.

figures—Byron to the glorious Apollo, Shelley to a Bacchus as well as an Apollo—this particular "Greekness" need not detain the critic of his poetry.

Serious mention of Keats in connection with the Greeks, therefore, refers either to his choice of subjects from Greek mythology, fable, and history, or else to the notion that he looked at the world in the spirit of the Greeks. *Endymion, Hyperion, Lamia,* and the odes reveal his fondness for classical themes; he turned continually and fruitfully to Greece. The idea that Keats possessed a Grecian spirit is more difficult to maintain; still, if a delight in sensory impressions constitutes a "Greek" (as many scholars and critics have argued), then Keats surely merits the label. Few poets have had so keen an interest in beauty apprehended directly by the senses and then passionately and sensuously described. Of course, to class Keats as a "Greek" may encourage unprofitable criticism; nevertheless, there is a definite value in pointing out some of the poet's "Greek" characteristics and affiliations. Though one learns little, if anything, about the Greeks, one gains in understanding of Keats and his poetry.

Keats himself gave both direct and indirect encouragement to this sort of speculation, since, like Landor, he invited comparison with the Greeks in that one of the major endeavors of his poetic career was to grow more Grecian. "To Hellenize is to know," someone has said, and Keats devoted himself in his most serious moments to a study of "the mighty abstract Idea I have of Beauty in all things." Again and again in the letters he expressed a "yearning Passion . . . for the beautiful, connected and made one with the ambition of my intellect." [12] In an earnest spirit, therefore, he studied the masterpieces of art and literature to discipline himself and to build up his store of knowledge. He wanted, in brief, to Grecianize himself: the progress of his mind was to be in the direction of antiquity.

The Grecianizing impulse displayed itself as early as the "Epistle to Clarke" (1816), where Keats thanked the teacher who

> Shew'd me that epic was of all the king,
> Round, vast, and spanning all like Saturn's ring (ll. 66–67).

[12] To George and Georgiana Keats, Oct., 1818 (*The Letters of John Keats,* ed. M. B. Forman [1931], I, 261–62).

Similarly under the influence of the Renaissance idea that the epic was the loftiest form of literature, other poets of the Romantic period attempted to body forth the mighty forms which floated through their dreams, with Landor being most obviously "classical." Keats, too, felt the attraction of epic heroes and their noble actions, and the only crown appropriate to the career which he began to desire for himself was a work of heroic proportions. He wished to be with Shakespeare in the drama and with poets in the epic or grand style like Milton and Homer, Spenser and Dante.

As things turned out, however, Keats had less originality or less force, apparently, than his contemporaries, so that in his various efforts to mold into shape the story of Hyperion, the theme of the poem which was to have been his masterpiece, he fluctuated between a mythological epic of the familiar and classic pattern and a more personal odyssey like *The Excursion*. No Wordsworth, he was not philosophical and rational enough to trace his own intellectual and spiritual development in an extended poem. He was unable either to work out an individual system of mythology of either Shelleyan or Blakeian proportions or to plunge deeply into the history of civilization, especially classical antiquity, in order to endow antique figures with his own characteristics, in the manner of Landor. His uneasiness about his career, training, and craftsmanship and his sensitive recording of experience, which make his letters so exciting for readers today, actually tended to weaken rather than to aid his poetic endeavor. In particular, his inability to sustain for any length of time the grandly epical or Shakespearean or sculptural or Miltonic or classical spirit—as he variously thought of the grand style revealed to him by his towering imagination—intensified his feeling of disappointment. Too often, perhaps, for the good of his poetry Keats heard ancestral voices reminding him that the poet must create on an elevated scale. In his own words, the bard was to be

> a sage;
> A humanist, Physician to all men.
> ("The Fall of Hyperion," Canto I, ll. 189–90.)

Conjecture aside, Greek sculpture was bound to excite a poet dreaming thus of epic shapes and mighty forms. Here he found works of art which had shown their beauty to the world for centuries; here were figures yet alive "in old marbles ever beautiful." To Keats, therefore, the sculpture of the Greeks—and he meant both the Hellenistic works and the Elgin Marbles, though the latter affected him more deeply—was not only a reminder of the classical world and its beautiful forms but also a stimulus to heroic activity on his part. In surveying the nature of Keats's response to the great art of the Greeks and his subsequent use of statuary in his poetry and criticism, one gains considerable insight into the mind and achievement of the poet.

KEATS AND THE ELGIN MARBLES

The growth of Keats's interest in Greek sculpture presents an engaging story. He was introduced to the arts, as the majority of English poets have been, through prints in his schoolbooks. In the library of the school of the Reverend John Clarke at Enfield, Spence's *Polymetis,* Tooke's *Pantheon,* and Lemprière's *Classical Dictionary* fell into appreciative hands. The Lemprière volume was the favorite, but traces of study in all three were to appear in the poetry.[13]

Like other poets of the Romantic period, Keats was first acquainted with the Hellenistic and Greco-Roman works familiar to the gentlemen of the eighteenth century, since he began to write before the Elgin Marbles were widely known. Therefore his earliest references to Grecian statuary were to the famous figures. The first evidence of his interest in classical art appeared in the description of Cynthia's bridal night in "I Stood Tip-Toe upon a Little Hill" (1816):

> The evening weather was so bright, and clear,
> That men of health were of unusual cheer;
> Stepping like Homer at the trumpet's call,

[13] On the basis of Charles Cowden Clarke's statement (*Recollections of Writers* [1878], p. 124) that Keats "appeared to learn" the *Classical Dictionary,* the emphasis has usually fallen upon that work. Recent critics, however, have tended to stress the influence of the *Polymetis,* to which Keats was clearly indebted for many images. See Maurice R. Ridley, *Keats' Craftsmanship* (1933), pp. 60–61, 299.

> Or young Apollo on the pedestal:
> And lovely women were as fair and warm,
> As Venus looking sideways in alarm (ll. 215-20).[14]

Keats was thinking of the Apollo Belvedere and the Venus de Medici pictured in Spence and Lemprière. The statues may have been more immediately in his mind as he remembered them in Hunt's cottage in the Vale of Health, the "poet's house" described at more length in *Sleep and Poetry* (1817). In that "poetic corner," Hunt told readers of his poetry, stood the Venus and perhaps an Apollo and a Mercury.

In a similar spirit, though with even less suggestion of a sculptural quality, were "The Lines on a Leander Gem Which Miss Reynolds, My Kind Friend, Gave Me" (written in 1816?). Since Keats always discovered life in the works of art which drew his attention, he portrayed the drama on the gem:

> Nigh swooning, he doth purse his weary lips
> For Hero's cheek, and smiles against her smile.
> O horrid dream! see how his body dips
>   Dead-heavy; arms and shoulders gleam awhile:
> He's gone: up bubbles all his amorous breath! [15]
>   (Lines 10-14.)

Notwithstanding this acquaintance of a sort with the Antique, Keats could have said with more honesty than Hazlitt that he had known almost nothing of the art of sculpture until he saw the Elgin Marbles. Through Haydon's efforts both critic and poet had their attention directed away from the Greco-Roman works to the Parthenon sculptures. Fortunately for Keats, he met those great works of art at the time of his first real awakening, between October, 1816, and April, 1817. Introduced by Hunt into the literary and artistic groups of London, the young poet became the friend of Hazlitt and Haydon, both of whom had recently been engaged in the defense of the Elgin Marbles. His admiration of Haydon in particular had al-

[14] See Bush, *Mythology and the Romantic Tradition in English Poetry*, p. 86, and H. W. Garrod, "Three Passages of Keats," *TLS*, March 5, 1925, p. 156.

[15] See also Finney, *The Evolution of Keats's Poetry*, I, 192, for Woodhouse's remark, "I believe it was once Keats's intention to write a series of *M.S.* sonnets and short poems on some of Tassie's gems." See below, pp. 265-66.

ready been celebrated in the "Sonnets Addressed to Haydon" ("High-mindedness, a Jealousy for Good" and "Great Spirits Now on Earth Are Sojourning") when in March, 1817, Haydon took Keats to behold the Marbles. Under the tutelage of the painter and, perhaps, of Severn and Hazlitt also, Keats immediately began to study the beauty of the figures from the Parthenon, and he soon sent two son-nets to his chief mentor.

The "Haydon" sonnets were not his finest sonnets, nor were they the best examples of his interest in the Antique. For one thing, they dealt very little with the actual works of art, since his intention did not permit in either case much description of the sculptures. The one stressed the feelings of the poet himself, and the other developed into a paean of praise of Haydon rather than the art. Of the two, the more personal sonnet was both more poetical and more successful as a response to the works of art.

On Seeing the Elgin Marbles

My spirit is too weak—mortality
    Weighs heavily on me like unwilling sleep,
    And each imagin'd pinnacle and steep
Of godlike hardship tells me I must die
Like a sick Eagle looking at the sky.
    Yet 'tis a gentle luxury to weep
    That I have not the cloudy winds to keep
Fresh for the opening of the morning's eye.
Such dim-conceived glories of the brain
    Bring round the heart an undescribable feud;
So do these wonders a most dizzy pain,
    That mingles Grecian grandeur with the rude
Wasting of old Time—with a billowy main—
    A sun—a shadow of a magnitude.

In this sonnet the rush of ideas and the rapid shifting from image to image give an impression of confusion; the thought is of a loose yet rich texture as in *Sleep and Poetry* and *Endymion*. Indeed, the sonnet seems to give the reader what was actually in the poet's mind; it is almost as though Keats had not known where the poem would end when he began. But for this very reason the sonnet represents the

crowding of images and thoughts Keats derived from actual sight of
the sculptures. The leading idea is not stated directly, for the main
thought is obscured by the sensations in his mind. The Marbles stir
his own hopes of becoming a great artist and torment him with
doubts whether he can match or rival their perfection. They remind
him that he is mortal, while the hardships he must endure in order to
scale the heights he sets for himself demand godlike or immortal qualities. His spirit, alas, may be too weak. And yet, as always with Keats,
the sensations are themselves a kind of pleasure—as Wordsworth
wrote in *The Excursion* (Book IV, l. 475), "there is a luxury in self-
dispraise"—and he enjoys the pain and dizzy whirl of thoughts
aroused by the new masterpieces he beholds. An ambitious young
poet, he is overpowered and sickened by the supreme examples of
the working of the artist's power, the power to which he has dedicated his own energies. He is a sick eagle looking at the Cliff of Poesy
towering above him, the heights he may never reach. Even as his mis-
givings about his poetical career bring on the feud in his mind, so
now the Elgin Marbles produce similar sensations; and another flow
of images almost drowns his thought in the sonnet. The sculpture
still enduring despite the ravages of old Time taunts the mortal poet.
The marble figures are akin to the constantly brilliant sun, whereas
mortal men and things are but waves which soon lose their identity in
the billowy ocean of time. Even the statuary is but a shadow or a small
part of the original magnitude of the beauty manifest in the Parthenon at Athens, as the sun itself is but a faint reflection or representation of a vaster power. In the presence of Grecian statues, magnificent
though in ruin, Keats can but tremble at what may happen to his own
perishable attempts to win glory.[16]

The other sonnet retains suggestions of the eagle motif, but Keats
is not so much sick as certain that he lacks the ability to thank Haydon
properly for having shown the Elgin Marbles to him.

---

[16] Severn's comments on Keats as reported by William Sharp in *The Life and
Letters of Joseph Severn* (1892), p. 32, offer some light on the "Haydon" sonnets.
"He went again and again to see the Elgin Marbles, and would sit for an hour or
more at a time beside them rapt in revery. On one such occasion Severn came upon
the young poet, with eyes shining so brightly and face so lit up by some visionary
rapture, that he stole quietly away without intrusion." See also pp. 28–29.

HERCULES, COMMONLY CALLED THE TORSO BELVEDERE

THESEUS, FROM PEDIMENT OF THE PARTHENON

To B. R. Haydon, with the Foregoing Sonnet on the Elgin Marbles

> Haydon! forgive me that I cannot speak
>   Definitively on these mighty things;
>   Forgive me that I have not Eagle's wings—
> That what I want I know not where to seek:
> And think that I would not be over meek
>   In rolling out upfollow'd thunderings,
>   Even to the steep of Heliconian springs,
> Were I of ample strength for such a freak—
> Think too, that all those numbers should be thine;
>   Who else? In this who touch thy vesture's hem?
> For when men star'd at what was most divine
>   With browless idiotism—o'erwise phlegm—
> Thou hadst beheld the Hesperean shine
>   Of their star in the East, and gone to worship them.

If he could, young Keats would roll poetic thunder up Mount Helicon (as he tagged along behind), all that Haydon might be well honored. To him alone belonged the praise; for when connoisseurs with "browless idiotism" and "o'erwise phlegm"—and these phrases were direct attacks on Knight—had questioned the merit of the Elgin Marbles, Haydon had long since recognized their merit and paid devout homage to the divine and mighty things. In knowledge of art Keats was hardly worthy to touch the hem of Haydon's garment.[17]

Keats was too overwhelmed, then, by the first sight of the Elgin Marbles to be able to write good poetry about his experience; he was greatly excited by beholding the definite evidence that other human

[17] Haydon's "Essay on the Judgment of Connoisseurs Being Preferred to That of Professional Men" (See *Autobiography and Memoirs*, I, 233 ff.) was in Keats's mind in this sonnet. "Browless [or "brainless"] idiotism" and "o'erwise phlegm" were direct attacks on detractors of the Marbles like Knight, who had criticized them in *Specimens of Antient Sculpture*. Keats turned against the connoisseurs the terms they had applied to Haydon. Once the sculptures were bought by the nation, Haydon exulted, "What became now of all the sneers at my senseless insanity about the Marbles?" In "Highmindedness, a Jealousy for Good," Keats praised Haydon as "a stout unbending champion" who "awes Envy, and Malice to their native sty." The language of the last two lines (which disturbs many readers) was inspired by Haydon. For the painter had referred to the Marbles as "divine things," had sworn never to "enter among them without bowing to the Great Spirit that reigns in them," and had stated that "pilgrims from the remotest corners of the earth will visit their shrine." Even the idea of the "thunderings" was in Haydon's essay. (See I, 237.)

beings had given enduring life to portions of their world. The Marbles were for him "truth," but a "truth" that overpowered him, not only because the statues were grandly beautiful in themselves, but also because they revealed how the imagination of Grecian artists had impressed itself so completely and effectively upon the material of their art that the figures thus created have seldom failed to enrapture beholders.

Keats now took his place in the front rank of poets who have drawn inspiration from the beauty made concrete in statues. Like the other "romantic" poets, he was clearly interested in the expressiveness of the ancient masterpieces. Though intoxicated by the beauty of their forms, he made no attempt in the "Haydon" sonnets to describe the statues and reliefs, and he entirely neglected technique in order to relate his sensations in the presence of the Elgin Marbles, or, in other words, his "soul-adventures." He was no Winckelmann, no Haydon, no Academic poet, trying to arrive at the principles by which he imagined the artists had achieved their striking effects; nor was he concerned with the details of the process of art. Besides, in poems presented to the sponsor of the Elgin Marbles he did not need to talk about the beauty of their form, had he been so presumptuous as to attempt it. As a young friend of "glorious" Haydon, but recently introduced to sculpture and lacking the apparatus of artists and critics, how could he speak definitively of the statues? It was enough for the young eagle to speak of those mighty things at all. He was merely a sensitive young man gratefully informing his artist-friend of the way in which the statues had moved him to ecstasy. "What the Imagination seizes as Beauty must be truth."

GREEK SCULPTURE IN *ENDYMION* AND *HYPERION*

The immediate effect of Keats's introduction to the Elgin Marbles was seen in *Endymion,* written during 1817 though not published until the following year, where references to the fine arts assumed the prominent place they enjoyed in all the later and greater works.

Though there were signs of his recent study of the Elgin Marbles, he referred as often to the Hellenistic and Greco-Roman works.

Directly after the splendid "Hymn to Pan" in *Endymion,* one of his finest lyrics, Keats described the dance of the young Greeks thus:

> those fair living forms swam heavenly
> To tunes forgotten—out of memory:
> Fair creatures! whose young children's children bred
> Thermopylae its heroes—not yet dead,
> But in old marbles ever beautiful. (Book I, ll. 315-19.)

The mere thought of Greek youth sent his mind rushing to the Parthenon sculptures which he had been studying, so that he saw the dancers in the shapes given by the ancient sculptors.

In the recreations, somewhat in the manner of the *Aeneid* or *Paradise Lost,* the archers made Keats think of Niobe, with the language indicating that he may have had the statue in mind in the following image:

> the trembling knee
> And frantic gape of lonely Niobe,
> Poor, lonely Niobe! when her lovely young
> Were dead and gone, and her caressing tongue
> Lay a lost thing upon her paly lip,
> And very, very deadliness did nip
> Her motherly cheeks. (*Endymion,* Book I, ll. 337-43.)

The scene was dramatic rather than sculptural—or, rather, sculpture dramatized—with the language more self-conscious than in later descriptions of statues. Still, the original posturing and the appearance of Niobe—"the trembling knee and frantic gape"—were sculptural. Moreover, Keats was following poets as different as Pope and Hunt in endowing such a figure with life. One discovers, too, that he presented all his sculptural figures as though they possessed lives of their own.

Sculpture also appeared in the "mimic temple" in the marble gallery found by Endymion in the "sparry hollows of the world." In this Lorrainesque shrine, reminiscent of Hunt's descriptions of similar buildings, there stood

on light tiptoe divine,
A quiver'd Dian. (Book II, ll. 261–62.)

Keats expected the reader to visualize the pillared aisles and the "niches old" with lovely figures of Grecian statuary.

The sleeping Adonis, revealed to Endymion as he followed his quest through the world, was an approximation to an Antinous or a Hermaphrodite—

> And coverlids . . .
> Fell sleek about him in a thousand folds—
> Not hiding up an Apollonian curve
> Of neck and shoulder, nor the tenting swerve
> Of knee from knee, nor ankles pointing light;
> But rather, giving them to the filled sight
> Officiously. Sideway his face repos'd
> On one white arm, and tenderly unclos'd,
> By tenderest pressure, a faint damask mouth
> To slumbery pout. (Book II, ll. 396, 398–406.)

" 'Tis might half slumb'ring on its own right arm" (*Sleep and Poetry,* l. 237) achieves a similar impression of sculpture.

Of the many suggestions of sculptural and architectural objects in *Endymion,* such as friezes, temples, and columns, only the vases need be singled out. Like Landor, Keats was always interested in urns, vases, embossed shields, and armor. In the marvelous treasury heaped on the shore Endymion found a "gold vase emboss'd with long-forgotten story" (Book III, ll. 126–27).[18] Keats first mentioned non-classical sculpture in this passage, and he continued to be eclectic in his taste in the arts as in many other matters. The

> sculptures rude
> In ponderous stone, developing the mood
> Of ancient Nox (ll. 131–33)

were presumably Egyptian, though they might also have been ancient Celtic or Druid monolithic figures.[19]

[18] Colvin showed (*John Keats,* p. 239) that Shelley imitated this passage in *Prometheus Unbound.* Landor may have remembered these lines in the *Hellenics;* see below, pp. 239–40.

[19] Keats owned (Colvin, *John Keats,* p. 557) a copy of Edward Davies, *Celtic Researches; on the Origin, Traditions & Language, of the Ancient Britons* (1804).

Even finer than these passages in *Endymion* was the sculptural posing or "stationing" which Keats employed in *Hyperion* and "The
Fall of Hyperion." The opening lines of *Hyperion,* in particular,
showed his ability to write "sculpture" more effectively than any
preceding English poet. Here, as in the "Ode on a Grecian Urn," the
poet created the effects of sculpture remarkably well. Though he
built his own figures without reference to specific statues, he certainly derived them from the Elgin Marbles. Saturn, nobly statuesque
in Olympian repose, was very much like the Elgin Theseus:

> Deep in the shady sadness of a vale
> Far sunken from the healthy breath of morn,
> Far from the fiery noon, and eve's one star,
> Sat gray-hair'd Saturn, quiet as a stone,
>
> . . .
>
> Upon the sodden ground
> His old right hand lay nerveless, listless, dead,
> Unsceptred; and his realmless eyes were closed;
> While his bow'd head seem'd list'ning to the Earth,
> His ancient mother, for some comfort yet. (Book I, ll. 1–4, 17–21.)

The goddess Thea, wed to Hyperion yet attempting to console
Saturn, suggested the so-called "Iris" of the Parthenon group. Sculpture, Egyptian as well as Grecian, contributed to Keats's conception
of this figure:

> She was a Goddess of the infant world;
>
> . . .
>
> Her face was large as that of Memphian sphinx,
> Pedestal'd haply in a palace court,
> When sages look'd to Egypt for their lore.[20]
> (*Hyperion*, Book I, ll. 26, 31–33.)

The pose of Thea was sculptural: one hand on her heart and the other
on Saturn's bended neck. She spoke sadly and then assumed another
similar posture, kneeling to spread her hair as a mat for the feet
of the god. Pausing to point the group, Keats commented,

Blake also possessed this work and showed considerable interest in the relationship
between the classical peoples and the ancient Britons, which Davies discussed.

[20] See Helen Darbishire, "Keats and Egypt," *RES*, III (1927), 1–11.

> Like natural sculpture in cathedral cavern;
> The frozen God still couchant on the earth
> And the sad Goddess weeping at his feet.
>   (*Hyperion,* Book I, ll. 86–89.)

Here, as in all his descriptions of pictures and statues, Keats gave life to the objects and persons presented. He never thought of sculptured figures as lifeless, and he was always interested in showing the emotions that had given rise to their external appearances. In both these respects he was in accord with the principles of "romantic" aesthetics which were concerned with relating the outer form to the spirit within. For Keats, too, wanted to explore

> all forms and substances
> Straight homeward to their symbol-essences.

The figures of his grandly dramatic epic had been created

> divine
> In sad demeanour, solemn, undisturb'd,
> Unruffled (Book I, ll. 329–31),

but the disintegration brought by the growth of the passions had destroyed their control of the world. Since they no longer lived and ruled "like high Gods," Hyperion now dominated the councils of the gods. Though destined to be supplanted by the true Apollo, Hyperion appeared in the guise of the sun-god of ancient statuary and poetry:

> Golden his hair of short Numidian curl,
> Regal his shape majestic. (Book II, ll. 371–72.)

The gods clustered about him in groups suggesting those of the Parthenon. The spirit of the Miltonic statuesque presided over these lines in the "naked and grecian manner." [21]

For the supernatural size of Hyperion, Keats turned again to Egyptian sculpture, referring this time to the well-known figure of Memnon, since the legend of the harp of Memnon sounding at break of day was a fitting symbol for the coming of Hyperion. Egyptian statuary was not for Keats the "barbarous" and "Gothic" monstrosity

---

[21] See above, pp. 60 ff., and below, pp. 230–31.

of superstition it had been to many eighteenth-century poets; instead, the darkness and mystery and ponderousness of its forms delighted him because they aroused visions of mighty romances long ago. Therefore he used Egyptian works when he pleased, and *Hyperion* reflected the complex and eclectic taste of the Romantic poets. The mingling of Greek and Egyptian did not offend his contemporaries, and one of his friends, Woodhouse, praised the "colossal" and "classical" qualities of *Hyperion* by remarking, "It is that in poetry which the Elgin and Egyptian marbles are in sculpture." [22]

Yet in contrast to the vaguely Oriental suggestiveness of the Memnon and the Sphinx, or "pyramids of glowing gold," or "bronzed obelisks," which have the quality of references drawn from literary sources, the descriptions of classical figures were more precise because the sight and study of antique representations of gods and heroes aided his imagination. A more significant difference between the Egyptian and the Greek in the poetry of Keats was that he based the human passions and actions of his sculptural figures on the statuary of Greece; their humanity and, hence, their richest expressive value was classical rather than Egyptian. In Book III of *Hyperion* (ll. 50 ff.) Apollo came with all the Belvedere figure's "immortal fairness." Mnemosyne of "antique mien and robed form" stood before an Apollo, who wondered at her beauty very much as Keats himself gazed at the figures of a frieze or an urn. With "ample skirts" in sculptural folds, she was a caryatid eternally calm in eyes and face.

Sculpture was even more conspicuous in "The Fall of Hyperion." Even though the revised work was fragmentary and the effects tentative, "The Fall of Hyperion" was more restrained and more carefully carved; for Keats tried even more than in *Hyperion* to achieve "a

<hr />

[22] Quoted by Helen Darbishire, "Keats and Egypt," p. 3. See also Bush, *Mythology and the Romantic Tradition in English Poetry*, pp. 116–17, and Ridley, *Keats' Craftsmanship*, pp. 64–65, 299–300. Bush's statement (p. 117) that in *Hyperion* "the results of Keats's familiarity with the Elgin Marbles are none the less important *for not being precisely demonstrable*" [italics added] is of questionable value; moreover, there is no reason to doubt Keats's debt to Egyptian statuary. He rightly points out the Oriental and Celtic elements that are mingled with the Greek and Egyptian in *Hyperion;* for the poem shows a characteristically "romantic" mixture of the sort found also in Blake or Southey or Peacock.

more naked and grecian manner." [23] That Grecian manner meant that the grandeur and epic scope of Keats's intended work required a Grecian precision and simplicity in the details. Sculptural imagery was in order, therefore, and the inspiration came largely from the Elgin Marbles. In Keats's mind may have been an account of the Grecian workmanship, such as that by Canova, to whom Severn, his companion on the ill-fated journey to Italy, carried a letter of introduction. Canova remarked,

I admire in them [the Elgin Marbles] the truth of nature combined with the choice of beautiful forms; everything about them breathes animation, with a singular truth of expression, and with a degree of skill which is the more exquisite, as it is without the least affectation of the pomp of art, which is concealed with admirable address. The naked figures are real flesh, in its native beauty.[24]

The poet might have subscribed to this view of the "naked and grecian manner" of sculpture as comparable to the works of the ancient epic poets.

In place of the direct action of the earlier version, Keats wrote a vision in which the mysteries of Hyperion were revealed to a poet who, like Keats himself, was peculiarly sensitive to beautiful objects. To introduce the vision, the poet drank of a marvelous potion:

> The cloudy swoon came on, and down I sunk
> Like a Silenus on an antique vase. (Canto I, ll. 55–56.)

Awakening in a pantheon-like temple, he perceived a carved image "huge of feature as a cloud," explained by the attendant Moneta,

> 'this old Image here,
> Whose carved features wrinkled as he fell,
> Is Saturn's' (ll. 224–26).

[23] Letter to B. R. Haydon, Jan. 23, 1818 (*Letters*, I, 88). See also Haydon's *Autobiography*, I, 235 ff. Keats was close to the official judgment of the Elgin Marbles given in the *Report from the Select Committee of the House of Commons on the Earl of Elgin's Collection of Sculptured Marbles* (1816): "It is surprising to observe in the best of these Marbles in how great a degree the *close imitation of Nature* is combined with *grandeur of style,* while the exact detail of the former, in no degree detracts from the effect and predominance of the latter" (p. 9).

[24] See *A Letter from the Chevalier Antonio Canova; and Two Memoirs Read to the Royal Institute of France on the Sculptures in the Collection of the Earl of Elgin; by the Chevalier E. Q. Visconti* (1816), pp. xxi–xxii.

Then a second shape appeared in the vision,

> an Image huge,
> Like to the Image pedestal'd so high
> In Saturn's Temple (ll. 298–300).

That Keats associated this figure with the Theseus-like Saturn of *Hyperion* was evident in Moneta's remark,

> 'So Saturn sat
> When he had lost his realms' (ll. 301–2),

followed by several lines unchanged from the earlier poem.

As a matter of fact, Keats presented this section of "The Fall" as a scene of "living" sculpture. In the dream he beheld a bas-relief showing Thea and Saturn, interpreting the activity and expression of the pair thus:

> The Goddess in fair statuary
> Surpassing wan Moneta by the head,
> And in her sorrow nearer woman's tears.
> There was a listening fear in her regard,
> As if calamity had but begun. (Canto I, ll. 336–40.)

Their attitudes were sculptural,

> Long, long, those two were postured motionless,
> Like sculpture builded up upon the grave
> Of their own power (ll. 382–84).

In short, the whole group was like an arrangement of the Elgin Marbles:

> still they were the same;
> The frozen God still bending to the Earth,
> And the sad Goddess weeping at his feet.
> Moneta silent (ll. 385–88).

Clearly, the "stationing" of figures in this manner was the finest illustration of Keats's successful use of Grecian sculpture in *Endymion* and the two versions of *Hyperion*.

SCULPTURE AND THE ODES

Without doubt the most famous as well as the best poem by an Englishman either upon a specific object of Greek sculpture or upon the history, theory, or morality associated with the art is the "Ode on a Grecian Urn" (1819). The ode is especially interesting for including both description of sculpture and theorizing about the art. No finer summary of the characteristic ideas of Keats concerning the fine arts can be found.

As in the case of many of Keats's references to the sculpture of the Ancients, one cannot be sure of the precise works of art he had in mind when he wrote. The "Ode on a Grecian Urn" has been read and studied for several generations; despite the painstaking investigation of numerous scholars, however, no definite urn or statue or vase has been found as the one source of Keats. Among the works of art on which the poet may have drawn are the following: vases seen at the British Museum, especially the Townley Vase with its bacchic dancing, including the lover "winning near the goal"; vases seen in books of engravings, such as the Musée Napoléon volumes with the "leaf-fring'd" Sosibios Vase, of which Keats himself made a tracing, or Piranesi's *Vasi e candelabri,* which showed the Borghese Vase with a bacchic dance, a piper, and a leafy fringe and the Holland House Vase showing a sacrifice; the Elgin Marbles, particularly the frieze showing the lowing heifer; paintings like Claude Lorrain's "Sacrifice to Apollo" or Raphael's "Sacrifice at Lystra." In poetry Homer's description of Achilles' shield (*Iliad,* Book XVIII), and the mazer-poems of Theocritus may also have contributed to the richness of the ode.[25]

To this impressive list of possible indebtedness one may add another non-sculptural source. Very similar to the decoration of the urn of Keats were the lines in Leigh Hunt's *The Story of Rimini* depicting a sacrifice in Poussin's "Polyphemus." While the animals in Hunt's poem were goats, the idea was very close to Keats, with several

[25] The classic discussions of the works of art represented in the ode are: Colvin, *John Keats,* 416 ff., de Selincourt, *Poems,* pp. 476 ff., and Paul Wolters, *Archiv fur des Studien der neurer Sprachen,* CXX (1908), 53–61. For a convenient summary, see Finney, *The Evolution of Keats's Poetry,* II, 639 ff. The Raphael painting was suggested by J. R. Macgillivray (*TLS,* July 9, 1938, pp. 465–66). In "More Concerning Chapman's Homer and Keats," (*PMLA,* XLII [1927], 1007–9), Grace W. Landrum concluded that, in respect to the "Ode on a Grecian Urn," "we must admit the Homeric passages could only have furnished the soil for the rich planting of other seeds of inspiration."

scenes of the woodland sacrifice and the groups of dancing figures, mainly nymphs. The spirit of *The Story of Rimini,* to which Keats was variously indebted, was similar to that of the second and third stanzas.[26] The lovers in stanza ii of the "Ode" seem likewise to have been partly suggested by Paolo and Francesca, not as Dante saw them but as Keats imagined them,

> For ever warm and still to be enjoy'd,
> For ever panting, and for ever young;
> All breathing human passion far above.

Less than a month before the "Ode on a Grecian Urn" he had identified, in a dream, his love for Fanny Brawne with the events of the fifth canto of Dante, "where . . . lovers need not tell their sorrows." A letter to his brother and sister-in-law (February 14, 1819) described the delights of the dream more fully, "I floated about the whirling atmosphere as it is described with a beautiful figure to whose lips mine were joined, at [as] it seemed for an age—and in the midst of all this cold and darkness I was warm—even flowery tree tops sprung up."[27] Very likely the events in Rimini and his own dream mingled in his mind with the figures he had seen on vases when he placed the lovers on the Grecian urn of his imagination, remembering too the sacrifice in *The Story of Rimini.*

Whatever the sculptured objects, paintings, and poetry which gave rise to the "Ode," Keats modeled a sculpturesque masterpiece of his own. If he took liberties with the Antique in carving a town and in mingling a bacchanal with a religious rite, he was working in the manner of the poet, selecting from his knowledge of ancient art the elements he wished for his literary and imaginary "sculpture." Writing on a congenial subject and trying to be antique in spirit, Keats wrote in his most sculptural style. The theme of the poem—that a thing of beauty is the expression of an enduring truth—was itself indicative of the influence Greek sculpture was exerting upon him. The "Ode" embodied, moreover, all his favorite ideas about sculpture, especially the naturalness and the expressiveness of the Elgin

---

[26] See *The Story of Rimini,* Book III, ll. 456–72, quoted below, pp. 253–54.
[27] See also "On a Dream," ll. 10–11.

Marbles. Behind it lay theories which he had learned from Haydon and Hazlitt and from poets, possibly Homer and Theocritus more than any others.

To Keats sculpture was above all an art expressing pathos and emotion and action. The figures on the imaginary Grecian urn were not static but teeming with life; they were expressive symbols showing the feelings within the bodies represented on the surface. Men or gods in "mad" pursuit of "loth" maidens—youths playing pipes and timbrels—the wild ecstasy of the struggle to capture or escape: they will hardly lie still on the urn. The young man will never cease his piping beneath the trees perpetually leafy with "happy, happy boughs"; the lover will never reach his goal but will retain the loved one in his arms, forever on the point of being kissed. The sacrificial procession (possibly the finest portion of the "Ode") is in motion: the priest leads the "lowing" heifer along the silent streets of some seaside or river town. The urn is alive with actual events from the lives of human and divine beings.

Cold and quiet was the actual urn, to be sure, but the passions of the figures on it were anything but cold. The gods and men on the urn enjoyed life forever in their marble "fairness"; in fact, theirs was a finer existence than that of ordinary beings, since they were not subject to the anguish and torture which annoy mortal creatures. Theirs was an everlasting passionless passion, if one can conceive of such a state of being. In other words, they lived in the condition to which Keats, puzzled by his own passions and tormented by sickness and sorrow, sought vainly to attain: they were steadfast in their actions, enjoying an unending and perennially painless emotional activity.

Because of that fair and lasting beauty the urn displayed to Keats the truth or essential beauty manifest in all supremely beautiful objects. Carried away by the thought of the centuries through which the urn had survived; thinking how fervidly he yearned to create a masterpiece embodying a beauty that should be eternally true and moving like the sculptures of the Greek masters; and in a spirit comparable to that in the sonnet "On Seeing the Elgin Marbles," Keats exclaimed that the message spoken by the urn with its "cold pastoral" scenes and figures was sufficient justification for its existence and a guarantee that it would continue to move men with its beauty long after the poet and his own generation were dead.

Obviously such sculpture as the Grecian urn, Keats felt, had made permanently beautiful the pulsing actions of real men and gods: the urn immortalized the actions and emotions of Grecian people and divinities, presenting the tale more directly, more sensuously, more immediately than Keats in his rhyme. Not only had the sculptor worked "more sweetly" than the poet, but he had also enjoyed the second advantage of using a material that resists the decaying forces of time. Though an object made by human hands, the urn had been adopted by "silence" and "slow time," which were preserving the beautiful moments of the dance and the sacrifice, seemingly forever.

How Keats envied the figures on the Grecian urn. Long after his burning forehead and parching tongue had been cooled, they would continue to inspire poets. All they knew—indeed, all they needed to know—on earth was that "Beauty is Truth, Truth Beauty"! Far different was the fate of the author of the "Ode on a Grecian Urn": the sick eagle knew that he was born for death. Though the urn had given him glimpses of a beauty which was also everlasting truth, he knew that the beauty he had experienced on earth was destined to die.[28]

In a second poem inspired by Greek sculpture, the "Ode on Indolence," likewise written in May, 1819, one finds perhaps the clearest commentary on the way in which Keats imagined the scenes in the "Ode on a Grecian Urn." Three figures appeared before him on a marble urn, Love, Poetry, and Ambition:

> One morn before me were three figures seen,
>   With bowed necks, and joined hands, side-faced;
> And one behind the other stepp'd serene,
>   In placid sandals, and in white robes graced;
> They pass'd, like figures on a marble urn,
>   When shifted round to see the other side;

[28] For a similar interpretation of the much-discussed last lines of the "Ode," see G. St. Quintin, "The Grecian Urn," *TLS*, Feb. 5, 1938, p. 92.

They came again; as when the urn once more
Is shifted round, the first seen shades return;
    And they were strange to me, as may betide
    With vases, to one deep in Phidian lore. (Stanza i, ll. 1–10.)

The ode was a kind of record of a puzzling yet pleasant daydream which he described to his brother and sister-in-law in a letter written on the day it occurred, March 19. "Neither Poetry, nor Ambition, nor Love have any alertness of countenance as they pass me: they seem rather like three figures on a greek vase—a Man and two women whom no one but myself could distinguish in their disguisement."

That Keats was recalling an engraving appears more clearly in the letter than in the ode. Apparently he had in mind a vase seen in Piranesi's *Vasi e candelabri,* very likely the one described thus by Colvin: "Draped figures of women, Seasons, it may be, or priestesses, walk with join'd hands behind a solemn Bacchus, or priest in the god's guise." [29] Keats tried to give the impression that he was puzzled by the figures on vases, since he thought of himself as one "deep in Phidian lore"; still, they suggest the Parthenon frieze as well as urns and vases. Moreover, they are not altogether unlike the three figures in both *Hyperion* and "The Fall of Hyperion."

Very much as Blake used classical figures to symbolize his own conflicts, and as Byron, Landor, Shelley, and Hunt at times identified themselves with ancient figures, so Keats in the "Ode on Indolence" read personal problems, thoughts, and feelings into the sculpture. Again he saw the mighty forms that came to him, the "huge cloudy symbols of a high romance" which appeared either in the dreams of sleep or in indolence. These dim-conceived glories coming in sculptural shapes were the equivalent of the outlines seen by Blake: they were the noble forms each poet wanted to put into an epic. Again the figures on the vase had a personal significance, turning to him and arousing his burning desire to follow them. Keats himself was the man on the vase in the letter, Ambition leading the muse and the loved one. He identified himself also with the Ambition of the "Ode on Indolence,"

[29] *John Keats,* p. 414.

> pale of cheek
> And ever watchful with fatigued eye,

marching between the "fair Maid" named Love and the other maiden
whom he loved the more, his "demon poesy." In fact, Keats saw on
the vase the tantalizing triangle of his personal problems: an ambitious
poet torn between a life of sensation and a life of thought. The dream,
however, was more pleasant than the reality, and the moment he
caught the living quality of the figures, he wished for calm and quiet,
begging them to

> be once more
> In masque-like figures on the dreamy urn.

The poet marveled at the beautiful shapes of the dreamlike pageantry
sculptured on ancient vases and urns; for they enjoyed the beauty
of form and the enduring peace which he wanted for himself and
his creations. Moreover, he envied the artists who had worked in stone,
since he could never quite convince himself that he had written in
anything but water.[30]

SCULPTURE IN *LAMIA* AND IN THE CRITICISM

After the splendid use of works of ancient art in *Endymion, Hyperion,* and the odes, the reader expects Keats to load *Lamia* (1819)
with similar classical ore, but the inspiration of sculpture, though
present, is less conspicuous. Only one image came from a specific
statue, and that was a work of Greco-Roman rather than fifth-century
art, a reversion to the Hellenistic strange in a poet who had proclaimed
himself "one deep in Phidian lore." Be that as it may, to describe
the features of the handsome Lycius as he reveled in the sorrows of
Lamia, Keats thought once more of the Apollo Belvedere he had seen

[30] For further consideration of this interpretation of the "Ode on Indolence" figures,
see the sonnet "Why Did I Laugh To-Night?" written at the time of the letter of
March 19. See also Finney, *The Evolution of Keats's Poetry,* II, 647–48, Lowell, *John
Keats,* II, 258, Clarence D. Thorpe, *The Mind of John Keats* (1926), pp. 64 ff., and
the letter to Benjamin Bailey, November 22, 1817 (*Letters,* I, 72 ff.). Colvin (p. 414)
thought the three figures were women, but the Ambition in the poem may have been
a man as in the dream.

in *Polymetis* and in the cottage of Hunt, presenting the figure with characteristic aptness of phrasing:

> Fine was the mitigated fury, like
> Apollo's presence when in act to strike
> The serpent. (Part II, ll. 78–80.)

Lamia was noteworthy, however, for the many suggestions of architectural and sculptural effects of the sort one usually thinks of as Landorian. The night scenes in Corinth,

> while many a light
> Flared, here and there, from wealthy festivals,
> And threw their moving shadows on the walls,
> Or found them cluster'd in the corniced shade
> Of some arch'd temple door, or dusky colonnade.
> (Part I, ll. 357–61.)

and Lamia's dreams were in the spirit of Tamar's vision of the Mediterranean lands in *Gebir* as well as Landor's accounts of Corinth. Again, there was a suggestion of sculpture in

> the young Corinthian Lycius
> Charioting foremost in the envious race,
> Like a young Jove with calm uneager face. (Part I, ll. 216–18.)

Even finer was the passage where Keats expressed the color and tactile sensations of marble in a fashion to delight the sculptor:

> A pillar'd porch, with lofty portal door,
> Where hung a silver lamp, whose phosphor glow
> Reflected in the slabbed steps below,
> Mild as a star in water; for so new,
> And so unsullied was the marble hue,
> So through the crystal polish, liquid fine,
> Ran the dark veins, that none but feet divine
> Could e'er have touch'd there. (Part I, ll. 379–86.)

Something of the same feeling appeared also at the banquet where sculpture was incidental,

> loaded with a feast the tables stood,
> Each shrining in the midst the image of a God.[31]
> (Part II, ll. 189–90.)

[31] Douglas Bush has shown (*Mythology and the Romantic Tradition in English Poetry*, pp. 113–15, and "Notes on Keats's Reading," *PMLA*, L [1935], 785 ff.) that

But since Keats was picturing a scene to vie in luxuriance with the banquet in *The Eve of Saint Agnes,* he made the accouterments of a lavish Oriental Alexandrian style. The "taste of Greek simplicity," to quote Hunt's description of certain lines in *Endymion,* may be seen more clearly in lines like

> A nymph . . .
> At whose white feet the languid Tritons poured
> Pearls (Part I, ll. 14–16)

than in the mere mention of columns, tripods, and censers. A good deal of *Lamia* also suggests that the poet was reverting to the manner of his earliest poems and to the poems on classical themes by Hunt and Mrs. Tighe.

For an interesting commentary on the difference between the odes and *Lamia* both in spirit and in texture, one may turn to "The Castle Builder," a fragment written in January, 1818. Notwithstanding the dramatic and familiar form of the lines, the speaker stated what may have been Keats's own confession that Grecian sculpture could not long please him. Partly from his inability to achieve the happiness of the lovers of whom he dreamed in the "Ode on Indolence" and then placed upon his Grecian urn, and partly from the torments arising out of his still unresolved personal problems, he felt often a restlessness in the presence of the perfection of the ancient works. Even though he was still to write his finest sculptural poetry, and though the fragment "The Castle Builder" coincided with his avowed intention of seeking a "more naked and grecian manner," the work suggests that less heroic kinds of art were also strongly attracting him:

> Greek busts and statuary have ever been
> Held, by the finest spirits, fitter far
> Than vase grotesque and Siamesian jar;
> Therefore 'tis sure a want of Attic taste
> That I should rather love a Gothic waste
> Of eyesight on cinque-coloured potter's clay
> Than on the marble fairness of old Greece (ll. 55–61).

"virtually all of the material background and customs described in *Lamia* appear to be drawn, sometimes with verbal echoes, from Potter" [the *Archaeologia Graeca,* which Keats owned]. See also Finney, *The Evolution of Keats's Poetry,* II, 674–77.

Yet as a critic Keats recognized that the Greek sculpture interpreted to him by Haydon and Hazlitt had had a part in checking his tendency to use excessive fancy. From the Elgin Marbles in particular he learned that grandeur of design and exactness of detail were compatible, and his own poetry gained from that knowledge. When he wrote his criticism, therefore, Greek sculpture sometimes came to mind, owing both to his personal experience and to the fact that Hazlitt and Hunt, from whom he adopted many ideas (at times doing little more than quote the former), had also given the plastic arts an important place in their critical writings. In reporting the performance of Kean in *Richard, Duke of York,* Keats turned very easily to a statue familiar to him, "We see nothing of Talbot, and missing him is like walking among the Elgin Marbles and seeing an empty place where the Theseus had reclined." [32]

More important, however, for the light it sheds upon his poetry was Keats's account of his discovery in Milton of the sculptural quality which Hazlitt and other critics had praised. "Milton in every instance pursues his imagination to the utmost. . . . But in no instance is this sort of perseverance more exemplified, than in what may be called his *stationing or statuary*. He is not content with simple description, he must station." [33] That lesson in "stationing" according to the principles of sculpture was, indeed, one of the chief inspirations Keats derived from the Elgin Marbles and from the critics who had described Milton as "heroic" and "Grecian" in his works. In their influence upon the poetry of Keats, especially *Endymion* and *Hyperion,* Greek sculpture and Milton were inseparably linked, and their influence was at least as strong as that of the other "heroic" art —Homer and Dante, Shakespeare and Spenser—which left marks upon his work.

To make his interpretation of Milton truly Keatsian, the critic stated the opinion that his predecessor had turned consciously from a life of sensation to a life of thought: the great poet had abandoned, he argued, "an exquisite passion for what is properly, in the sense of ease and pleasure, poetical Luxury," and had deliberately aimed

[32] *Works,* ed. H. B. Forman (1883), III, 10.
[33] *Ibid.,* pp. 28–29. See above, pp. 60 ff., pp. 218–19, and Hazlitt, *Works* (Howe), IV, 38 ff.; V, 60 ff.

at the lofty goal of an epic in the grand or severe style. The finest praise he could give *Paradise Lost* was that its "management" was truly "Apollonian." Having thus described the "progress" of Milton in the very terms which he used in the plans for his own poetical development, Keats hoped his masterpieces would also be "Apollonian." In so far as they measure up to that standard, he was in a considerable degree indebted to his study of the sculpture as well as the literature of the Greeks.

Keats enriched English poetry with more good lines inspired by Greek sculpture than any other poet. As in the case of the Homeric poetry found in Chapman, Keats heard the Ancients "speak out loud and bold." When he was under the spell of the ancient marbles, he wrote in a spirit akin to that of the Greeks, except in the "Haydon" sonnets, where he gave a direct account of his emotional response to the mighty works, or, in other words, the adventures of his soul in their presence. In *Endymion,* the "Ode on a Grecian Urn," and the "Ode on Indolence" he described statues and vases, and drew from them images to achieve sculptural effects, that is, to re-create the feeling of sculpture in the medium of the poet. Largely under the influence of the Elgin Marbles, he began in *Hyperion* to place his figures in the manner of statuary, until he created a whole scene in "The Fall of Hyperion" as though he were a sculptor. Nonclassical sculpture likewise had its place in the poetry of Keats, but the Greek alone expressed the perfect beauty of human life and passion which teased him out of thought. No Romantic poet learned more from Greek statues than Keats, in whose poetry a definitely sculptural quality developed from his first intuitive appreciation and his later study of the masterpieces to which Haydon introduced him.

In a sonnet on the tranquilizing and purifying effect of the South Wind, Keats gave a kind of allegory of the place of Greek sculpture in his poetry:

> After dark vapours have oppress'd our plains
>> For a long dreary season, comes a day
>> Born of the gentle South, and clears away
> From the sick heavens all unseemly stains.

In a similar fashion on many occasions the sculpture of the Greeks cleared his heavens. There he found "incarnate Delight," Severn reported, and the Greek spirit was for him "the Religion of the Beautiful, the Religion of Joy."

'Keats,' Severn remarked once to a friend, 'made me in love with the real living Spirit of the past. He was the first to point out to me how essentially modern that Spirit is: "It's an immortal youth," he would say, "just as there is no *Now* or *Then* for the Holy Ghost." ' [34]

Frequently, under the influence of that living spirit of Greece, calm thoughts and epic shapes came round him. The poet then sang, for a time, in full-throated ease. More than anything else, Keats wanted finally to rank among "the mighty ones," sculptors and poets,

> who have made eternal day
> For Greece and England.

[34] See Sharp, *The Life and Letters of Joseph Severn*, p. 29.

X. LANDOR AND HUNT

LANDOR AND GREECE

WALTER SAVAGE LANDOR was the most consciously "classical" artist among poets of the Romantic period in England: he frequently strove to write as "a Grecian would have written." Exceeding most of his contemporaries in his admiration of Greek art, he was nevertheless, like them, an eclectic. If he was regarded as anything else, he was offended; moreover, on several occasions he went out of his way to defend his eclecticism. Severely criticized for neglecting the living in his preference for the illustrious dead, Landor calmly replied,

> but let me ask in turn
> Whether, whene'er Corinthian urn
> With ivied Faun upon the rim
> Invites, I may not gaze on him?
> I love all beauty. ("Apology for Gebir," ll. 53–57.)

At other times he took great pains to correct the impression that he was entirely classical in taste. He was particularly irritated when Emerson reported his tastes in *English Traits* (1856) as follows: "In art he loves the Greeks, and in sculpture them only. He prefers the Venus to everything else, and after that, the head of Alexander in the gallery [at Florence]." [1] Replying in his "Letter to Emerson," Landor remonstrated, "I share with [Horatio Greenough, the American sculptor and a mutual friend] my enthusiastic love of ancient art; but I am no *exclusive,* as you seem to hint I am."

For a lover of old Greece, too, Landor was remarkably sympathetic toward the classicistic sculptors of his own day. Like Byron he could praise both Canova and Phidias; he surpassed Coleridge and Blake in praising Flaxman with the enthusiasm reserved for his greatest

[1] Page 13.

favorites in art and literature. Even Horatio Greenough seemed a great artist, and Landor encouraged Emerson's American "votary of the Greeks" to imitate the Antique, in this advice offering an illuminating contrast to Coleridge, who in Rome had urged another student from America, Washington Allston the painter, to avoid the forms of the Classical Revivals.

On the other hand, Landor would have shuddered at the thought of being considered a poet of the Neo-Classical camp, since he hated anything however remotely associated with France, the country which had set the pattern of the Academic tradition for his countrymen. This prejudice is nowhere more vividly seen than in the following incident of his visit to France in 1802 with Charles James Fox. The two friends had gone to the Louvre to behold the antiques plundered from Italy by Napoleon; but Landor soon forgot the sculptures in his rage against tyrannical kings and "the stupidity of men who could not in the whole course of their existence have given birth to any thing equal to the smallest of the works" produced by the Ancients.[2] French painting, with the notable exceptions of works by Claude Lorrain and Nicolas Poussin, he likewise condemned as primarily servile copying from the Antique.

Still, though he praised Flaxman and Greenough and "complimented" Canova, and though he was fond of the Venus and other Hellenistic statues, Landor was familiar with the earlier Greek works as far as they were known then. Phidias was the sculptor to whom he referred most often, while the sculptures from the Parthenon appeared frequently in his poetry and prose. Never long absent from his thought, the golden age of Pericles, Sophocles, and Phidias was indeed his favorite period in the history of the world. Upon that time of Apollonian glory Landor founded lofty hopes similar to those of Shelley and Byron for the political freedom and moral regeneration of the modern world—in Greece, Italy, Spain, Hungary, all Europe. He likewise agreed with Milton and the Augustans and with Collins and many Romantic poets that freedom in the political body is the condition essential to the flourishing of the fine arts. Therefore the

2 *Charles James Fox; a Commentary on His Life and Character by Walter Savage Landor,* ed. Stephen Wheeler (1907), pp. 167–68.

poets turned to intellectual Greece rather than to imperial and commercial Rome.

After the great figures of the Periclean age Landor was most interested in men who, like himself, acknowledged their indebtedness
to Greece—in Romans who bowed in matters of culture to their
predecessors; in Italian poets and artists and scholars who had created
the rebirth of freedom and the arts; and in Milton and in workers
for liberty in the early nineteenth century. In the noble discourse
between P. Scipio Aemilianus and his learned Greek friends, Polybius
and Panaetius—one of the finest in *Imaginary Conversations*—the
Roman conqueror of Carthage hears the gifts of Greece enumerated
as Panaetius declaims a glowing tribute to the country that "taught
the Romans all beyond the rudiments of war." [3] To Michelangelo
Buonarotti, conversing with Machiavelli, Landor attributed the following ambition:

O that by any exertion of my art I could turn the eyes of my countrymen
towards Greece! I wish to excell in painting or in sculpture, partly for
my glory, partly for my sustenance, being poor, but greatly more to arouse
in their breasts the recollection of what was higher (III, 4).

Similarly consecrating himself to Liberty in the spirit of Milton, his
idol among English poets, Landor looked toward Greece, asserting
that whoever

beholds the skies of Italy
Sees ancient Rome reflected, sees beyond,
Into more glorious Hellas, nurse of Gods
And godlike men: dwarfs people other lands. ("To Shelley," ll. 13-16.)

LANDOR AND THE SCULPTURESQUE

The sculpture of the Greeks was not only the favorite art of Landor
but it was also a major source of his inspiration. When the Aspasia
of his novelette *Pericles and Aspasia* remarked (Letter XLVIII) that
"coldness is experienced in the highest beauty," that brilliant lady expressed a sentiment which her creator largely derived from the cold
and regular perfection of Grecian statuary. Landor had those noble

[3] *The Complete Works of Walter Savage Landor*, ed. T. Earle Welby and S.
Wheeler (1927–36), II, 88.

and simple forms in mind, moreover, when he announced that in poetry the passions should be presented with a dignity suggestive of sculpture: they should be displayed in idealized figures "naked, like the heroes and the Gods." [4] In the best antiques, such as the Theseus, he found the expression of true simplicity, adding that many of his contemporaries would profit from studying the lesson manifested by the statues, namely, the greatness of design coupled with economy in execution. He wished, moreover, to bring back into poetry "scenes and figures" of a kind with which "Sculpture and Painting have never ceased to be occupied." Poetry, the first of the arts, ought also, he felt, to make use of subjects continuously employed by its sister-arts.

Landor felt also that in the poetry of his maturity, such as the series of splendid idylls, the *Hellenics,* he had achieved a beauty akin to that of the Grecian artists; for this reason he confidently appropriated the Horatian boast of the immortality of his own poetry:

> He who sees rising from some open down
>   A column, stately, beautiful, and pure,
> Its rich expansive capital would crown
>   With glorious statue, which might long endure,
> And bring men under it to gaze and sigh
>   And wish that honour'd creature they had known,
> Whose name the deep inscription lets not die.
>   I raise that statue and inscribe that stone.[5]

Landor's aim and classical inspiration did not escape the attention of his contemporaries. De Quincey, for example, early pointed out his "sculpturesque faculty," emphasizing thus the quality which has always been associated with his works.[6] The critic was thinking, how-

---

[4] Quoted by Sidney Colvin, *Landor,* "English Men of Letters" series (1909 ed.), p. 61. See also Keats, above, pp. 217 ff.

[5] *Works,* XVI, 81. See also the Preface to the *Hellenics* (1847), *Works,* XIV, 315, where Landor termed his works "rude frescoes, delineated on an old wall high up, and sadly weak in coloring."

[6] See "Notes on Walter Savage Landor," *Collected Writings of De Quincey,* ed. David Masson (Edinburgh, 1889–90), XI, 404; the Introduction in E. C. Stedman and T. B. Aldrich, *Cameos Selected from the Works of Walter Savage Landor* (Boston, 1873); and such a characteristic criticism as Ernest de Selincourt's remark: "Landor's [art] is essentially statuesque rather than pictorial. We feel the emotion of his char-

ever, not so much of the total effect of Landor's writing—the lucidity
and sculptural beauty of the poetry itself, which appeals to the so-
called "objective" critics of the early twentieth century—as of the
numerous clean-cut or relief-like descriptions of festal processions,
storied streets with paneled gates and porticoes, and sculptured vases
in his work. In other words, De Quincey was primarily interested in
Landor's classical subject matter, while today critics study his "sculptural" style.

To represent the "sculpturesque faculty" of Landor the following
characteristically neat and polished account of the dwelling in *Cory-
thos* may be chosen, because it shows a happy blending of classical
subject and sculptural style in the story of the son of Paris and Oenone.

> The palace now they reach where Paris dwelt;
> They wonder at the wide and lofty dome,
> The polisht columns and the brazen forms
> Of heroes and of Gods, and marble steps,
> And valves resounding at the gates unbarr'd.
> They enter them. What ivory! and what gold!
> What breathing images depicted there! [7]
> > (Part I, ll. 193–99 [1859].)

Within the palace, sculptures adorned the chamber where Paris slew
his son in the very presence of Helena:

> Around the chamber shone the images
> Of boys and maidens robed in vest succinct,
> And holding burnisht lamps, whence incense wreath'd

---

acters in the pose and gesture of their figures far more than in any words they may
speak." ("Classicism and Romanticism in the Poetry of Walter Savage Landor,"
England und die Antike, ed. Fritz Saxl, *Vorträge der Bibliothek Warburg, 1930–31*
[Leipzig and Berlin, 1932], p. 243.)

[7] In 1847 the lines read:
> "At last to Parisis abode they come.
> Bidden to enter here, the spacious courts,
> The lofty columns, the resplendent gods
> Of brass and marble, the smooth steps and wide,
> And the vast portals and resounding valves,
> Strike them with admiration and with awe.
> How many ivory statues breathe around!
> How many golden! nor do fewer move
> In the warm colours emulous of life" (ll. 198–206).

Its heavy cloud whitened with cedar oil,
And under them the purple gleam'd forth,
And over was the residence of Gods,
And nectar-bearing youth, in light serene.[8]

(Part II, ll. 59–65 [1859].)

Similar sculpturesque lines were to have closed *The Phocaeans.*
Here Landor carefully described a scene of sacrifice as an Hellenic
bas-relief of maidenly figures, which is somewhat suggestive of
Shelley's groups in *The Revolt of Islam.*

Here stood three maidens, who seem'd ministers
To nine more stately, standing somewhat higher
Than these demure ones of the downcast smile:
Silent they seem'd; not silent all the nine.
One sang aloud, one was absorb'd in grief
Apparently for youths who lately bled;
Others there were who, standing more elate,
Their eyes upturn'd, their nostrils wide expanded,
Their lips archt largely; and to raise the hymn
Were lifted lyres; so seemed it; but the skill
Of art Hellenic forged the grand deceit.

(Sequel to *The Phocaeans,* ll. 16–26.)

To the *Heroic Idylls* (1863) Landor appended a mythological piece
on the Niobe. His eye was so definitely upon the statuary group (even
though he altered the number of figures) that the work almost merits
being called a "sculpture-poem." The Niobe statue, still alive among
the slaughtered Niobids, makes a final prayer desiring the last arrow
to kill herself:

Amid nine daughters slain by Artemis
Stood Niobe: she rais'd her head above
Those beauteous forms which had brought down the scath
Whence all nine fell, rais'd it, and stood erect (ll. 1–4).

In picturing scenes from antiquity in this fashion Landor utilized
the fine arts for several reasons. First of all, endowed (according to

---

[8] Here the improvement over the 1847 lines was greater:
　　"Now censers burning all around reflect
　　　The images that hold them, images
　　　Of youths whose left-hand holds long garments back."

(Lines 385–87.)

Emerson) "with an English appetite for action and heroes," [9] he delighted to show the backdrop against which the drama of the *Idylls* and the *Conversations* was enacted; for noble Greek and Roman heroes merited at least a decorated stage. Moreover, such descriptions gave the veneer of culture and learning expected by many readers in the early years of the nineteenth century. Music, painting, architecture, and especially sculpture extended the range of the classical associations. Again, like many contemporary writers, Landor reflected the widespread interest in classical art by using ancient works, not only for the purposes of decoration and learning already mentioned, but also for illustration of every sort of statement, aphorism, or critical remark. For example, Landor's Pericles sharpened an epigram (Letter LXII) by an analogy from art: "Religion and Power, like the Cariatides in sculpture, never face one another; they sometimes look the same way, but oftener stand back to back." The poet himself found, we have seen, that the art of sculpture frequently illuminated his critical principles.

But his fondness for describing and referring to works of art was above all the badge of membership in the company of Alexandrian poets. With Theocritus, Catullus, and Propertius among the Ancients, with the poets of the Italian Renaissance, and with Chaucer, Spenser, Pope, Thomson, Keats, and Shelley—to name but a few of his countrymen—Landor shared a delight in the craftsmanship of all the arts. Poets, Diogenes told Plato in the *Imaginary Conversations,* are the children of Enthusiasm; they are therefore "fond of festivals, of wine, of beauty, and of glory." [10] To that fellowship of poets Landor

---

[9] *English Traits,* p. 14.

[10] *Works,* I, 99. For Landor's use of statues in miscellaneous poems and epigrams, see the Theocritean "Inscription on a Statue of Love" (XVI, 137), the verses on a statue in *Pericles and Aspasia* (Letter CLIX), and the somewhat Byronic protest against the desecration of statues by travelers, "Observing a Vulgar Name on the Plinth of an Ancient Statue" (XVI, 31).

> "O Venus! in thy Tuscan dome
>   May every God watch over thee!
> Apollo! bend thy bow o'er Rome
>   And guard thy sister's chastity.
> Let Britons taint their bodies blue
>   As formerly, but touch not you."

See also "An Alabaster Hand; Presented by Lord Elgin" (XV, 349).

belonged, and in the *Hellenics* he invited his readers along with the
poets to Athens, promising drafts of the blushful Hippocrene,

> such as anciently the Aegaean isles
> Pour'd in libation at their solemn feasts:
> And the same goblets shall ye grasp, embost
> With no vile figures of loose languid boors,
> But such as Gods have lived with, and have led.
>   ("Thrasymedes and Eunöe," ll. 8–12.)

Vases and urns, porticoes and gates, ancient statues (or even casts
from them) and classical temples, works of art such as the paintings
of Poussin with "nymph-frequented woods . . . templed highths
and long-drawn solitudes" or a "warm sunset of Ausonian Claude"—
all these mementos of antiquity carried him to the golden age of
European man, to Greece and the reign of Apollonian freedom,
reason, and the arts. With many contemporary poets he cried, "Who
will away to Athens with me?" [11] Thus Landor dreamed, as have
many English poets, among them Shakespeare and Keats, of a beautiful Athens and a Greece of high romance, which existed only in
their quick-conceiving imaginations.

THE THEORY OF SCULPTURE

To the Parthenon, therefore, for many reasons the thoughts of
Landor were continually reverting. No archaeologist and not much
of a connoisseur, he knew very little about the architectural detail
of the great work; yet he responded immediately to the magic of its
name. The very word "Parthenon" was a bell arousing a complex
set of feelings associated with Greece. As enduring as any work built
by human hands, the Parthenon survived as a perpetual reminder
of the age of Pericles, and Landor enthusiastically praised that great
achievement of Greek art for its perfection beyond cavil and for its
eloquent testimony to the genius that men had once displayed. Certainly by the time of the dialogue between Pericles and Sophocles
(published 1824) he felt an especial attraction to fifth-century Greece

---

[11] "First Bring Me Raffael, Who Alone Hath Seen," and *Hellenics,* "Thrasymedes
and Eunöe" (*Works,* XIV, 292; XVI, 80).

so that with the voices of the great Athenians he was expressing his own sentiments.

PERICLES. O Sophocles! is there in the world a city so beautiful as Athens? . . .

SOPHOCLES. And it arises, O Pericles, the more majestically from the rich and delightful plain of equal laws. The gods have bestowed on our statuaries and painters a mighty power, enabling them to restore our ancestors unto us, some in the calm of thought, others in the tumult of battle, and to present them before our children when we are gone (I, 56).

Out of this dialogue—one of the best of the early "conversations"—sprang the longer work *Pericles and Aspasia* (begun in 1835), without doubt the finest exposition of Landor's ideas by means of a Grecian framework. In dedicating to Julius Hare this book in which he attempted to participate in the loftiest moment of Greek civilization, Landor gave the Parthenon a prominent place.

> Aspasia comes
> With him, high-helmeted and trumpet-tongued,
> Who loved her.
>   . . .
>
> The stone that flew
> In splinters from the chisel when the hand
> Of Phidias wielded it, the chips of stone
> Weigh with me more than they [sycophantic poets]
>   do. To thy house
> Comes Pericles. Receive the friend of him
> Whose horses started from the Parthenon
> To traverse seas and neigh upon our strand.
>   ("To Julius Hare," ll. 2–4, 10–16.)

Charged with scorn of tyrannical and corrupt kings, the lines show that the poet valued the monuments of Greek art, such as the Parthenon sculptures, not only for their intrinsic greatness but also for the associations of peace, freedom, and noble heroism clustering about them.

In *Pericles and Aspasia,* besides discoursing upon love and statecraft and literature, Landor did not neglect the opportunity to set forth his ideas concerning the arts of the Greeks. In the novelette he gave long and serious consideration to ancient art, particularly sculpture;

for the "mighty power" of the sculptors excited him as much as anything in Greece—Aspasia alone excepted! Therefore, nothing if not gallant, he bestowed upon the fascinating Aspasia the honor of describing the building of the Parthenon, putting his own theories of art into her letters. Since he was constantly expressing his own ideas through the voices of the several characters, passages like the discussions of sculpture in *Pericles and Aspasia* clearly revealed his opinions on the arts.

The central element in the remarks on the art of sculpture was his insistence on the temporal limitation of the art. Sculpture, maintained Aspasia (Letter LXX), when surrounded by the masterpieces newly created by the great Greeks, was a static art: it was capable of showing but one situation or action, and even that had to be concentrated into one moment.[12] The sculptor was destined to be exasperated more often than the poet or painter, she continued, by subjects which would not submit to such compression. Thus Landor agreed with the poets that sculpture, even the Antique, is less expressive than poetry, which seemingly has no curbs to freedom of action, time, and place.

Even more eloquently Landor advanced the same argument in some opinions of Pericles (Letter LXVI):

"There are things, Aspasia, beyond the art of Phidias. He may represent Love leaning upon his bow and listening to Philosophy; but not for hours together: he may represent Love, while he is giving her a kiss for her lesson, tying her arms behind her: loosing them must be upon another marble." [13]

On another occasion (Letter LXXII) the Athenian compared the relative expressiveness of the sister-arts of sculpture, painting, and poetry so vividly that part of his argument merits quotation, because it is one of the best statements of a group of sentiments which have engaged the interest of many English poets.

[12] Landor was using some of the arguments of the critics of the "paragone" discussions; see above, pp. 40*n*, 47 ff. Lessing's *Laokoon* comes to mind at once as the most likely source of these statements; yet Landor may have drawn them from his own feelings about the art of sculpture.

[13] See also Letter LXX.

"Sculpture has made great advances in my time; Painting still greater: for until the last forty years it was inelegant and rude. Sculpture can go no farther; Painting can: she may add scenery and climate to her forms. . . . Her reign is boundless, but the fairer and richer part of her dominions lies within the Odyssea. Painting by degrees will perceive her advantages over Sculpture; but if there are paces between Sculpture and Painting, there are parasangs between Painting and Poetry. The difference is that of a lake confined by mountains, and a river running on through all the varieties of scenery, perpetual and unimpeded. Sculpture and Painting are moments of life; Poetry is life itself, and every thing around it and above it." [14]

One is not surprised that Landor, portraying Pericles amid the masterpieces at Athens, should represent him as believing that the art had reached its ultimate with the school of Phidias. Indeed, of all the sculptors from the dimness surrounding the origin of the art until the time he was writing, only Michelangelo had been allowed (and even he sometimes grudgingly) to stand unabashed in the presence of the sculptors of Pericles' acquaintance. On the other hand, in poetry Virgil, Dante, Shakespeare, and Milton had all found places beside Homer and the tragedians. With considerable justice Landor felt that since the fifth century in Greece there had been a greater variety of achievement in poetry than in sculpture. Therefore, in assuming the position indicated in the remarks of Pericles, he was repeating a familiar doctrine of the "romantic" poets, namely, that poetry is life or action while sculpture is simple grandeur and calm repose without the pulse of living beings. Nevertheless, the sculpture of the Parthenon was a great achievement; even though less expressive to the "romantic" poets than the masterpieces of their own art, the Grecian statuary showed that the sculptors had been able to put the beliefs and ideals of their own age into forms of an almost perfect beauty. In the fifth century their works had been alive with meaning for their beholders; in their own day the great Grecian sculptors had been "romantic."

Landor made Pericles recognize that there was, moreover, a permanence in the materials of sculpture which the poet, working with paper and ink, might well envy. Apparently it was the sculptor rather

<hr />

[14] For other discussions of the relative merits of the arts, see above, p. 34n.

than the poet who gave the most lasting form to the gods worshiped by mankind.

"But let us . . . offer due reverence to the truest diviners of the Gods. Phidias in ten days is capable of producing what would outlive ten thousand years, if man were not resolved to be the subverter of man's glory. The Gods themselves will vanish away before their images."

For this reason the sculptor could be more influential than the poet, partly because his works stood a better chance of surviving to be seen by a larger number of human beings over a greater extent of years, and partly because the limitations already mentioned forced the artist to select the most essential and most expressive moment. The temporal limitation therefore might give the sculptor an ultimate advantage over the poet.

Again, very much in the spirit of Akenside and Thomson, Landor described the process of art as mind giving form to the ideas it had conceived. One of the few English poets who have violently attacked Plato, he nevertheless wrote lines with the distinctly Platonic ring of the following:

> From heaven descend two gifts alone;
> The graceful line's eternal zone
>   And Beauty, that too soon must die.
>
>   . . .
>
> For mutual succor Heaven designed
> The lovely form and vigorous mind
>   To seek each other and unite.
>   ("Ianthe," *Gebir* [1831], ll. 1–3, 7–10.)

Here the perfect forms existing within the appearances of nature await the mind of the artist who can endow them with substance and life. For Landor as for Shelley and Keats—of whom he was perhaps thinking when he penned these lines—Greek art, especially sculpture, was the supreme example of the way "genius" expresses itself in "lovely forms" of enduring beauty.

Like the poets of the seventeenth and eighteenth centuries, Landor displayed interest also in the history of the arts. The early work entitled "The Birth of Poesy" (1795) was a "progress" of the art in-

spired by Gray and written in couplets recalling Pope. Later he several times mentioned the origin of the plastic arts given by Pliny: the
quaint notion that a maiden first traced on a wall the shadow of her
loved one's features.[15] Landor paid homage to the illustrious city of
Corinth as the scene of that momentous discovery, relating the account of the "shadow origin" of art as a part of the bird's-eye view
of the isles of Greece in *Gebir*—a passage undoubtedly suggested by
the visions of the Mediterranean regions with which Satan tempted
Christ in *Paradise Regained*.

He [Tamar] saw the land of Pelops, host of Gods;
Saw the steep ridge where Corinth after stood,
Beck'ning the serious with the smiling Arts
Into her sunbright bay: unborn the maid
That, to assure the bent-up hand unskill'd,
Look'd oft; but oft'ner fearing who might wake. (Book VI, ll. 148–53.)

The same incident appeared again in "To Corinth," a poetical ap-
pendage to the 1824 "imaginary conversation" between Maurocordato
and Colocotroni, heroes of the Greek Revolution. Honor was due
the city because

> To give the inertest masses of our Earth
> Her loveliest forms was thine, to fix the Gods
> Within thy walls, and hang their tripods round
> With fruits and foliage knowing not decay (ll. 36–39).[16]

In Landor's comments on the history or "progress" of the arts the
most noteworthy element was, however, his interest in Egyptian art,
since he shared the curiosity of the Greeks themselves regarding their

---

[15] Landor's note in *Gebir*, Book VI, ll. 151 ff. (1803 ed.), reads: "The story of the
maid of Corinth is too celebrated for repetition. Drawing the lines of her lover's face
against the wall, I have represented her as equally fearful of drawing them amiss,
and being discovered by his awakening" (*Works*, XIII, 348–49). See Pliny, *Nat.
Hist.*, XXXV, 12, and also Landor's caustic remarks on Isaac D'Israeli's use of the
story in "The Lovers; or, Origin of the Fine Arts" in *Romances* (1799), *Works*, XIII,
362. (The "birth" of sculpture occurs in *Romances* at pp. 289–90.) Landor also might
have read the account of the Sicyonian maid in Hayley's "Essay on Painting," *Poems
and Plays* (1785), I, 124 ff. The story is outlined by James Montgomery in "The
Molehill" [1807] (*Poetical Works* [1841], pp. 217–18) and by John Ward in *The
Potter's Art; a Poem . . .* (Burslem, 1828).

[16] See also Akenside, p. 83, and Wordsworth, pp. 127–28, above.

predecessors. Very appropriate, therefore, was the passage (Letter LXXII) in which Pericles discussed the differences between the sculptures of the Egyptians, "the inventers of all durable colours, and indeed of everything else that is durable in the arts," and those of the Greeks, who "refined" the earlier forms.

"Judgment and perception of the true and beautiful will never allow our statuaries to represent the human countenance, as they have done, in granite, porphyry, and basalt. Their statues have resisted Time and War; ours will vanquish Envy and Malice."

No longer subject to the prejudice of such gentlemen as Shaftesbury, Thomson, and Walpole against Egyptian or "barbaric" art, Landor belonged with the more eclectic Romantics. The statue of Memnon, referred to by Pericles and used elsewhere by Landor as a symbol of the resistance of genius to Philistine onslaughts, was in particular a favorite with his contemporaries.[17]

Though never systematized, Landor's theories of art were, then, consistent; and, when brilliantly stated, as in *Pericles and Aspasia,* they hold a high place among the similar passages of criticism indulged in during several centuries by English men of letters. Unlike most of the major Romantic poets, however, he derived his information about art primarily from ancient writers, especially the historians, instead of from the actual works of art which inspired Thomson, Byron, Keats, and Shelley, or from the learned tomes, such as Spence's *Polymetis* and Tooke's *Pantheon,* used by William Mason, Keats, and Hunt. For contemporary critics like A. W. Schlegel and, for that matter, their Academic predecessors, Landor had small respect and less use.[18] Apparently he knew little of Winckelmann and of the

---

[17] See *Pericles and Aspasia,* Letter LXXII, with the reference to Cambyses's attempt to destroy the figure. See also above, pp. 122–23, 218–19, and *Don Juan,* Canto XIII, stanza lxiv.

[18] Henry Crabb Robinson, who had been reading Goethe's *Winckelmann* in 1832, reported some of Landor's opinions thus: "Landor was most extravagant in his praise [of Flaxman],—would rather have one of Flaxman's drawings than the whole of the group of the Niobe. Indeed, 'most of those figures, all but three, are worthless,' and Winckelmann he abuses for praising this sculpture, and Goethe, he says, must be an ignoramus for praising Winckelmann" (*Diary, Reminiscences, and Correspondence,* ed. T. Sadler [2d ed., 1869], III, 11). See also *Last Days, Letters and Correspondence,* ed. H. C. Minchin (1934), p. 69, for a letter to Browning (1860) where Landor

vast body of aesthetic and archaeological speculation in the eighteenth century. At the time when he was writing, of course, most of those theories about sculpture had become commonplaces—in no small measure from their frequent use by the poets; but the similarities between the ideas advanced by Landor and those expressed by other English poets are to be explained by way of the ancient writers, such as Pliny, Pausanias, and Plutarch, whose statements about art had filtered throughout European aesthetics, rather than by way of English intermediaries like Spence, Reynolds, or Haydon. Of the Romantic poets, Wordsworth was closest to Landor in drawing thus more often on ancient sources than on actual works of art or modern criticism.

MORALITY AND THE ARTS

More important to Landor than history and theory, and fully as significant in a study of his mind, was his strong belief in the intimate connection between the arts and the political and moral temperature of a state. "Systems of poetry, of philosophy, of government, form and model us to their own proportions," the Petrarca of his *Pentameron* (1837) remarked, adding that "as our systems want the grandeur, the light, and the symmetry of the ancient, we can not hope for poets, philosophers, or statesmen, of equal dignity." [19] Though more optimistic than the Italian humanist in maintaining that modern men could approach the *dignitas* of the Ancients, Landor likewise measured the poets, artists, philosophers, and statesmen of his own day by the standards of Greece and Rome.

In the philhellenism of the Romantic writers one of the principal elements, one scarcely needs to be reminded, was the conviction—inherited from the Augustan poets—that literature and the arts can flourish only in the genial atmosphere of Liberty. They demanded no more proof of this doctrine than the indisputable greatness of the Greeks in matters of mind. Nevertheless, even while looking back

---

ridiculed Schlegel's famous remark that Sophocles can best be understood when one stands before the Niobe or the Laocoön. Landor protested: "These noble works afford no help whatever to the comprehension and appreciation of the glorious poet."

[19] *Works,* IX, 172.

to the Periclean age, they were dreaming of a new golden age in the nineteenth century: the hope for freedom in their own time was always coupled with the Ancients. First of all, the War for Independence was to found a new great age in Greece. In 1826 Landor wrote, "Her old heroic age was less heroic than the present: grant her another, and our children may see a Phidias and a Sophocles." [20]

Landor's devotion to the ideal of Liberty was present in both poetry and prose. In *The Phocaeans,* an early work (1802), the voice was unmistakably his own:

> Heroes of old would I commemorate.
>
> . . .
>
> And, borne amidst them, I would dedicate
> To thee O Liberty the golden spoils (ll. 1, 5–6).

Liberty was the burden of "Regeneration" (1821), the companion of "To Corinth," and in these two poems Landor gave the most poetic expression of his hatred of tyranny, repeating the themes of the 1802 volume in more violent form. Thermopylae, Salamis, and Marathon—glorious names reminding the English poets of the valiant Greeks—were the banners of his enthusiasm for the War for Independence.

> The Marathonian columns never told
> A tale more glorious, never Salamis (ll. 54–55).[21]

Summoned to the struggle for freedom, the Romantic poets were to fight tyranny everywhere with a valor comparable to that of the heroic Greeks still living in ancient art and in the hearts of modern men like Landor himself.

[20] Dedication of *Imaginary Conversations,* Series 3 (published 1829 and later suppressed), *Works,* X, 255.

[21] The tale on the columns was the celebrated mural painting of the Battle of Marathon, formerly attributed to Panainos. Wordsworth had had in mind the same work in the 1816 ode ("When the Soft Hand of Sleep"), and the poem may have called it to Landor's attention; see above, p. 130. Like Wordsworth, Landor was familiar with Pliny and Pausanias, the chief sources of information about the painting, while the mention of Panainos in *Pericles and Aspasia* suggests that Landor was following Pausanias. Also noteworthy is the fact that the dialogue between Pericles and Sophocles takes place on the day when the decorations for the Poecile at Athens were completed. See also *Pericles and Aspasia,* Letter CVIII.

But of the many paeans to Liberty and the arts following in its train, none was finer than the sentiments expressed in the *Imaginary Conversations* by the greatest of the Florentine artists.

MICHEL-ANGELO. The Arts cannot long exist without the advent of Freedom. From every new excavation whence a statue rises, there rises simultaneously a bright vision of the age that produced it; a strong desire to bring it back again; a throbbing love, an inflaming regret, a resolute despair, beautiful as Hope herself; and Hope comes too behind.

Men are not our fellow-creatures because hands and articulate voices belong to them in common with us: they are then, and then only, when they precede us, or accompany us, or follow us, contemplating one grand luminary, periodically obscured, but eternally existent in the highest heaven of the soul, without which all lesser lights would lose their brightness, their station, their existence.

If these things should ever come to pass, how bold shall be the step, how exalted the head, of Genius. Clothed in glorified bodies of living marble, instructors shall rise out of the earth, deriders of Barbarism, conquerors of Time, heirs and coequals of Eternity. Led on by these, again shall man mount the ladder that touches heaven; again shall he wrestle with the angels (III, 16).

Michelangelo's eloquence was Landor's, and the passage crystallized the spirit of the Renaissance in a fashion surpassed by few writers. For Italian artist and English poet the rediscovery of the Antique was an inspiration—rather, a command—to create beauty: both hoped that "Sculpture awaits but the dawn of Freedom to rise up before new worshippers in the fulness of her glory." Landor, convinced that the liberty being achieved in his day guaranteed the flourishing of the arts, even went so far as to assert that the sculpture of his own age surpassed everything but the masterpieces of the Greeks! "Sculpture at the present day flourishes more than it ever did since the days of Pericles; and America is not cast into the shade by Europe," he wrote Emerson in 1856. The American sculptor who equaled Europe's best and was to rival Phidias was none other than his old friend Horatio Greenough!

Devoted as he was to the Greeks, Landor did not forget that he lived in another age. He was, Havelock Ellis rightly said, "an unmistakable Englishman . . . intensely alive to the influences of his own age." [22] Since Greece and things Grecian exerted a powerful influence upon Englishmen in the first half of the nineteenth century, Landor and many of his compatriots, ardent philhellenists, were conscious of a peculiar share in the destiny of the Greeks. For this reason Elizabeth Barrett, writing in 1839, could propound the notion that "of all living writers" Landor had proved himself in *Pericles and Aspasia* "the most unconventional in thought and word, the most classical, because the freest from mere classicalism, *the most Greek because pre-eminently and purely English*"! [23] Surely the poetess surpassed all her brother-poets in identifying Englishmen with the Greeks.

Landor was a "Greek," then, not only because he often concerned himself with Grecian subject matter, mythology, history, and art, but also because he tried to make great art out of the thoughts, aspirations, and beliefs of Englishmen in the very same way in which he conceived the Greeks as having worked. Moreover, to the Greeks he gave the sentiments of his countrymen, expressing thus the ideals they liked to associate with the ancient land of liberty, peace, and the arts. Yet he always returned from the Ancients to his own age, and he summarized his feeling for the antique world in the words of Andrew Marvell in his "imaginary conversation" with Milton:

Our admiration of Antiquity is in part extraneous from her merits: yet even this part, strange as the assertion may appear, is well founded. We learn many things from the ancients which it cost them no trouble to teach, and upon which they employed no imagination, no learning, no time. Those among us who have copied them, have not succeeded. To produce any effect on morals or on manners, or indeed to attract any attention, which, whatever be the pretext, is the principal if not the only aim of most writers, and certainly of all the comic, we must employ the language and consult the habits of our age (IV, 181).

Like other "romantic" writers, Landor felt that he must deal with matters of interest to his contemporaries. In replying to the speech of

---

[22] Introduction to *Pericles and Aspasia*, "Camelot Series" (1893), p. vi.
[23] Quoted by John Forster, *Walter Savage Landor* (1869), II, 298.

Marvell just quoted, Milton pointed out the principal lesson which the truly great English writers have learned from their study of classical literature and art, namely, "Write on the same principles as guided them"; and that was Landor's final advice, too. Reynolds and Blake, Pope and Shelley, could all agree with such guides. As steadily as any Romantic poet, Landor strove to capture the heroic elements in the life about him—even though he sometimes presented them in the guise of antiquity—with the simplicity and nobility which writers of every period since the Renaissance had found in the literature and sculpture of the ancient Greeks.

HUNT'S DESCRIPTIONS OF STATUES

Friend at some time of all the great Romantics except Blake, Leigh Hunt was both poet and critic in his own right. Trying his hand at various sorts of poetic endeavor—narratives and sonnets, lyrics of sentiment and *vers de société,* didactic verse and translations from Greek, Latin, Medieval Latin, and Italian—at some times he was a lesser Byron, at others a lesser Landor or Keats. In political opinions he was closest to Shelley, while the curious mixture of rationality and sentimentality in his critical judgments recalls Hazlitt. His *Autobiography* is a splendid picture of the most thoroughgoing "Liberal" among the English Romantic writers.

When a Deputy Grecian at Christ's Hospital, young Hunt began a lifelong attachment to poetry and the fine arts. Tooke's *Pantheon,* Lemprière's *Classical Dictionary,* and Spence's *Polymetis,* along with poetry, were the chief items in his aesthetic fare as in that of Keats. The glimpses of antiquity presented by those Neo-Classical gentlemen so delighted the impressionable scholar that he transfigured three young ladies of his acquaintance into goddesses from the *Pantheon.* In the studio of the celebrated Benjamin West he also familiarized himself with pictures and with "the tranquil, intent beauty" of the ancient statues. From the Academician the sensitive boy heard the story of Napoleon's eagerness in welcoming the Venus de Medici to

Paris. "Bonaparte, Mr. West said, turned round to those about him, and said, with his eyes lit up, 'She's coming!' as if he had been talking of a living person." [24] In such incidents Hunt early found the interests which later gave the aesthetic flavor to all his works.

Traveling to Italy, "the land of the fine arts," in 1821, Hunt responded to the magic of the South in the fashion of the true children of the Enlightenment. The very word "Mediterranean" haunted him like a passion, and he incanted a prose paean to the region which Dr. Johnson had termed "the grand object of travelling." Hunt reveled in the reminders of the classical world and felt that "Antiquity refuses to look ancient in Italy . . . you discover that Italy is the land, not of the venerable, but the beautiful; and cease to look for old age in the chosen land of the Apollo and the Venus." [25] Even more striking was his conclusion that the works of Dante and the painters of the early Italian Renaissance were "the only real antiquities" in contrast to the classical objects of timeless beauty.

In Florence this passionate pilgrim met the heaviest disappointment of the visit when the Venus de Medici—by whom, he said, more pilgrims were drawn to Italy than "by the Virgin herself"—failed to meet his expectations. In relating the incident in the *Autobiography,* Hunt reluctantly admitted that he had been forced to side with Smollett and Hazlitt, the severe critics of the famous statue, rather than with Thomson, Sterne, and her admirers. Prefacing his remarks with the same sort of humble apology employed by the earlier detractors of the Venus, Hunt confessed that he had been unable to agree with "the poetical Scotchman" Thomson in regard to "the statue that enchants the world." The Venus, he maintained, was immodest both in countenance and in gesture. Hers was "the face of a foolish young woman, who thinks highly of herself, and is prepared to be sarcastic on all her acquaintance." The expression suited the gesture: it was "pert, pretty, insolent, and fastidious." As a matter of fact the renowned Venus was, in Hunt's opinion, a fine statue only when compared with the "lank and insipid" goddess of love by Canova, which

---

[24] *The Autobiography of Leigh Hunt,* ed. Roger Ingpen (1903), I, 97.
[25] *Ibid.,* II, 108.

Byron and others had showered with superlatives. Hunt argued, "Venus, above all goddesses, ought to be a woman; whereas the statue of Canova, with its straight sides and Frenchified head of hair, is the image (if of anything at all) of Fashion affecting Modesty." [26] A true-born English Romantic poet, he had little use for the classicality of the world of fashion.

Like Hazlitt and Gibbon, in Florence Hunt was most interested in the portrait busts of the Roman emperors. These Romans, both the heroic and the commonplace, convinced him of the justice of Hazlitt's identification of Englishmen with the Ancients. Yet Hunt soon tired of the pageant of art and history in Italy. At heart no more a wanderer than Wordsworth, he preferred to have sight of classical nymphs and goddesses at home among his books and friends in the Arcadian English countryside where he had first imagined the ancient world in reading his beloved poets. The life of Childe Harold was not for him, and the antique statues no longer signified to him what they had to the eighteenth-century poets and connoisseurs or, indeed, to many of his contemporaries. Still, he was man of taste enough to embellish his writings with references to the Antique.

Like Shelley and Peacock, Hunt was fond of adorning with statuary the houses and pavilions in his poetry. The classical summerhouse in *The Story of Rimini* (1816), a poem in the lush manner of his favorite Italian poets, was

> a delicious sight,
> Small, marble, well-proportioned, mellowy white,
> With yellow vine-leaves sprinkled,

in surroundings reminiscent of Claude Lorrain.

> It was a beauteous piece of ancient skill,
> Spared from the rage of war, and perfect still;
> By most supposed the work of fairy hands,
> Famed for luxurious taste, and choice of lands,
>
> . . .
>
> But 'twas a temple, as its sculpture told,
> Built to the Nymphs that haunted there of old;

[26] *Ibid.*, pp. 160 ff.

For o'er the door was carved a sacrifice
By girls and shepherds brought, with reverent eyes,
Of sylvan drinks and foods, simple and sweet,
And goats with struggling horns and planted feet:
And on a line with this ran round about
A like relief, touched exquisitely out,
That shewed, in various scenes, the nymphs themselves.
(Book III, ll. 64–72, 448–50, 456–59.)

In this description of sculptured reliefs Hunt was at his best, since the classical subject may have prevented him from slipping into the flaccidity often found in his works. Among his contemporaries only Keats, Landor, and Shelley surpassed him in similar passages.

Involved most of his life in the helter-skelter of journalism and caught several times in the turmoil of political strife, Hunt dreamed often of a retreat far from the world, a finer version of the cottage in the Vale of Health described by Keats in *Sleep and Poetry* and by himself in "Fancy's Party" as a

poetic corner
With books about and o'er us,
With busts and flowers,
And pictured bowers (ll. 1–4).

One of his statues was the Venus (presumably the Medici figure), Hunt told his readers in "To the Lares," in which he also promised to honor the household spirits with

some divine antique . . .
Which ye may whisper Greek to.

In "The 'Choice' " (1823), a poem in couplets suggesting the familiar verse of other Romantic poets as well as that of Pomfret and numerous Horatian poets of the eighteenth century, Hunt showed the good taste of a connoisseur like Samuel Rogers. Describing the house of his choice, he remarked,

And yet to show I had a taste withal,
I'd have some casts of statues in the hall,
Or rather entrance, whose sweet steady eyes
Should touch the comers with a mild surprise (ll. 108–11).

In the study was to be a bust of Mercury; in the chapel were to be found both "Greek beauty" and "Gothic shade." [27]

Statues of Apollo, god of Poesy, were Hunt's favorites, if one judges from his poetry. In the satirical "Feast of the Poets" (1811) he described the god himself with a statue in mind, presumably that in the Belvedere.

> Imagine, however, if shape there must be,
> A figure sublimed above mortal degree,
> His limbs the perfection of elegant strength,—
> A fine flowing roundness inclining to length,—
> A back dropping in,—an expansion of chest,
> (For the God, you'll observe, like his statues was drest)
> His throat like a pillar for smoothness and grace,
> His curls in a cluster,—and then such a face,
> As marked him at once the true offspring of Jove,
> The brow all of wisdom, and lips all of love (ll. 51–60).

In contrast to that Browningesque account, the poet maintained in a more serious and conventional passage in "Apollo and the Sunbeams" that the ancient god still lived:

> he has shrines
> And marble incarnations in hushed rooms,
> Where, as he stands, he seems as though he need
> Never move more, reposing on his truth,
> And the air loves him (ll. 32–36).[28]

Hunt found greatest satisfaction in the reposeful beauty of both the Apollos and the busts. Throughout his life the antique statues possessed, for him, the gentle beauty and the calm perfection which he had discovered in his boyhood visits to West's studio. The fondness for the tranquillity of the Antique is most clearly seen, perhaps, in the third of the sonnets to Dr. Batty in appreciation of his gift of Milton's "Apollonian tresses," where Hunt specifically mentioned

> the placid power
> Of those old Grecian busts.

[27] With this poem compare Rogers, "An Epistle to a Friend" (1798); see below, p. 258.

[28] Hunt's note indicated his indebtedness to *The Excursion* (Book IV, ll. 858 ff.) for his "old imagination" which "shaped forth a god."

On at least one occasion Hunt was critical, however, of even his favorite statues. As a "romantic" poet, he feared to give one definite form to an artist's fancies, since he felt that a rigid form or "fixed shape" never does justice to the original conception.

> We hurt the stories of the antique world
> By thinking of our school-books,
>
> . . .
>
> Or sculptures, which from Roman 'studios' thrown,
> Turn back Deucalion's flesh and blood to stone.
>   (*Hero and Leander,* ll. 8–9, 11–12 [1832–60].)

Since his early taste was formed on the familiar Greco-Roman antiques, Hunt apparently concerned himself with the Elgin Marbles but little. In an essay in the *Examiner* in 1821, however, he assumed that all Englishmen had been "enraptured" with those works of sculpture.[29] He also continued the tradition of Pope and other satirists of the fashionable zeal for antiquities. When Apollo visited the revels of the Blue-Stockings, he found an amusing scene:

> The buxom, uniting both tastes, filled the doors
> With their shoulders and frills, *à la Louis Quatorze;*
> O with robes *à l'antique,* and with crowns from their graperies:
> Blest were the eyes that beheld their broad draperies!
>   (*Blue-Stocking Revels,* Book I, ll. 156–59.)

Nevertheless, under the spell of the Grecian struggle for independence and of his philhellenic friends, Hunt confessed the modern world's debt to the Greeks.

All that is best in our very dress and fashions comes from Greece; the draperies of our women; and the heads, rescued from the powderer and the peruke-maker, of our men. . . . We cannot elegantly amuse ourselves, we cannot paint, sculpture, write poetry or music, we cannot be school-boys, be patriots, be orators, be useful or ornamental members of society, be human beings in a high state of cultivation, be persons living and moving and having their being in other worlds besides those of the idiot who only sees before him, without having a debt of gratitude to the Greeks.[30]

---

[29] "The Greeks," Oct. 7, 1821 (conveniently found in R. B. Johnson, *Shelley–Leigh Hunt* [1928], p. 325).
[30] *Ibid.,* pp. 323–24.

XI. THE LESSER POETS

THE "OLD ANTIQUE"

FOR THE LESSER POETS of the Romantic period the Antique still exerted great attraction; hardly a poet failed at some time to respond to the "marvellous power" of Grecian sculpture. What Haydon termed the "old antique" in contrast to the Parthenon figures remained popular, especially with poets who saw ancient sculpture principally in books or in Paris and Italy. The ideas associated with the Antique in the eighteenth century likewise survived in many poems of the early nineteenth century, while the characteristically "romantic" responses of Coleridge and Wordsworth spread somewhat slowly among the poets. For a number of reasons, then, the "old antique" more than held its own against the Elgin Marbles in the first third of the nineteenth century.

Travel on the Continent was still almost a necessity for both poet and gentleman. The familiar Greco-Roman statues became more accessible to Englishmen than ever before, when Napoleon brought the Apollo Belvedere, the Venus de Medici, the Laocoön, the Torso Belvedere, and the Horses of Lysippus to France as part of the spoil of his Italian campaigns. After the Peace of Amiens in 1802 many Englishmen scurried across the Channel to behold those miracles of ancient art. In *Elements of Art; a Poem; in Six Cantos; with Notes and a Preface; Including Strictures on the State of the Arts, Criticism, Patronage, and Public Taste* (1809) Martin Shee, R.A., related the story of the installation of the Apollo in the Louvre in what became known as the Salle d'Apollon. He regretted, too, that the English had not succeeded in marching to Paris in order to pillage the Louvre:

The author confesses, that he would have seen with a very patriotic exultation, a detachment of the committee of Taste under some adventurous virtuoso, or a well selected rifle corps of the Royal Academy, appointed to

invade all the recesses of the Louvre—to dislodge its most illustrious in-
habitants, and as prisoners of war, conduct them to assist in adorning the
triumph, and advancing the arts of his country.[1]

Benjamin West was present at the reception of the Venus de Medici,
and his glowing account of Napoleon awaiting the goddess left a
lasting impression on Leigh Hunt. Flaxman alone among the English
artists, ruled by great scorn for the tyrant, refused to look at the
statues, though Landor also raged at Napoleon so violently that he
was unable to appreciate the statuary.[2] Of Englishmen who beheld
the Venus, Hazlitt, then a student of art in Paris, was almost the
only one whose response was not ecstatic.

Samuel Rogers was so moved by the statuary that he wrote, on the
spot as it were, the sonnet entitled "To the Fragment of a Statue of
Hercules, Commonly Called the Torso," in which he continued the
prosaic vein of his earlier works:

> And dost thou still, thou mass of breathing stone,
> (Thy giant limbs to night and chaos hurled)
> Still sit as on the fragment of the world;
> Surviving all, majestic and alone? [3]

The enthusiasm of Thomas Campbell, who saw the famous statues
with Mrs. Siddons in 1814, probably represented the feelings of the
majority of poetic travelers during this period. Campbell gloried in
the antiques:

[1] See the notes to the descriptions of the Apollo and the Venus, Canto II, ll. 187 ff.,
223 ff.

[2] See above, p. 234.

[3] The beginnings of Rogers's interest in art (aroused by a visit to Paris in 1791
and by the final lecture of Reynolds) were evident in the description of the processes
of art in "The Pleasures of Memory" (1792) and in "An Epistle to a Friend" (1798).
> "Thy gallery, Florence, gilds my humble walls;
> And my low roof the Vatican recalls!"
Flaxman, Fuseli, and Wedgwood were among his mentors (with what different
results were they acquainted with Blake!), and his artist friends aided him in dec-
orating his rooms with classical statuary. In 1803 Rogers built the mansion in St.
James's Place, which became a literary salon for many Romantics, with classical
decorations by Flaxman. The staircase had a frieze from the Parthenon, derived from
Stuart and Revett's *Antiquities of Athens*. See *The Poetical Works of Samuel Rogers*,
ed. Edward Bell (1892), pp. xxv ff.

Far from wondering at the madness of the female, who fell in love with the Apollo, I thought her only a reasonable enthusiast. I could not command myself, and left Mrs. Siddons—glad to indulge the most absurd and pleasing of all tears. I know it is all *imagination*. Perhaps, unless told of it, I could not even discover either the Apollo or the Venus; yet, when convinced that I really saw the statues that enchant the world—the prodigies of two thousand years!—such associations rushed upon me, that I thought myself far transported into another world.[4]

John Scott, friend of many writers of the Romantic period, described his impressions in *A Visit to Paris in 1814,* reporting that "if I were condemned to a solitude [on a desert isle?], . . . I would much rather surround myself with these sublime marbles than with the canvasses up stairs . . . the triumphant Godhead of the Apollo, the delicacy and beauty of the Venus, the terrors and agony of the Laocoön, the symmetry of the Hermaphrodite. . . ."[5]

In 1815 when Napoleon was vanquished and the art treasures sent back to Florence, Rome, and Venice, there was a flood of poetry. George Croly, an enthusiast for things Grecian, wrote a long poem in Spenserians entitled *Paris in 1815* with full accounts of the Halls of Sculpture at the Louvre. "The glorious Grecian steeds" from Venice drew the most lines; but the Apollo, the Laocoön, the Dying Gladiator, and the Venus—"a being of grace and placid beauty"— were sufficiently described. Croly gave a picture also of the removal of the statues.[6]

Felicia Hemans, that dependable barometer of taste, celebrated the return of the sculpture in *The Restoration of the Works of Art to Italy* (1816), "so sweet a song of triumph of their return" that her

[4] *Life and Letters of Thomas Campbell,* ed. William Beattie (1849), II, 254. Both actress and poet found the Apollo the most overpowering statue, while Campbell added that later in the day the tragedienne, "exhausted with admiring the Apollo, fell asleep."

[5] Page 225 (Philadelphia, 1815). For Wordsworth's interest in this book and its successor, *Paris Revisited in 1815,* see the letters to Scott, May 15, 1815, and Feb. 22, 1816.

[6] *Paris in 1815* drew the laconic praise of "good" from Byron; see *Letters* (Prothero), IV, 164. For Croly's debt to *Childe Harold,* Cantos I and II, and in turn Byron's debt to *Paris in 1815* in Canto IV, see S. C. Chew, Jr., "Byron and Croly," *MLN,* XXVIII (1913), 201–3.

couplets were warmly praised by Byron and the poem went through
at least two editions. With information gathered mainly from Winckelmann and Alison, she gave full play to her enthusiasm by praising
the

> Grecian skill sublime
> Inspiring young genius

with a parade of the statues: the Torso Belvedere, "triumphant
wreck"; the Horses of Lysippus; the Apollo Belvedere; the Laocoön;
the Venus de Medici,

> Love's radiant goddess, Idol of mankind!
> Once the brightest object of Devotion's vow,
> Shall claim from taste a kindred worship now.

Once again in the possession of Italy, these antiques later called
forth the praises of Byron in *Childe Harold* and elsewhere, Shelley
in his *Notes* and poetry, Hunt in his *Autobiography,* Hazlitt, Landor,
and many other poets. After *Childe Harold* the most famous poem
on Italy and its cultural associations and shrines was Samuel Rogers's
Italy (1822–28). At Florence, having paid his first homage to Virtue,
the poet turned to the Venus de Medici,

> worshipping,
> In her small temple of rich workmanship,
> Venus herself, who, when she left the skies,
> Came hither.

William Sotheby followed Byron and Rogers in *Italy and Other
Poems* (1828). At the Vatican he "sympathized" with the Torso, the
Apollo (relating, of course, the story of the maid who died for love
of the statue); at Venice with the Horses; at Florence with the Venus,
the Niobe, and the Dancing Faun.[7]

Most of this poetry on travel and the arts was fully supplied with
notes out of the familiar accounts also read by the better poets. Forsyth's *Remarks on Antiquities, Arts, and Letters, during an Excursion
in Italy in 1802–3* (1813) and Eustace's *Classical Tour through Italy*

---

[7] In *The Elements* Sotheby gave an "origin" and "progress" of the arts in phrases
suggestive of Milton (pp. 263 ff.), while Virgil's tomb (pp. 157 ff.) drew from the
poet a Wordsworthian passage on the pagan embodiment of nymphs.

(1813), for example, supplied information to Shelley, Wordsworth, and Byron, and to Mrs. Hemans. The many books of archaeological findings were similarly employed by important poet and poetaster. The ideas of Winckelmann, often as advanced by later critics like A. W. Schlegel, were common in minor Romantic poetry. Handbooks of mythology and general books on the arts, culture, and history of Greece, like Potter's *Archaeologia Graeca* and Barthélémy's *Les Voyages du jeune Anacharsis,* had places on the writing-tables of the poets. A popular book with the Romantic poets was Madame de Staël's *Corinne,* a mixture of love story, guidebook, and herald of Italomania.

The universities also encouraged poets to acquaint themselves with the antiquities. The Newdigate Prize at Oxford was established in 1806 for "fifty lines and no more in recommendation of the ancient Greek and Roman remains of architecture, sculpture, and painting." The initial award went to "A Recommendation of the Study of the Remains of Ancient Grecian and Roman Architecture, Sculpture, and Painting," with references to Flaxman and Mrs. Damer as well as to the Venus, Urania, Apollo, and Laocoön. The pugilistic skill of the poet John Wilson ("Christopher North") may have aided him in winning the prize against his competitors, numbered by the author of his *Memoir* in the Galignani edition (Paris, 1829) of his work as three thousand! Were the number of poets decimated, a considerable body of poetical recommendation of antiquities would still remain.

The following titles show that the collegiate poets of the early nineteenth century were following earlier masters than the "romantic" poets.

1810, G. R. Chinnery,	"The Statue of the Dying Gladiator."
1811, Richard Burden,	"Parthenon."
1812, H. H. Milman,	"The Belvidere Apollo."
1814, J. L. Adolphus,	"Niobe."
1815, Samuel Richards,	"Temple of Theseus."
1816, Alexander Macdonnell,	"Horses of Lysippus."
1817, J. S. Boone,	"The Farnese Hercules."
1826, W. W. Tireman,	"Trajan's Pillar."

Milman's "Belvidere Apollo" was apparently the most widely read of these poems, for it was printed in several journals. The poet claimed, moreover, that Byron borrowed from the prize poem in his account of the Apollo in *Childe Harold*. Milman may have been the chief propagator of the story of the French maiden who died for love of the Apollo. Hartley Coleridge failed to win the Newdigate in three competitions. Two lines in his "Farnese Hercules" were criticized as "Lakish," when they were actually by Theocritus! [8]

The poets of Cambridge were not to be outshone in praising the Antique, and several Medal Poems may be mentioned.

1819,	T. B. Macaulay,	"Pompeii."
1822,	J. H. Bright,	"Palmyra."
1824,	W. M. Praed,	"Athens."
	T. M[arshall],	"Athens."
1825,	E. G. L. Bulwer,	"Sculpture."

The Cambridge poets took more comprehensive subjects than individual statues or temples, perhaps because they were not limited to fifty lines. Bulwer-Lytton's "Sculpture" exceeds the others in interest in the present study, because it was in the tradition of the "progress" of sculpture in eighteenth-century poetry. The story here went from Greece to nineteenth-century classicistic artists like Thorwaldsen, Dannecker, Chantrey, and Canova. The sculptor was imagined as carving the idea-in-the-mind—"the hand sculptured what the fancy drew." The Venus stood in no less than "breathing, palpable, embodied love." Yet the poet was aware of the difference between the pagan and Christian worlds, the South and the North:

[8] For the several prize poems on statues, see *Oxford Prize Poems, with Illustrations, Historical and Descriptive, of the Newdigate Poems* (1827). The remarks of Hartley Coleridge occur in "Ignoramus on the Fine Arts," *Essays and Marginalia*, ed. Derwent Coleridge (1851), I, 188–89. His "Horses of Lysippus" may be found in *Complete Poetical Works*, ed. Ramsay Colles, "Muses' Library," pp. xxx–xxxi. The failure to win the Newdigate Prize was the turning-point in the young poet's life; see *Letters of Hartley Coleridge,* ed. Grace E. Griggs and Earl L. Griggs (1936), pp. 17–18. Mr. Robert H. Super has called my attention to a rival of the 1810 Newdigate poem, "The Statue of the Dying Gladiator; a Poem, by a Non-Academic," which appeared that year.

> I pause—a Northern votary's wreath to twine,
> Land of the Roman round thy ruin'd shrine.[9]

The traditions of the eighteenth century endured in the art world as in the universities, and the "old antique" still ruled the affections of many gentlemen and artists. As "ideal forms" the Venus and the Apollo were still unchallenged. For many a gentleman accustomed to the Greco-Roman works, the Elgin Marbles seemed less "perfect" and hence inferior. Poets continued to describe the familiar statues long after the Parthenon figures were at rest in the British Museum.

The spirit and matter of Hayley's *Essay on Sculpture* was renewed (or continued) in some of the versified theorizing about art in the Romantic period. Martin Shee's *Rhymes on Art* (1805) and *Elements of Art* (1809) were essays on the criticism of art in Popeian couplets. "Advent'rous on didactick wings," he sought to impart information and stimulate appreciation of the arts. He was a complete Grecian:

> To form your Taste, and educate your eye,
> In Beauty's School, to polished Greece apply.
>
> . . .
>
> Be yours the task, with faithful hand to trace
> Her forms of symmetry—her turns of grace.

His "progress" of sculpture was a long and detailed account out of Pausanias and Winckelmann. The Venus was the "unrivall'd Form" as she appeared in Paris:

> To thee the Bard, as erst on Ida's hill
> Like Paris, would present the Apple still,

and the Apollo was "the noblest image of a God below . . . through every age the idol of Virtù." In the number of his notes Shee surpassed even Hayley, and his learning crowded the verses off many

---

[9] See *Cambridge Medal Poems 1813–27* (1827) and *Poetical Works of the Rev. H. H. Milman* (1839), II, 297. Bulwer-Lytton's poem was published separately at least twice (Cambridge, 1825; New York, 1831). He referred, like many poets, to Milman's Apollo and to the maid of France; moreover, he sketched the scene in the sculpture galleries of the Louvre in 1815, when the troops of the Allies went there in large numbers.

a page. Like Pope and Byron, he could satirize the affectations of the connoisseurs:

> On Tiber's banks have they but passed a week!
> They ever after rave of the antique.
> In loud delirium Nature's charms disown,
> And like Pygmalion, fall in love with stone.[10]

THE USES OF SCULPTURE

The Antique was also the source, as it had been for poets in the eighteenth century like Prior, Robert Lloyd, or Walpole, of decorative detail, classical allusions, epigrams, and *vers de société*. Romantic poets from Byron and Landor to Mrs. Hemans and Henry Neele imitated the Greek anthologists and more recent makers of highly polished, cameo-like verses. Thomas Moore showed this interest in ancient sculpture as well, perhaps, as any Romantic poet. In "A Kiss *à l'Antique"* Moore described a kiss modeled on the amorous interchange of passion of Cupid and Psyche, seen in this case in the gem on a maiden's ring.

> Look, darling, what a sweet design!
>   . . .
>
> Thou seest, it is a simple youth
>   By some enamoured nymph embraced–
> Look, Nea, love! and say, in sooth,
>   Is not her hand most dearly placed?

---

[10] *Elements of Art,* Canto V, ll. 121–24. Yet Shee elsewhere expressed sentiments like these spoken by the Torso Belvedere:

> " 'On Attic wings alone, attempt the skies,
>   Nor look at Nature but through Grecian eyes.
>   . . .
>
> To copy Nature! Precept vain and weak!
> Can vulgar Nature vie with the Antique?
> Can models cull'd from Drury, or Rag-fair,
>   Rival the Medici, or Belvedere?' " (Canto I.)

Shee was in part anti-Winckelmann, and he carefully answered the arguments concerning climate, government, religion, athletic games as influences upon Grecian art. He praised the Elgin Marbles, but felt that one should go slowly before decking "the brows, even of Theseus himself, with those wreaths which are to be plucked from the Torso, the Hercules, and the Laocoön." As a member of the Royal Academy, he placed art above poetry: "Can the airy shadows of poetical imagery be compared to the embodied realities of Art?"

Upon his curled head behind
　　It seems in careless play to lie,
Yet presses gently, half inclined
　　To bring his lip of nectar nigh!

Oh happy maid! too happy boy!
　　The one so fond and faintly loth,
The other yielding slow to joy—
　　Oh, rare indeed, but blissful both!

Imagine, love, that I am he,
　　And just as warm as he is chilling;
Imagine too that thou art she,
　　But quite as cold as she is willing:

So may we try the graceful way
　　In which their gentle arms are twined,
And thus, like her, my hand I lay
　　Upon thy wreathed hair behind:

And thus I feel thee breathing sweet,
　　As slow to mine thy head I move;
And thus our lips together meet,
　　And—thus I kiss thee—oh, my love!

Moore entirely forgot the gem and the sculpture in reviving the ancient passion in the spirit of Elizabethan or Renaissance Ovidianism or, shall one say, of Byron, Hunt, and young Keats?

In the note explaining that he had in mind the Cupid and Psyche at Florence, Moore added, "I know of very few subjects in which poetry could be more interestingly employed, than in illustrating some of the ancient statues and gems." [11] Ever since Addison and Spence had pointed out parallels between poetry and statuary, gems, and coins, poets in England had "illustrated" ancient statues by both

[11] *Works,* ed. A. D. Godley (1915), p. 109. He was drawing his figures from the *Museum Florentinum,* Vol. II, Plates XLIII, XLIV. Moore's lines may have contributed to Byron's "antique" embrace of Don Juan and Haidée, while the language of the third stanza quoted suggests the lovers on Keats's Grecian urn; see above, pp. 166–67, 222–23. There are several poems in this vein in *The Literary Remains of the Late Henry Neele* (1829). See also "A Tale; Addressed to a Sybarite," in Isaac D'Israeli's *Narrative Poems* (1803), where a lover employs a statue of himself by "skilled Praxiteles" to soften his loved one's coldness until she cries, "Oh, be not twice a Statue to my sigh!"

ancient and modern poetry and vice versa, while connoisseurs had long been interested in antique gems. Winckelmann's work on the collection of Baron de Stosch, which drew the praise of Goethe, was well known throughout Europe. Of English publications *A Select Collection of Drawings from Curious Antique Gems* by T. Worlidge (1768) and *A Descriptive Catalogue of a General Collection of Ancient and Modern Engraved Gems, Cameos as Well as Intaglios, Taken from the Most Celebrated Cabinets in Europe* by James Tassie and R. E. Raspe (1791) may be singled out here. The volumes on outlines by Cumberland and the drawings of Cipriani also drew attention to gems and to other works of art related to them.

Blake became interested in gems through his early studies and through his association with Cumberland, Flaxman, and the Wedgwoods, and several of the leading poets of the Romantic period responded likewise to cameos, intaglios, gems, and so forth. Not only Rogers but also Coleridge possessed a collection of engraved gems, and the young Keats wrote a sonnet on a Leander gem and also planned to "illustrate" Tassie's gems. Yet from Moore rather than the greater poets very likely stemmed the several volumes of "illustrations" of antique and other gems in the Romantic period.

Gems, Principally from the Antique, Drawn and Etched by Richard Dagley . . . (1822) was a popular book. George Croly contributed the verse "illustrations" of the gems, which were chosen, in language reminiscent of Addison, Pope, and Spence, with an eye to their "capability of supplying topics for poetry." Poets and men of taste would find them valuable for the many reasons announced in the preface:

Gems illustrate the attributes and tales of mythology, the costumes of antiquity, the fine romances of the poets, the characters of the early languages, the great historic events, and the progress of the arts . . . they offer an endless treasure of the brilliant thoughts, and buried wisdom, the forgotten skill, and the vanished beauty, of a time when the mind and form of man reached their perfection.[12]

---

[12] See above, pp. 109*n*, 140–41, 210, and Croly's *Works* (1830), I, 251–52. After reading several "illustrations," one is inclined to accept Hazlitt's description of Croly's work as *"auctioneer-*poetry" (*Works* [Howe], XII, 104–5).

Not many years later appeared (1831) a work entitled *Illustrations of Modern Sculpture. A Series of Engravings, with Descriptive Prose, and Illustrative Poetry,* by T. K. Hervey. Hayley's poetical "Sketch of Modern Sculpture" had not been written, but now Flaxman, Canova, and Westmacott received "illustration" in poetry from Hervey. At last these classicists were with the Ancients!

The Ovidian tale was popular with Romantic poets, and it is not surprising that the story of Pygmalion should be retold. With his extreme admiration of the Elizabethans, Thomas Lovell Beddoes was the poet for the task. In "Pygmalion, the Cyprian Statuary" (1825) the sculptural presence was of minor emphasis in the poem, the major interest being the sensations of Pygmalion and, it may be, the poet's identification of himself with the statuary. In a city of Cyprus stood a lavish palace of Keatsian architectural effects, though the rhythms and texture of the poem suggest a mixture of Landor and Shelley quite as often as Keats.

> There stood and sate or made rough steeds their throne
> Immortal generations wrung from stone
> Alike too beautiful for life and death
> And bodies that a soul of mortal breath
> Would be the dross of.

There dwelt also lonely Pygmalion, loving no earthly creature but dreaming of an ideal spirit such as Shelley imagined. Out of a marble fragment, in a fury of "light creative" the sculptor shaped "a delicate delight"; and this shining marvel

> was smooth and full, as if one gush
> Of life had washed her.

The "loved image stepping from his breast" had entered the stone. Yet his prayers in Faustian agony for the life of his "she-rock" went unheard. Pygmalion went insane, and then ironically the statue came to life.

A second story of a human being who died for love of a statue concerned a maid of France. Of Ovidian inspiration though also documented by the reports of eyewitnesses, the sad tale proved that modern lovers were as sensitive as the ancient. Procter gave the most appreciative as well as the longest treatment of the story in Romantic poetry in *The Girl of Provence* (1823), using it as a pendant to the title poem. Eva, the girl of Provence, who dreamed in the fashion of Byron's "solitary nymph" (*Childe Harold,* Canto IV, stanza clxii) of Apollo in a setting reminiscent of *The Eve of Saint Agnes,* went on an *Endymion*-like visit to a marvelous palace where she became the bride of Phoebus. On awaking—"for 'twas a dream," the poet took the pains of reminding us—the poor girl pined and presumably died. Then Procter added seventeen stanzas about the actual French maid whose love for the Apollo Belvedere drove her to death. In the language of Byron partly modified by Keats, the poet described "the marble dream" with an abundance of mythological reference.

> Life in each limb is seen, and on the brow
> Absolute God;—no stone nor mockery shape
> But the resistless *Sun,*
>
> . . .
>
> And round his head and round his limbs have clung
> Life and the flush of Heaven, and youth divine,
> And in the breathed nostril backwards flung,
> And in the terrors of his face, that shine
> Right through the marble, which will never pine
> To paleness though a thousand years have fled,
> But looks above all fate, and mocks the dead.[13]

The fond idolatress strewed flowers before the god, "worshipping in amorous pain," until one day she was gone from the Louvre and died in raving madness.

Thomas Moore's "The Ring" was a ballad based on the medieval legend of a young man betrothed to the statue of Venus. The inspiration here was mainly from Gothic romances and ballads, with the statue incidental of course. Moore was even more ambiguous than medieval narrators of the episode:

> It was a heathen goddess, or
> Perhaps a heathen queen.

[13] Stanzas lxxxvii–lxxxviii (*The Flood of Thessaly, The Girl of Provence, and Other Poems* [1823], pp. 114–15). See also Richard W. Armour, *Barry Cornwall* (Boston, 1935), p. 159, and above, pp. 163–64, 262.

The general use of sculpture for a variety of effects survived among poets like Peacock, Southey, and Campbell. The first, Thomas Love Peacock, was the deepest in the arts. *Rhododaphne* (1818) presented a partly Shelleyan treatment of Grecian sculpture; hence, the criticism by the greater poet was sympathetic. "It is a Greek and Pagan poem. In sentiment and scenery it is essentially antique. We stand in the marble temples of the Gods, and see their sculptured forms gazing and almost breathing around." Throughout the poem statuary was conspicuous in imagery and in references to the life imagined in the figures.

We visit the solitudes of Thessalian magic, and tremble with new wonder to hear statues speak and move and to see the shaggy changelings minister to their witch queen with the shape of beasts and the reason of men, and move among the animated statues who people her inchanted palaces and gardens.[14]

Southey showed relatively little interest in the arts, though he drew Oriental ruins in *Thalaba* (1800) and elsewhere used some of the popularized information about "all-glorious Greece." Phrases about the freedom and the arts of the Greeks were more generously sprinkled through Campbell's poetry. With his fondness for seeing resemblances between actual persons, including Indians, and works of art, the ancient sculptures came in handy. His lectures on the poetry of Greece he "enriched by frequent allusions to her sculptures." [15]

GREECE AND THE ELGIN MARBLES

Greece came into its own in the topographical poetry of the Romantic period, thanks to Byron and Shelley and their general praise of Greece and their enthusiasm for the War of Independence and also, in a lesser degree, to Wordsworth and Keats and their interest in the myths of the Greeks. Even before them there were such poems as

[14] See particularly, Canto I, ll. 9 ff.; the Temple to Love with the three statues with "sculptured emblems fair" of Creative, Heavenly, and Earthly Love, ll. 98–106; Canto III, ll. 64–65; Canto VI, ll. 298–301; and Shelley, *Prose*, VI, 273. See also the incident in *Crotchet Castle* (chap. vii) where Mr. Crotchet filled his house with Venuses and defended the nude against the Rev. Dr. Folliot: "Sir, ancient sculpture is the true school of modesty. But where the Greeks had modesty, we have cant. . . ."

[15] See *Life and Letters* (Beattie), II, 255–56, 341–42. Mrs. Siddons made him "proud of English beauty—even in the presence of Grecian sculpture" (II, 270).

Richard Polwhele's *Grecian Prospects: a Poem, in Two Cantos* (Helston, 1799), Joseph D. Carlyle's *Poems, Suggested Chiefly by Scenes in Asia-Minor, Syria, and Greece* (1805), Henry Boyd's "Ruins of Athens" (1807), and Waller R. Wright's *Horae Ionicae* (1809). Carlyle, who had accompanied the Earl of Elgin to the East in 1799, proved himself a traveler of deep feeling in "On Viewing Athens from the Pnyx, by the Light of a Waning Moon." [16]

More than anything else, Byron's devotion to Greece set the tone for the lesser poets. Even in the narrative poems and in *Don Juan* he praised the land of freedom, glory, and the arts in ancient times and the region of blue skies, olive fields, and classical monuments in modern days. Throughout his work Greece was ever the Idea of Greece, a land once free and living and productive of great art and heroes but now dead until reawakened by the freedom soon to sweep the earth. Shelley, too, used Grecian names to evoke a similar set of emotions in a fashion suggesting the symbols of the later school of English poetry. The lesser poets imitated Byron and Shelley, of course, but in general they were less successful because they made too explicit the feelings which Byron and Shelley, like the Symbolists, were content to arouse without exactly defining. In contrast to such general praise of Grecian landscape and antiquities, Wordsworth's account of Greek mythology in *The Excursion* led a number of poets to consider the spirit of Grecian religion, mythology, and art. To this stream of Grecian interest the poetry of Keats also contributed. Thus, the minor poets who wrote of Greece followed either or both of these groups of greater poets, sometimes describing Grecian scenery and art for general purposes and sometimes reflecting rather seriously upon the nature of the mythology and religion of the Greeks. Every poet who wrote of Greece responded at some time to the Parthenon.

Besides the statues known to the poets of the two preceding centuries, the sculptures from the Parthenon were now in England. Re-

[16] In the eighteenth century poets like Thomson and Falconer and Thomas Warton had written descriptions of Greece; yet it is interesting that Aubin, *Topographical Poetry in XVIII-Century England,* lists only one topographical poem on Greece before 1800; see pp. 366, 307, and entries under "Greece" in his Index. Wright's work (3d ed., 1816) and Carlyle's *Poems* belong in Aubin's list.

moved by Lord Elgin and his agents in the years 1801–6 and finally purchased for the British Museum in 1816, these great works were destined, as their zealous proponent Haydon prophesied, "as completely [to] overthrow the old antique, as ever one system of philosophy overthrew another more [un?] enlightened." Critics like Hazlitt soon wrote of the Marbles as "the finest remains of Grecian art . . . the paragons of sculpture and the mould of form." [17]

Two lesser poets paralleled Byron's attacks in *The Curse of Minerva* and *Childe Harold* on the Parthenon Marbles and their thief. In 1813 Horace Smith printed "The Parthenon; on the Dilapidation of the Temple of Minerva at Athens" in the work entitled *Horace in London,* written by him and his brother James. In the six Spenserian stanzas of "The Parthenon" Smith was following *Childe Harold,* and he may also have seen the manuscript of *The Curse of Minerva.* Though disparate in length, the two poems were similar in plan.[18] In Smith's poem,

> As Elgin o'er the violated wave,
> Spoil'd Parthenon, thy marble glories bore,
> While modern Greeks, alas! too weak to save,
> With silent tears his sacrilege deplore,

the gods and goddesses arose to utter their maledictions on the Scot's unlucky head. Pallas enjoyed the privilege of giving the curse, screaming in a spirit similar to that of Byron's goddess that a baneful life awaited Elgin. One of the ships bearing the spoils sinks, and Poseidon "snatches the relics" to "deck his coral palaces."

> The sea-nymphs sound their shells as they regain
> The shipwreck'd trophies of their monarch's fane.

Soon too, the poet states, "a titled bard from Britain's Isle" is going to "fire with Athens' wrongs an angry age." Smith gave no indication whatsoever of the merit of the sculpture. "The Parthenon" won praise from Byron himself in a letter to John Murray (February 20, 1813), but two years later he was forced to disown some verses on "The

---

[17] See Haydon, *Autobiography* (Taylor, Huxley), I, 235, and Hazlitt, *Works* (Howe), XVIII, 160.

[18] See Claude M. Fuess, *Lord Byron as a Satirist in Verse* (New York, 1912), p. 90.

Malediction of Minerva, or the Athenian Marble-Market" signed "Steropes" in the *New Monthly Magazine,* April, 1815.[19]

A second poet, John Galt, claimed that his own "Atheniad," a poem written at Athens about 1810 and read by Byron during his travels in the eastern Mediterranean, had been the source of the plan and some of the ideas of *The Curse of Minerva.* That the charge has little truth can be seen from even a brief glance at "The Atheniad." Elgin or Brucides is prodded to his crime by the "crafty" Mercury; for Galt, a Scot, stresses the mercenary aspects of the transactions instead of the Scottish nationality of the thief. The winds sink one of the ships. Minerva gets her revenge in making Brucides bring disgrace upon himself by writing strange messages which offend statesmen at home. Recalled, Elgin travels through Italy and France where Minerva as Talleyrand urges France to seize both Elgin and the statues. Later Fauvel, the French consul at Athens and a friend of Galt and Byron, who had "made much ado to stop such an atrocious robbery" as Elgin's theft in order to secure the sculptures for his own nation, was sent a four-wheeled "Byzantian" cart, but the Turks gave it to the English when the French invaded Egypt. The cart is being taken away by Dontitos,

> chieftain of the cords and crew
> That from their frames the sacred sculptures drew,

when Fauvel claims the work of art, and Dontitos surrenders it. Thus have the gods "avenged their fane"! [20]

Apparently the first favorable description of the Elgin Marbles— to balance the attacks by Byron, Horace Smith, and Galt—was the passage in *Greece* (1814) by a little-known poet. William Haygarth

[19] To Murray, Byron described (*Letters,* III, 270–71) "The Malediction" as "stolen and published in the miserable and villainous copy in the Magazine." The text was used in various pirated editions.

[20] See *The Autobiography of John Galt* (1833), I, 154–69, and also above, pp. 151 ff. "The Atheniad" first appeared in the *Monthly Magazine,* XLIX (1820), 51–54. More interesting than the poem is Galt's account of how he almost gained possession of the Elgin Marbles for his own profit (p. 158). In his authoritative article "Lord Elgin and His Collection" (*Journal of Hellenic Studies,* XXXVI [1916], 163 ff.), A. H. Smith fails to mention Galt's activities. Though Galt's abilities in fiction may have suggested his "tall tale," the financial arrangements concerning the Marbles at Malta may very well have allowed him to act somewhat as he reports.

belonged in the tradition of Byron (with whom he had been acquainted in Greece in 1811) both in seeing resemblances between actual women and antique statues and in responding to the associations of the Idea of Greece. The poem was in part the versification of his experiences in Greece. Also something of a Wordsworthian, the poet pointed out the spirit of Greek art and mythology:

> In them a spirit still survives, in them
> The soul of Athens seems to live again.

Haygarth imaginatively described the Elgin Marbles as he thought they must have appeared on the Parthenon to the believing Greeks, and he attempted to convey the impression of seeing them.

>   the pond'rous architrave
> Leans on its capital; the metopés
> Start into ambient air, and breathe with life.
> Fall back with white upturned wond'ring eyes
> To gaze upon the sculptur'd frize; the long
> Procession moves—light female forms array'd
> In stole and modest peplus bear the load
> Of sacred urns and torches; fir'd with rage
> The bull glares wildly by; with bended knees,
> And firm projected arms, the struggling boy
> Draws the tight cord; till to the altar dragg'd,
> It backward bends its dewlapp'd throat, to meet
> The blow. There youths and warlike bands are seen—
> Some grasp the ringing buckler; some bind on
> The martial greave; some guide the dusty car;
> Or seated graceful on their snowy steeds,
> Whose eye-balls flash and nostrils snort with fire,
> They press the foaming curb, and give their vests
> To stream in careless folds upon the wind.[21] (Part II, ll. 623-41.)

In the spirit of Thomson, these lines are more readable than the accounts of sculpture by Darwin and Hayley.

Felicia Hemans, who kept in touch with every topic of interest, wrote another poem on Greece. With an epigraph from Thomson's

[21] In Part III, l. 48, Haygarth described an alto-relievo in the Elgin collection from Stuart and Revett's *Antiquities*, and he several times mentioned Elgin. The poet was moved by Milton's ideals of Liberty and by the hope of regenerating Greece.

Liberty, her *Modern Greece* (1817) employed Byronic Spenserians to sing the glories of the "fair land of Phidias." A touching picture of Greek emigrants in the savannahs of America dreaming of their homeland introduced the view of the Greece that was no more, "realm of sad beauty!" An imaginary excursion through Greece, where

> Grace, beauty, grandeur, strength, and symmetry
> Blend in decay,

led finally to the Parthenon and its sculpture. For thirteen stanzas she tediously described the beauty of the Elgin Marbles, citing Canova, West, and Haydon as her authorities.

> in those fragments, though by time defaced,
> And rude insensate conquerors, yet remains
> All that may charm th' enlighten'd eye of taste,
> On shores where still aspiring freedom reigns.
> (Stanza xci, ll. 1–4.)

From studying the Elgin sculptures, a "British Angelo" might arise; for England had the "power to be what Athens e'er hath been." [22]

Bryan Waller Procter ("Barry Cornwall") wrote one of the few Romantic poems solely on the Elgin Marbles. His "On the Statue of Theseus" needed the explicit subtitle "One of the Elgin Marbles," because the statue aroused a flood of mythological impressions of the sort often found in nineteenth-century poetry.

> AYE, this is he,
> A proud and mighty spirit: how fine his form
> Gigantic! moulded like the race that strove
> To take Jove's heav'n by storm and scare him from
> Olympus. There he sits, a demigod,
> Stern as when he of yore forsook the maid
> Who doating saved him from the Cretan toil,
> Where he had slain the Minotaur. Alas!
> Fond Ariadne, thee did he desert
> And heartless left thee on the Naxos shore,
> To languish.—This is he who dared to roam
> The world infernal, and on Pluto's queen,

---

[22] See stanza lxii ff. for a Wordsworthian passage on the mythological spirit "peopling with shadowy powers each dell and grot."

Ceres' own lost Proserpina, did lay
His hand: thence was he prison'd in the vaults
Beneath, 'till freed by Hercules. Methinks,
(So perfect is the Phidian stone) his sire,
The sea-god Neptune, hath in anger stopped
The current of life, and with his trident-touch
Hath struck him into marble.

Of greater interest, perhaps, were the poet's numerous figurative and decorative uses of the sculptures of Phidias,

> whose carved thoughts
> Threw beauty o'er the years of Pericles.

His devotion to the age of Pericles suggests that of Landor, even as his poetry suggests the *Hellenics*. In "Portraits," too, Procter looked at Aspasia with the eyes of Landor:

Behind her the Roman Cornelia followed an Athenian dame,
(The pale and elegant Aspasia)
Like some fair marble carved by Phidias' hand,
And meant to imitate the nymph or muse: . . .
And fit to be beloved of Pericles.
(*A Sicilian Story, and Other Poems* [1820], pp. 151–52.)

In *The Flood of Thessaly* (1823) the glories of Greece arose in a vision of the kind which poets of the Romantic period liked to unfold. In a "progress" of the arts and philosophy came

> Praxiteles, and Phidias, and the rest
> Whose Promethean touch awaken'd life
> In the cold marble.[23]

In *Athens* (1824) W. M. Praed echoed Byron's lyrical praise of Grecian scenery with only an offhand glance at "Art's creations." Thomas Moore dreamed in *Evenings in Greece* (1825) of the early Greece where the "mute poesy" of nature "illum'd that land of bards to be":

> While yet undream'd, her seeds of Art
> Lay sleeping in the marble mine—

[23] Page 69. See also "Ludovico Sforza," *Dramatic Scenes and Other Poems* (1819), p. 16, and the Shelleyan figures in *The Flood of Thessaly* (pp. 58–60), which contrast with the usual Keatsian and Landorian shapes in the poetry of Procter.

Sleeping till Genius bade them start
    To all but life, in shapes divine;
Till deified the quarry shone
And all Olympus stood in stone.[24]

Richard Monckton Milnes continued the tradition in *Memorials of a Tour in Some Parts of Greece, Chiefly Poetical* (1834). But no minor Romantic poet more charmingly described the ideal Greece which exerted such attraction for the poets, great and small, of the day than did Horace Smith in his sonnet "On the Statue of a Piping Faun." Sculpture evoked the realms of faëry, and the marble piper led him back to an early and simple Greece of perfect Arcadian bliss.

O happy Greece! while thy blest sons were rovers,
Thro' all the loveliness this earth discovers,
    They in their minds a brighter region founded,
Haunted by gods and sylvans, nymphs and lovers,
    Where forms of grace thro' sunny landscapes bounded,
    By music and enchantment all surrounded.

24 *Works* (Godley), p. 287.

XII. CONCLUSION

During the romantic period in England poets responded to the sculpture of Greece in a variety of ways. Many of them stated directly the sensations felt when they beheld works of art. In recording in verse the actual experience of seeing sculptured works, Byron and Keats surpassed other poets of the time. A man of taste almost in spite of himself, in *Childe Harold* Byron described the "old antique" in the visits of his hero to the Italian galleries. The familiar Greco-Roman works had been somewhat staled by countless gentlemen who had marveled at their canons of proportion and Ideal Beauty. None the less, Byron gave the Apollo and the Venus a show of significance through his easy rhetoric and passionate sentimentality. In *The Curse of Minerva* a different method of statement appeared, with the imagined sensations of prize fighters and dainty maidens reflecting the poet's own experience and opinion of the Elgin Marbles. Keats, on the other hand, in the "Haydon" sonnets reported almost too accurately his experiencing of the "mighty things" from the Parthenon. A young poet untutored in the arts, he transferred to paper the dizzying rush of sensations with which he saw before him a new realm of artistic achievement in the grand style of the Greek sculptures.

Two lesser poets offered parallel statements. In *Paris in 1815* George Croly, a disciple of Byron, enumerated the antiques in the Halls of Sculpture at the Louvre and minutely described their appearance. William Haygarth in *Greece* imagined the Elgin friezes in their original places on the Parthenon, even turning his eyes upward to gaze upon the "long procession" of marble men and maidens moving to the sacrifice.

Other poets left glowing accounts of their "soul-adventures" in the presence of Greek sculpture, but more often in letters or journals, in criticism, or in miscellaneous prose than in poetry. Again Keats and, in a lesser degree, Byron gave very personal reports, though Shelley easily outdid them in prose statements of his interest in ancient art. The comments in Shelley's *Notes on Sculptures in Rome and Florence* were the most vivid record by any Romantic poet of stimulating hours in galleries. Shelley represented all poets, perhaps, when he remarked, "These things are best spoken of when the mind has drunk in the spirit of their forms." [1]

For "romantic" poets, as indeed for certain poets as far back as the twelfth century, the most exciting element in seeing Grecian statuary was the feeling that the forms or figures of sculpture were expressive. Statues were not "bodies" but "breathers." After making that discovery, the poets went beyond their own sensations to revel in and to describe the "life" of the sculptured forms. To show the vitality and lifelike qualities of a statue, the "romantic" poet often termed it a "breathing stone" in the manner of earlier poets. He was more likely, however, to grant the statue a more complex set of activities than merely being a counterfeit of nature or the embodiment of a typical trait or characteristic. Many statues were imagined as enjoying finer lives than those of human beings, in passionate moments made enduring in the lasting material of marble. Whether stones "warmed to life," whether "incarnations," in the language of Shelley, "of all the finest minds have conceived of beauty," or whether "cold pastoral" scenes of bacchanales or sacrifices, Greek sculpture had to reveal vital or living or emotional qualities in order to stir the feelings and imaginations of poets.

The discovery of "life" in statues was the prerequisite of poetry throughout the long tradition of interest in Greek sculpture among English poets. In the Romantic period the imaginative "animation" or "energizing" or "emotionalizing" of Grecian statues took a greater variety of forms than previously. There was little evidence of aesthetic appreciation of sculpture, of course, in the factual or informational accounts, which remained fairly numerous. The minor poets, such as the collegiate winners of Newdigate Prizes and Chancellor's Medals,

[1] See letter to Peacock, March 23, 1819 (*Letters*, X, 37), and above, pp. 167 ff.

tended to assert the "life" of sculptures and to describe little more than the positions of the figures and the activities represented. Byron, Wordsworth, and Coleridge at times wrote verse of this more rhetorical and "academic" nature.

The emphasis on the "life" of statuary also led to a rehearsal of episodes from the mythological history of the subject. In the Romantic period poets turned on many occasions from statues to mythological tales, legends, and fancies. Procter's "Theseus" was perhaps the finest example of a purely mythological sketch suggested by a statue. The Pygmalion myth still attracted the poets, along with a somewhat similar modern story of the maid of France who died from unrequited love for the Apollo Belvedere.

As far as the description in poetry of the "life" found in sculpture was concerned, Keats held the foremost position among "romantic" poets, largely because he vitalized the sculpture itself instead of presenting incidents and episodes other than those represented in the subjects of his poems. In the "Ode on a Grecian Urn" and the "Ode on Indolence," for example, he concerned himself with the emotions and passions of the figures, in other words, with the drama arrested in the sculpture instead of with extraneous incidents. The continuously blissful future of the lovers (along with the "happy boughs" and the "melodist, unwearied,") was mentioned, to be sure, but always as an ever living, because sculptured, passionate activity. Since Keats kept his attention on the figures themselves as they were upon the urn and the vase, the two odes approached the ideal of the poetic endowing of sculpture with "life," the re-creation of the feeling of sculpture in the medium of poetry.

The identification of himself with a sculptural figure imagined to possess great vitality and emotional activity was easy for almost every "romantic" poet. At some time all the major poets except Wordsworth and Coleridge identified their own feelings with the "life" in Grecian statues. The Apollo statues, especially the Belvedere figure whose arrow has perhaps just felled a tyrant, was a particular favorite. Apollo also symbolized various aspects of the beau ideal of manly beauty for Shelley, Byron, and Hunt. The statue was admired, too, as the form of the poet's god, the symbol of poesy, reason, thought, and everything muselike. Byron saw the love of Juan and Haidée in a sculptured group as an idealized version of one of his own amours. Shelley identified himself with Bacchus; Byron associated himself sometimes with Hercules and again with Apollo. Blake could find in the Laocoön group an allegory of his struggles with the world of art. Keats interpreted figures on vases in relation to his personal problems.

"Romantic" poets likewise gave peculiarly personal descriptions of Grecian statues. The Venus de Medici still served for the beau ideal of feminine grace. Byron in particular tended to judge many of his friends by their similarity to the darling of the Uffizi. Shelley responded to Praxitelean shapes of an eager lightness and a soft ideality. Landor's feeling in sculpture was for coldness, grandeur, and restraint. Hunt, Keats, De Quincey, and Hazlitt carried their ideas of sculpture into the theater, writing criticism of actors and acting in the terms of sculpture.

Yet the imaginative re-creation of sculptural scenes and figures presented the best reflection of the interest of poets of the Romantic period in the "life" which they found in ancient art. These re-creations of the feeling of sculpture ranged from Byron's Zuleika postured as a younger Niobe to Shelley's hermaphrodites in *The Witch of Atlas* and *Epipsychidion;* from Keats's statuesque "stationings" in *Hyperion* and *Endymion* to the flower in Wordsworth's "Love Lies Bleeding" drooping in the fashion of the Dying Gladiator, or to Moore's "Kiss" *à la* Cupid and Psyche; and from the sculpturesque scenes in the poetry of Keats and Landor to the visionary sculptures of Blake and the linear, dreamlike reliefs seen by Shelley.

Landor, Keats, and Shelley excelled in re-creating sculptural scenes and relief-like figures, with Hunt and Byron nearest them, though at some distance. Somewhat apart from the other poets in his conscious checking of emotional suggestiveness, Landor was most nearly the "classical" sculptor. Nevertheless, he was only slightly more appreciative of the decorative values of sculpture than were Keats and Shelley. The three of them were the early nineteenth-century poets most concerned with sculpturesque qualities. Keats possessed the ability to make his descriptions of sculpture convey the feeling of the art to a degree unequaled by any contemporary English poet. Shelley had similar powers of intuition and expression, but he often clothed his figures in Shelleyan garments. His sculptural figures became rather too unsubstantial, too dreamlike, or too linear for sculpture. Byron was sensitive to sculptural qualities, though he was inclined either to be too serious and too sentimental or else to distrust his feelings. His imaginative use of sculptures for comical and satirical purposes was unequaled in Romantic poetry. In a few lines Hunt alone rivaled him in poetry of this kind.

A similar richness and variety appeared in the poetry of the Romantic period which dealt with the complex group of "ideas" concerning society, the arts, and culture associated, as we have seen, with Greek sculpture by poets from the seventeenth century onward. The Grecian enthusiasm of Shelley, Byron, Hunt, and Landor led them to relate social and political ideals to sculpture more often than the other poets. They were the leading Hellenists of the Romantic period in respect to social and political matters, and they admired the state where sculpture had flourished under the tutelage of Liberty.

Blake, Shelley (and through him Byron to a small degree), Landor, Wordsworth, and Coleridge were interested in the Grecian workmanship revealed in sculpture for the light shed upon the poetical faculty or power and upon the nature of the artistic or creative processes. Landor again stood somewhat apart from the other poets in that he failed to advance the distinctive "romantic" theory of art, namely, the theory in which the stress fell upon the inner meaning and organic form of the ancient statues. Shelley more than compensated for Landor's silence, however, in his numerous treatments in poetry of various aspects of that view of the Antique.

Excluding Landor, then, these poets might be called Hellenists in regard to morality and aesthetics, were it not that one hesitates to apply the term to Blake, Wordsworth, and Coleridge. The three poets were such staunch defenders of the Christian and the Modern against the Pagan and the Ancient that they scarcely merit the label of Hellenist. They would probably have agreed with Horace Smith, whose "Moral Ruins" related a kind of "progress" of sculpture and the other arts in the light of their morality, in which the highest and the one true and abiding religion proved to be the Christian.

> The marble miracles of Greece and Rome,
>   Temple and Dome,
> Art's masterpieces, awful in the excess
>   Of loveliness,
> Hallowed by statued Gods which might be thought
> To be themselves by the Celestials wrought,—
> Where are they now?—their majesty august
>   Grovels in dust.[2]

However, they were concerned with the moral and religious influences upon Grecian art almost as much as Shelley. Though convinced that the mythological fables of Greece expressed pagan creeds and outworn sentiments, this trio might have been willing occasionally to join the poetaster T. K. Hervey, whom Williams's *Select Views in Greece* (1829) moved to exclaim,

> The heart that owns a better faith may kneel,
> Nor wrong his creed, while bending o'er the sod
> Where gods—and men *like* gods, in act and will,—
> Are made immortal, by the wizard rod
> Of him whose every thought aspired to be a god![3]

Moreover, like Shelley, each poet interpreted the Greek works as illustrating his personal and "romantic" conceptions of the creative power. Blake imagined that the Grecian artists had sculptured visions. Wordsworth and Coleridge saw in Grecian art the working of the Neo-Platonic plastic process by which spiritual belief reveals itself in sensuous and intelligible material forms. Shelley felt that the ancient artists had made sculpture into a vehicle for the expression of thought and intellectual beauty. The Greek statues were of great beauty and external loveliness; but, for all four poets, their true glory lay in the

---

[2] *Poetical Works* (1857 ed.), pp. 40–41.
[3] See "The Temple of Jupiter Olympius at Athens" and "The Acropolis, at Athens," *The Poetical Sketch-Book* (1829), pp. 14, 120–21. Hervey's note explained that the wielder of the "wizard rod" was none other than Phidias!

mental or intellectual or spiritual elements which the sculptors had expressed in "fixed shapes" of stone.

Great artists, the Greek sculptors too, apparently, had been "romantic." In the words of Blake, they had bodied forth "spiritual existences." Or, as a minor "romantic" poet, Charles Lloyd, succinctly stated this view of art:

> 'Tis not the form that is th' essential thing,
> It is the soul, the spirit, that is there.[4]

Yet the all-important spirit or soul needed a shape or material form in which to reveal itself, and the statues of Greece presented something close to an ideal fusion of spirit and matter, the Idea made manifest in sensible form. In sculpture, as practised by the Greeks in particular, Coleridge found that "the perfection of form is an outward symbol of inward perfection and the most elevated ideas, where the body is wholly penetrated by the soul, and spiritualized even to a state of glory." Expressive symbols, the statues were living forms whose external beauty resulted from the spirit within.

With such a view of art, the admiration of external forms is already on the decline. Their praise of the spirit of Grecian workmanship actually led Blake, Wordsworth, and Coleridge away from the Antique—to such an extent that one ordinarily excludes them from the ranks of the Hellenists. These "romantic" poets valued statues, not for their perfect forms—whether reposeful or grandly simple or teeming with emotional activity—but for the spirit or soul operating within the marble forms. Wordsworth gave the finest statement in poetry of this view of sculpture in *The Excursion,* where he explicitly turned from the "fixed shapes" of statuary to the spiritual or immaterial essence. Coleridge expressed a similar view in his carefully worded warning against excessive imitation of the Antique in *On Poesy or Art.* Clearly the stress on the spirit operating within a work of sculpture—both the plastic power felt by Shelley and the organic or inner form in the aesthetics of Wordsworth and Coleridge—tended to make poets slight the individual masterpieces of sculpture.

Only Shelley, the thoroughgoing Hellenist of this group of Roman-

[4] *Desultory Thoughts in London* (1821), p. 41.

tic poets, failed to warn against too great a liking for the "fixed shapes"
of the Antique. In his poetry, however, Shelley showed more often
than either Wordsworth or Coleridge how a poet would use this
theory; for he always read the spiritual (and intellectual and emotional) qualities expressed in a statue from its external form. Under
the influence of both Shelley and Wordsworth, Byron also reflected at
times a somewhat similar feeling for the spirit of ancient statues. Keats
presented in his re-creations of sculpture an even finer illustration of
the ways in which a poet imaginatively seizes upon the spirit operating within external appearances. Accordingly, had he explicitly stated
a theory of sculpture, he would probably have equated the spirit in
statues with emotions and passions or sensations rather than with
intellectual and spiritual elements. Yet Keats, too, wished to explore

> all forms and substances
> Straight homeward to their symbol-essences.

Strange as it seems, the Elgin Marbles were yet another influence
which, to some extent, at least, directed poets away from the Antique.
At the time of the controversy over their merit in 1815 and 1816,
critics like Hazlitt, artists like Canova, West, and Haydon, and poets
like Keats regarded the sculptures as "natural" in contrast to the "old
antique" of the idealized Greco-Roman figures. The Elgin Marbles
presented the forms of nature. The great beauty of the Parthenon
sculptures resulted from a grandeur of style employed in displaying
actual human beings engaged in the activities of real life. This "naturalness" showed that the Greek sculptors had made beautiful sculpture out of the circumstances of their age and out of the deeds of
heroes and the actions of gods which were instinct with meaning for
the Greeks. The lesson taught by the Elgin Marbles was that "romantic" poets should treat the life of the early nineteenth century in
the spirit of the Greek artists, or in the "naked and Grecian manner"
of grand design achieved with care and precision in detail. Thus the
Elgin Marbles contributed the force of their antique example to the
"romantic" theories about art: fifth-century Greece joined hands with
Wordsworth and Coleridge in urging writers to use the circumstances
and spirit of their own age.

Yet the familiar forms of Ideal Beauty of the "old antique" lingered in the minds of many Romantic poets even after the "new antique" of the Elgin Marbles had been placed in the British Museum. The opposition between the Greco-Roman and the Parthenon figures remained, for the most part, a subject for discussion among critics and gentlemen rather than poets, with the notable exceptions of Keats and Byron. Although Haydon belabored the Greco-Roman favorites of the connoisseurs, and although Hazlitt and other critics ridiculed the Ideal Beauty of the Neo-Classical and Academic theorists, the Elgin Marbles failed to displace the "old antique" from the affections of the English poets. Most of them continued to think of the statues which they had seen in books like Spence's *Polymetis* at school or at the universities and elsewhere. In Italy the poets, like Shelley and Byron and Landor, still studied the Greco-Roman works after the Elgin Marbles had been accepted in England.

Of course, a good deal of the Romantic poetry inspired by Greek statuary was primarily sculpturesque decoration, in which poets were little concerned, if at all, with theories of art. Interested in the poetic or imaginative and emotional values in the sculpture of Greece, Landor, Hunt, Shelley, and especially Keats liked to describe the beautiful objects of the art of the sculptor—from gems to friezes, from urns and vases to heroic statues. They were the heirs of the Alexandrian poets of classical antiquity and of the Renaissance. Landor, Keats, and, to a lesser degree, Shelley took pleasure in ornamenting and adorning the stages upon which occurred the moving drama of their poetry.

But classical details and architectural and sculptural effects alone satisfied few Romantic poets. Landor, Keats, Byron, Shelley—in fact, almost every poet of the time—poured modern feelings into ancient forms, since they felt that the forms or "fixed shapes" of classical sculpture, history, mythology, and poetry offered poor vehicles for modern themes and feelings. Largely for that very reason, Wordsworth and Coleridge pointed out the difference between the fancy, with which a poet might treat classical motifs, and a higher power, the imagination, with which he expressed the vital articles of his beliefs. Their analysis of the opposition between fancy and the imagination reflected the growing realization among "romantic" writers of the conflict between

> the Grecian dream
> Of Beauty perfect in a finite mould [5]

and the indefinable, intangible, and spiritual sentiments of the Christian and modern (or "romantic") genius—the conflict which profoundly disturbed the poets of the later nineteenth century.

What these foreshadowings of the conflict between the Grecian or pagan and the modern or Christian meant in the Romantic period may be seen by reference to two admirers of Wordsworth and Coleridge. Charles Lloyd versified the opposition between fancy and imagination in relation to sculpture thus:

> Beauty, to the ancients, was a love, devotion:
>   Power was their symbol of sublimity!
> Attitude, Passion, Symmetry, and Motion,
>   With them were fix'd in forms of statuary!
>   . . .
>
> But, at the same time, howe'er much I prize,
>   And much I prize it, classical tradition,
> I still must feel what difference there lies
>   'Twixt it, and gospel truth's sublimer mission.
> From one for fancy many charms may rise;
>   To the sense grateful is its exhibition!
>   . . .
>
> But, in the gospel page, Imagination.[6]

George Dyer announced that he could feel the spirit or soul or genius of the lakes of Westmoreland and Cumberland, which he had visited with Wordsworth and Southey, with greater force

> 'Mid falling water's solemn sound,
> 'Mid pathless rocks, and mountains rude,

[5] Aubrey de Vere, *The Waldenses* (1842), p. 292.

[6] *Desultory Thoughts in London,* "On the Connection between Different Degrees of Spiritualization, in Religion, and a Taste for the Arts in General, and a Material or Metaphysical Taste in Poetry," and "Parallel between the Imagery of Heathenism and That of the Bible," pp. 71, 155. Lloyd had in mind *The Excursion* (see above, pp. 124 ff.) and Coleridge's lines on mythology in *The Piccolomini* (see above, pp. 143–44).

And all yon deep opaque of wood,
Than if, enshrin'd aloft I saw thee stand,
Glittering in robes of gold, and shap'd by Phidias' hand.[7]

Moreover, though they had inherited a preference for things classical, especially Grecian, "romantic" poets and critics determined to find subject matter and means of presentation appropriate to their age. Because the Greeks and Romans had been silent concerning many emotions, sentiments, and experiences which were of great importance and of frequent occurrence in the nineteenth century, these writers found it difficult to "coöperate" fully with the Ancients. "Romantic" poets must create the forms which would possess significance for their own age.

The "romantic" poets in England continued, nevertheless, to look to the past and to Greek sculpture, but not as their immediate predecessors of the Academies had turned to antiquity. Many gentlemen, connoisseurs, and poets of the eighteenth century had refined themselves according to classical antiquity, where they found the perfect or correct taste—first of Rome and then of Greece—by which they became urbane, reasonable, and enlightened. "Romantic" poets saw themselves, rather, as links new-forged in the golden chain of poets; and they hailed the sculpture of Greece as a stimulus to creative activity on their own part. They wished to emulate the Greeks in making great art from the circumstances of their time. In other words, they were to do "for Britain what the artists of old did for Greece: their works are classical—not from being the offspring of a classic land, but because they were the embodied poetry of its actual beauty and sentiment."[8]

Among the poets and critics of the Romantic period, therefore, description of antique forms was supplemented and largely replaced by imaginative and poetic interpretation, and admiration of the canons of proportion of the Antique gave way to study of the inner harmony and organic form. Wordsworth and Coleridge presented this position

[7] *Poetics; or, A Series of Poems, and Disquisitions on Poetry* (1812), p. 231. See above, pp. 127 ff.

[8] Allan Cunningham, criticizing the classicistic forms painted by James Barry, *Lives of the Most Eminent British Painters, Sculptors, and Architects* (2d ed., 1830), II; 140.

most clearly—a position which had developed almost inevitably from the Platonic theories of Shaftesbury, Winckelmann, and Reynolds and from the pioneer versification of an aesthetic response to sculpture by Thomson and Akenside. Accordingly the "romantic" poets treated the spirit of works of ancient art more often than their external forms.

At the same time that Wordsworth and Coleridge, through their stress upon the inner qualities of art, to some extent directed poets away from the Antique, they encouraged the study of the nature of the artistic processes, including what they considered to have been the spirit of the Grecian workmanship. The finest poetic re-creations of sculpture in the Romantic period sprang, indeed, from the concern with the spirit within the ancient works—that is, with the intellectual and mental and emotional qualities which poets imaginatively discovered in sculpture. The emphasis upon the internal and poetic and imaginative qualities in Greek sculpture paralleled the renewed interest in the spirit of ancient religion and mythology. Again, poets sometimes sought to understand the Ancients by studying how the sculptors had presented the beliefs of Greece in their statues, vases, and friezes of gods and men and heroes.

Wordsworth set the pattern for succeeding poets—with his early toying with classical motifs in the manner of the Academic poets; with his original creations of the great decade from 1798 to 1807 in which he showed how a modern poet made poetry from the familiar matter of his day with a "classical" simplicity inherited from the eighteenth century; with his analysis in *The Excursion* and elsewhere of a spirit within the "fixed shapes" of Grecian sculpture which possessed more beauty than stone or marble; and, finally, with several poems on classical subjects where his fancy could make use of the forms of ancient art.

Then, too, Wordsworth joined with Coleridge in advancing the "romantic" theory by which the two of them as well as other poets, both in the Romantic period and later, might hope to create works of art comparable in formal beauty and spiritual significance to

the works
Of Grecian Art and purest Poetry.

LIST OF CRITICAL TERMS

Since the use of several words which are commonly employed with a variety of meanings is unavoidable in this book, I wish to indicate the sense in which they appear here. This list need not be memorized or even consulted to enjoy the book. Still, it may prove useful to students of the terminology of criticism.

ROMANTIC. A chronological term referring to the years commonly thought of as "The Romantic Revival" or "Movement," roughly from 1798 (*Lyrical Ballads*) to 1832 (death of Sir Walter Scott). In short, "Romantic" is a synonym and an abbreviation for "belonging to the first third of the nineteenth century."

"ROMANTIC." "Sharing, or possessing, or characterized by the distinctive traits, qualities, and beliefs of writers and thinkers of the Romantic period." Thus, a "romantic" poet, in contrast to "academic" writers who followed the standards of the Academies or to "classicists" devoted to the Ancients, was one who consciously (or, perhaps, unconsciously) concerned himself with expressing the spirit of the age. He found the inner or essential spirit of the early nineteenth century by a thorough examination of, or an imaginative participation in, its activities and thoughts. A "romantic" poet shared all four "ideals" which Professor Arthur O. Lovejoy has termed the "essentials of the aesthetic creed of Romanticism" (" 'Nature' as an Aesthetic Norm," *MLN*, XLII [1927], 450). A fifth "ideal"—Professor Lovejoy's 'Nature' in sense *t*—also belongs to the aesthetic creed of the English poets treated in this study. This is the "ideal" of *"Naturgefühl;* expression of emotions derived from the contemplation of the sensible world external to man [including works of art, such as statues], especially when this is conceived as a source of moral teaching or as a manifestation of, or means of contact with, some pervasive spiritual Presence . . . but the function of the artist is here conceived to be, not 'imitating' the external world [not describing with factual or informational details], but expressing his subjective response [giving his impressions or sensations] to it or interpreting its supposed inner meaning." See Chapter I, above, pp. 9–10.

ACADEMIC. A chronological term referring to the second half of the eighteenth century. Though Academies of the arts and sciences had

been founded in the previous century on the Continent, in England
the conscientious imitation of the works and principles of the Ancients,
as conceived by the Academies, did not prevail until the latter years of
the eighteenth century.

"ACADEMIC." "Devoted to, or characterized by the standards of the
Academies."

CLASSICAL. "Of the standard Greek and Roman writers; belonging to
the literature or art of Greek and Roman antiquity" (OED "classical,"
adj. 2, 4; also "classic," adj. 2, 3).

"CLASSICAL." Applied to subjects or works, other than Greek and Roman, which the Ancients might have used or created, or to writers who
consciously strove to write as though they were "classical." When applied to human beings, "classical" is closest to "would-be classical."

CLASSICISTIC, and CLASSICIST. "Characterized by an adherence to, adoption of, or close imitation of classical material or style," (based on OED
"classicism"). Both terms, but especially "classicistic," have chronological overtones, since "classicists" flourished particularly in the latter (or
Academic) half of the eighteenth century and in the early nineteenth
century.

NEO-CLASSICAL. A chronological term referring to the last forty years of
the seventeenth century, when the aesthetic standards, theories, and
principles of the classicizing Academies of the Continent (aided to some
extent by the classicizing tendencies of late Elizabethan and Stuart
authors and artists) began to dominate English poetry and art. "Neo-
Classical" standards continued to be important throughout the Augustan and Academic periods of the eighteenth century; but the word itself
refers to the Age of Dryden.

SCULPTURAL. "Possessing, or suggesting the qualities of sculpture." "Sculptural" is a general word and, when applied to poetry, refers to the
suggestion of any work of sculpture or of the materials, instruments,
or distinctive manner of expression belonging to the art.

SCULPTURESQUE. "Like sculpture, having the qualities of sculpture"
(OED). "Sculpturesque" is more limited than "sculptural," since it
suggests the "lesser" (?) branches of the art, the ornamental and
decorative kinds of sculpture, such as reliefs, vases, carvings, gems,
cameos, etc. Used figuratively, "sculpturesque" refers to any impression of sculpture, but primarily to suggestions of reliefs, vases, carving,
etc.—that is, to sculpture which tends in the direction of the linear
and pictorial rather than the "statuesque."

STATUESQUE. "Having the qualities of a statue or of sculpture" (OED).
"Statuesque" refers in particular to statuary proper—free-standing fig-

ures, torsos, busts, etc., either of considerable size or grandeur, or of unusually pleasing symmetry or proportions. Applied to literature, "statuesque" refers to figures or groups arranged like, or suggestive of "statues."

A SELECTIVE BIBLIOGRAPHY

IN THE FOLLOWING bibliography there is no attempt to run through the extensive fields of Romanticism, Hellenism, and Greek sculpture. Rather, I list the more important titles for the investigation of the present and allied topics or subjects. Since the notes are heavily documented, specialized studies, as a rule, will be found there. The place of publication is London, unless some other reference is given.

Agard, Walter R. The Greek Tradition in Sculpture. Baltimore, 1930.

Angeli, Diego. Le cronache del Caffè Greco. Milan, 1930.

Aron, Erich. Die deutsche Erweckung des Griechentums durch Winckelmann und Herder. Heidelberg, 1929.

Aubin, Robert A. Topographical Poetry in XVIII-Century England. New York, 1936.

Baker, C. H. Collins. "The Sources of Blake's Pictorial Expression," *Huntington Library Quarterly,* IV (1941), 359–67.

Baldwin, Edward [William Godwin]. The Pantheon; or, Ancient History of the Gods of Greece and Rome. 1806.

Bell, John. Bell's New Pantheon; or, Historical Dictionary of the Gods, Demi-Gods, Heroes, &c. 1790.

Bertrand, Louis. La Fin du classicisme et le retour à l'antique dans la seconde moitié du XVIII⁰ siècle et les premières années du XIX⁰, en France. Paris, 1897.

Borinski, Karl. Die Antike in Poetik und Kunsttheorie von Ausgang des klassischen Altertums bis auf Goethe und Wilhelm von Humboldt. Leipzig, 1914–24.

Bosanquet, Bernard. A History of Aesthetics. 1892.

Boyse, Samuel. A New Pantheon; or, Fabulous History of the Heathen Gods, Heroes, Goddesses, &c. Explain'd in a Manner Intirely New. 1753.

Bray, René. La Formation de la doctrine classique en France. Paris, 1927.

Bredvold, Louis I. "The Tendency toward Platonism in Neo-Classical Esthetics," *ELH,* I (1934), 91 ff.

Brown, Huntington. "The Classical Tradition in English Literature; A Bibliography," *Harvard Studies and Notes in Philology and Literature,* XVIII (1935), 7–46.

Burrow, E. J. The Elgin Marbles; with an Abridged Historical and Topographical Account of Athens. 1817.

Bush, Douglas. Mythology and the Renaissance Tradition in English Poetry. Minneapolis and London, 1932.

―――― Mythology and the Romantic Tradition in English Poetry. Cambridge, Mass., 1937.

Butler, E. M. The Tyranny of Greece over Germany. 1935.

Carpenter, Rhys. The Aesthetic Basis of Greek Art. New York, 1921.

Chambers, Frank P. Cycles of Taste. Cambridge, Mass., 1928.

―――― The History of Taste. New York, 1932.

Chislett, William. The Classical Influence in English Literature in the Nineteenth Century. Boston, 1918.

Clarke, Helen A. Ancient Myths in Modern Poets. New York, 1910.

Collins, J. Churton. Greek Influence on English Poetry. 1910.

Collison-Morley, Lacy. Italy after the Renaissance; Decadence and Display in the Seventeenth Century. 1930.

Combe, Taylor. A Description of the Collection of Ancient Marbles in the British Museum; with Engravings. . . . 1812–61.

Croce, Benedetto. Aesthetic, translated by Douglas Ainslie. 2d ed., 1922.

Cust, Lionel Henry. History of the Society of Dilettanti, edited by Sidney Colvin. 1914.

Dallaway, James. Of Statuary and Sculpture among the Antients. 1816.

Davies, Cicely. "Ut Pictura Poesis," *MLR*, XXX (1935), 159–69.

Dewey, Malcolm. Herder's Relation to the Aesthetic Theory of His Time. Chicago, 1920.

Draper, John W. Eighteenth Century English Aesthetics: A Bibliography. "Anglistische Forschungen," Vol. LXXI (1931).

DuBos, Jean Baptiste. Réflexions critiques sur la poesie et sur la peinture. Paris, 1719.

Durham, Willard H. Critical Essays of the Eighteenth Century, 1700–1725. New Haven, 1915.

Elton, Oliver. A Survey of English Literature, 1730–1780. 1928.

―――― A Survey of English Literature, 1780–1880. 1920.

Fairbanks, Arthur. Greek Art, the Basis of Later European Art, "Our Debt to Greece and Rome" series, No. 39. New York, 1933.

Félibien, Jean François. Conférences de l'Academie Royale de Peinture et de Sculpture. 1705.

Folkierski, Wladyslaw. Entre le classicisme et la romanticisme. Paris, 1925.

Gardner, Ernest A. A Handbook of Greek Sculpture. 1896–97.

―――― Art of Greece. 1925.

Gayley, Charles M.   The Classic Myths in English Literature and in Art. Boston and New York, 1911.

Goldmark, Ruth I.   Studies in the Influence of the Classics on English Literature. New York, 1918.

Greene, Theodore Meyer.   The Arts and the Art of Criticism. Princeton, 1940.

Griffith, Reginald H.   "The Progress Pieces of the Eighteenth Century," *Texas Review*, V (1920), 218 ff.

Gutteling, Johanna F. C.   Hellenic Influence on the English Poetry of the Nineteenth Century. Amsterdam [1922].

[Hamilton, William Richard.]   Memorandum on the Subject of the Earl of Elgin's Pursuits in Greece. Edinburgh, 1810, 1811; 2d ed., corrected, 1815.

Hogarth, William.   The Analysis of Beauty. 1753.

Hourticq, Louis.   De Poussin à Watteau. Paris, 1921.

Howard, William G.   "Burke among the Forerunners of Lessing," *PMLA*, XXII (1907), 608 ff.

——— "Ut Pictura Poesis," *PMLA*, XXIV (1909), 40 ff.

Hyde, Walter W.   "The Place of Winckelmann in the History of Classical Scholarship," *Classical Weekly*, XII (1918–19), 75–79.

Jones, H. S.   Select Passages from Ancient Writers Illustrative of the History of Greek Sculpture. 1895.

Justi, Karl.   Winckelmann und seine Zeitgenossen. Leipzig, 1898.

Kellett, E. E.   The Whirligig of Taste. 1929.

——— Fashion in Literature; A Study in Changing Taste. 1931.

Knight, G. Wilson.   The Burning Oracle. 1939.

Kraemer, Caspar J.   "The Influence of the Classics on English Literature," *Classical Journal*, XXII (1926–27), 485–97.

Landré, Louis.   Leigh Hunt (1784–1859); Contribution à l'histoire du romanticisme anglais. Paris, 1936.

Lawrence, Lesley.   "Stuart and Revett; Their Literary and Architectural Careers," *Warburg Institute Journal*, II (1938), 128–46.

Lawrence, Mrs. [Rose d'A.].   Cameos from the Antique; or, The Cabinet of Mythology: Selections Illustrative of the Mythology of Greece and Italy, for the Use of Children, and Intended as a Sequel to the Poetical Primer. Liverpool and London, 1831.

Lemprière, J.   A Classical Dictionary. 6th ed., corrected, 1806; A New Edition, Revised and Considerably Enlarged, by Rev. T. Smith. 1847.

Lessing, Gotthold Ephraim.   Laokoon, edited with English notes, by A. Hamann, revised by L. E. Upcott.

Lessing, Gotthold Ephraim. Selected Prose Works, translated by E. C. Beasley and Helen Zimmern, edited by Edward Bell. 1890.

—— Laokoon; Lessing, Herder, Goethe. Selections edited by W. G. Howard. New York, 1910.

Levin, Harry. The Broken Column; A Study in Romantic Hellenism. Cambridge, Mass., 1931.

Lovejoy, Arthur O. "On the Meaning of 'Romantic' in Early German Romanticism," Part I, *MLN*, XXXI (1916), 385 ff.; Part II, *ibid.*, XXXII (1917), 65 ff.

—— "Schiller and the Genesis of Romanticism," *MLN*, XXXV (1920), 1 ff.; Part II, *ibid.*, 136 ff.

—— "On the Discrimination of Romanticisms," *PLMA*, XXXIX (1924), 229 ff.

—— " 'Nature' as an Aesthetic Norm," *MLN*, XLII (1927), 444 ff.

Manwaring, Elizabeth W. Italian Landscape in Eighteenth Century England. 1925.

Mayoux, Jean-Jacques. Richard Payne Knight et le pittoresque; essai sur une phase ésthetique. Paris, 1932.

Mead, William E. The Grand Tour in the Eighteenth Century. Boston and New York, 1914.

Michaelis, Adolf T. F. Ancient Marbles in Great Britain, translated by C. A. M. Fennell. 1882.

—— A Century of Archaeological Discoveries, translated by Bettina Kalmweiler. 1908.

Miller, Walter. Daedalus and Thespis; The Contributions of the Ancient Dramatic Poets to Our Knowledge of the Arts and Crafts of Greece. Vol. II, Sculpture. Columbia, Mo., 1931; Vol. III, Painting and Allied Arts. Columbia, 1932.

Monk, Samuel H. The Sublime; A Study of Critical Theories in XVIII-Century England. New York, 1935.

Montgomery, Marshall. Friedrich Hölderlin and the German Neo-Hellenic Movement. 1923.

Murray, Gilbert. The Classical Tradition in Poetry. Cambridge, Mass., 1927.

"Newdigate, The." *TLS*, June 14, 1934, pp. 413 ff.

Panofsky, Erwin. 'Idea'; ein Beitrag zur Begriffsgeschichte der älteren Kunsttheorie, "Studien der Bibliothek Warburg," No. 5. Leipzig and Berlin, 1924.

—— Studies in Iconology; Humanistic Themes in the Art of the Renaissance. 1939.

Pierce, Frederick E. "The Hellenic Current in English Nineteenth Century Poetry," *JEGP*, XVI (1917), 103 ff.

—— Currents and Eddies in the English Romantic Generation. New Haven, 1918.

Pollock, Courtenay. "Lord Elgin and the Marbles," *Essays by Divers Hands: Being the Transactions of the Royal Society of Literature,* N.S., XI (1932), 41 ff.

Pughe, F. H. "Byron, Wordsworth, und die Antike," chap. iii, in his Studien über Byron und Wordsworth, "Anglistische Forschungen," VIII (1902), 40–54.

Read, Herbert. In Defence of Shelley and Other Essays. 1936.

Reynolds, Sir Joshua. The Works, edited by Edmond Malone. 1797.

—— The Discourses, edited by Helen Zimmern, 1887; edited by Roger Fry, 1905; edited with an Introduction by Austin Dobson, "World's Classics," 1907.

Richardson, Jonathan. The Works, edited by his son Mr. J. Richardson. 1773.

Richter, Gisela M. A. The Sculpture and Sculptors of the Greeks. New Haven, 1930.

Robb, Nesca A. Neoplatonism of the Italian Renaissance. 1935.

Robertson, John G. The Gods of Greece in German Poetry. 1924.

Rocheblave, Samuel. "L'Art français au XVIIᵉ siècle dans ses rapports avec la littérature," chap. xii, Vol. V, Histoire de la langue et la littérature française, edited by L. Petit de Julleville. Paris, 1898.

Sargeaunt, G. M. Classical Studies. 1929.

Saxl, Fritz, ed. England und die Antike. "Vorträge der Bibliothek Warburg," 1930–31. Leipzig and Berlin, 1932.

Scheffer, John D. "The Idea of Decline in Literature and the Fine Arts in Eighteenth-Century England," *MP,* XXXIV (1936–37), 155 ff.

Schlegel, August Wilhelm von. Lectures on Dramatic Art and Literature, translated by J. Black. 2d ed., revised by A. W. Morison. Bohn, 1894.

Schlosser, Julius von. Die Kunstliteratur. Wien, 1924.

Schneider, Elisabeth. The Aesthetics of William Hazlitt. Philadelphia, 1933.

Sherwood, Margaret. Undercurrents of Influence in English Romantic Poetry. Cambridge, Mass., 1934.

Smith, A. H. "Lord Elgin and His Collection," *Journal of Hellenic Studies,* XXXVI (1916), 163 ff.

Spence, Joseph. Polymetis; or, An Enquiry concerning the Agreement between the Works of the Roman Poets, and the Remains of the Antient Artists. Being an Attempt to Illustrate Them Mutually from One Another. 3d ed., 1774.

Spence, Joseph.   Crito; or, A Dialogue on Beauty, by Sir Harry Beaumont (pseud.), edited by Edmund Goldsmid. Edinburgh, 1885.

Spender, Harold.   Byron and Greece. 1924.

Steegman, John.   The Rule of Taste from George I to George IV. 1936.

Stern, Bernard H.   The Rise of Romantic Hellenism in English Literature, 1732–1786. Menasha, Wis., 1940.

Templeman, William D.   "Contributions to the Bibliography of Eighteenth-Century Aesthetics," *MP*, XXX (1933), 309–16.

Texte, Joseph.   "Keats et le néo-hellénisme dans la poésie anglaise," *Études de littérature européenne* (Paris, 1898), pp. 95–145.

Tooke, Andrew.   The Pantheon, Representing the Fabulous Histories of the Heathen Gods, and Most Illustrious Heroes. . . . 1781.

Trevelyan, Humphry.   The Popular Background of Goethe's Hellenism. 1934.

Venturi, Lionello.   History of Art Criticism, translated by Charles Marriott. New York, 1936.

Vines, Sherard.   The Course of English Classicism from the Tudor to the Victorian Age. 1930.

Walpole, Horace.   Anecdotes of Painting in England; with Some Account of the Principal Artists; with additions by the Rev. James Dallaway . . . A new ed., revised, with additional notes by Ralph N. Wornum. 1876.

Warburg, Bibliothek.   .Kulturwissenschaftliche Bibliographie zum Nachleben der Antike, edited by Hans Meier, Richard Newald, Edgar Wind. Vol. I, 1931; Leipzig and Berlin, 1934.

Whitley, William T.   Artists and Their Friends in England, 1700–1799. 1928.

——— Art in England, 1800–1820. 1928.

——— Art in England, 1820–1837. 1930.

Winckelmann, Johann Joachim.   Werke, edited by C. L. Fernow. Dresden, 1908.

——— History of Ancient Art, translated by G. Henry Lodge. Boston, 1872–73. 4 vols.

——— History of Ancient Art among the Greeks, translated by Lodge. 1850.

INDEX

Academic, term, 289
"Adam Naming the Beasts" (Blake), 102
Addison, 11, 66-75, 84, 97, 265; Pope's praise of, 12; visit to Italy: preference for statuary, 66
Adolphus, J. L., 261
Adonais (Shelley), 197, 201
Aeneis, The, 58
Age of Bronze, The (Byron), 166
Akenside, Mark, 7, 44, 75-84, 87, 97, 114n, 288; emotional approach to works of art, 82; satirical thrusts at fashionable taste for Antique, 83
"Alaric in Italy" (Hemans), 19
Alaric in Rome (Arnold), 19
Alcuin, of York, 20
Allston, Washington, 137, 234
Ampelus, 198
Ancient and Modern Rome (Keate), 88
"Ancients," Blake's disciples, 113
Ancients-Moderns controversy, 140
Annus Mirabilis (Dryden), 12, 58
Antinous, 4
Antique, satirical thrusts at fashionable interest in, 74, 83; English interest in, during late eighteenth century, 89; forms of the Ancients unsuitable vehicles for modern expression, 141; the "old antique," 257-69; *see also under* Sculpture
Antiquitez de Rome (Du Bellay), 35
Antiquities of Athens, The (Stuart and Revett), 87, 99; Blake's engravings for, 104
Antiquities of Rome (Palladio), 69
Antony, Mark, 164
Antony and Cleopatra (Shakespeare), 40
Apollo, Hunt's partiality for statues of, 255
"Apollo and the Sunbeams" (Hunt), 255
Apollo Belvedere, 3, 4, 81, 139, 142, 151, 156, 196, 210, 227, 259 ff. *passim,* 279; Byron's interpretation of, 163; taken to

France by Napoleon, 257; French maid who died for love of, 260, 267, 269, 279
Apologie for Poetrie, An (Sidney), 34
"Apology for Gebir" (Landor), 233
Archaeologia Graeca (Potter), 261
Archaeology, poets' use of books on, 261
Architecture, Greek revival, 87
Aristotle, theory of ideal imitation, 57
Armstrong, John, 90
Arnold, Matthew, 19, 60, 205
Art, fostered by spirit of Liberty, 15, 178 ff., 234, 247, 281; morality, history, and theory of, 15; plastic arts the equals of poetry, 42; Italians awarded prize for expressiveness to, 42, 48; movement to encourage in England, 43; tradition of collecting begun, 45; the "aping" of nature, 47; speaks to senses, 47; discussions popularized history and theory of, 52; aesthetics of, adopted by English, 54; mental dignity of, 91; Neo-Classical and Academic theories transformed into romantic aesthetics, 98, 105; heroic, and Grecian workmanship, 99-105; role of mind in, 106; task of dedicated spirits, 113; ancient and modern divided into parcels, 114; religion and morality of Greeks, 131; Coleridgean antithesis between Gothic and Grecian, 137, 139; civilization comparable to progress of, 178 ff.; and morality, 247-51; placed above poetry, 264n; *see also* Sculpture
Artists, imitation of classical models, 88; Shelley's account of Florentine, 185
Art of Preserving Health, The (Armstrong), 90
Art-process, effort to explain nature of, 14; primarily mental or intellectual, 56; described by Landor, 244
Ascham, Roger, 32
Astraea Redux (Dryden), 54
As You Like It (Shakespeare), 41